More praise for *Leaders of Their Own Learning*

"*Leaders of Their Own Learning* points the way toward a dramatically better system for assessing the skills that matter most and motivating our students to achieve mastery. This important book should be read by every parent, educator, and policy maker."

—Tony Wagner, Harvard University; author, *The Global Achievement Gap* and *Creating Innovators*

"*Leaders of Their Own Learning* represents nothing less than a sea change in how to think about the assessment process. Assessment is frequently seen as something done to teachers and students; this book puts the powerful tools of measuring progress back in the hands of the learners themselves. Chock-full of examples, tips, and video illustrations, this masterful book achieves the remarkable feat of being both a practical how-to guide for how students, teachers, and school leaders can use student-engaged assessment, and a visionary argument for how we can invert the school reform pyramid and put students in charge of their own learning."

—Jal Mehta, associate professor, Harvard Graduate School of Education; author, *The Allure of Order: High Hopes, Dashed Expectations, and the Troubled Quest to Remake American Schooling*

"Student-engaged assessment practices are at the core of our school's success. Our graduates—100 percent of whom are accepted to college every year—are better prepared for college and life with the skills and attitudes they developed because of the strategies described in *Leaders of Their Own Learning*. Any teacher or school leader committed to every student being successful should read this book."

—Stephen R. Mahoney, principal, Springfield Renaissance School, Springfield, MA

"With increasing emphasis on students leading their learning, EL Education has been consistently turning this lofty aspiration into proven classroom practice. *Leaders of Their Own Learning* is an essential guide for practitioners about how meaningful assessment processes truly are a valuable learning tool. This book uses experience and data to show how reaching college- and career-ready goals is accomplished by comparing individual performance to standards, not by comparing students to each other. While written for teachers and school leaders, this book will also be invaluable to policy makers seeking to implement the intentions of college- and career-ready standards."

—Bob Wise, president, Alliance for Excellent Education; governor of West Virginia, 2001–2005

"*Leaders of Their Own Learning* stretches our educational thinking to tackle the most important issue for schools today: creating an assessment system that engages students in understanding and improving their learning. If we know we've been doing the wrong kind of teaching to the wrong kinds of tests, this book sets us on the right path to the right kinds of teaching and learning."

—Milton Chen, chairman, Panasonic Foundation; senior fellow, The George Lucas Educational Foundation; author, *Education Nation: Six Leading Edges of Innovation in Our Schools*

"What if testing were not something done to our students but for and with them? What if student reflection, revision, and improvement were what teachers and school leaders were held accountable for? If more meaningful assessment is your aspiration, this is the book for you."

—Barbara Chow, education program director, The William and Flora Hewlett Foundation

"In this remarkable 'user's manual' for student-engaged assessment, students and educators have given us the keys to the ample store of EL Education. What a gift!"

—Roland S. Barth, author, former school educator, faculty member, and director of the Harvard University Principals' Center

"Anyone interested in how to engage students more authentically and effectively in the assessment of their own learning will love this book. It is full of practical and respectful ways of increasing rigor and improving results by enhancing student agency. Thanks to Ron Berger and his colleagues at EL Education for leading us forward on this essential issue."

—Nicholas C. Donohue, president and CEO, Nellie Mae Education Foundation

LEADERS OF THEIR OWN LEARNING

Transforming Schools Through Student-Engaged Assessment

Ron Berger
Leah Rugen
Libby Woodfin

Foreword by Mike Johnston

Director of Video Production: David Grant

EL Education

JB JOSSEY-BASS™
A Wiley Brand

Cover design by Jeff Puda
Cover art supplied by Ron Berger
Published by Jossey-Bass
A Wiley Imprint

One Montgomery Street, Suite 1200, San Francisco, CA 94104-4594—www.josseybass.com

Jossey-Bass books and products are available through most bookstores. To contact Jossey-Bass directly call our Customer Care Department within the U.S. at 800-956-7739, outside the U.S. at 317-572-3986, or fax 317-572-4002.

Wiley also publishes its books in a variety of electronic formats and by print-on-demand. Some material included with standard print versions of this book may not be included in e-books or in print-on-demand. If the version of this book that you purchased references media such as CD or DVD that was not included in your purchase, you may download this material at http://booksupport.wiley.com. For more information about Wiley products, visit www.wiley.com.

Library of Congress Cataloging-in-Publication Data has been applied for.

ISBN: 978-1-118-65544-3 (paper);
978-1-118-65577-1(ebk.);
978-1-118-65581-8 (ebk.)

Printed in the United States of America
SECOND EDITION
PB Printing 10 9 8 7

Contents

DVD Contents

On the DVD in the back of this book you'll find our *Core Practices in Action* video series. These videos—which we will direct you to at various points throughout the book—show key practices in action with students and teachers in schools throughout the United States.

1. Using a Learning Target throughout a Lesson
2. Students Unpack a Learning Target and Discuss Academic Vocabulary
3. Students Unpack a Learning Target
4. Students Discuss the Power of Learning Targets
5. Instructional Strategies That Support Learning—Checking for Understanding
6. Kids Like Cold Call and No Opt Out—Checking for Understanding
7. Strategies for Monitoring Progress—Checking for Understanding
8. Promoting Student Ownership and Engagement in Math—Checking for Understanding
9. Schoolwide Structures for Checking for Understanding
10. Goal Setting for Achievement in Reading—Using Data with Students
11. Students Own Their Progress—Using Data with Students
12. Schoolwide Structures for Using Data
13. Grade-Level Data Meeting with Third-Grade Teachers—Using Data with Students
14. A Group Critique Lesson—Models, Critique, and Descriptive Feedback
15. Descriptive Feedback Helps All Students Meet Proficiency—Standards-Based Grading

16. Austin's Butterfly: Building Excellence in Student Work—Models, Critique, and Descriptive Feedback
17. Middle School Student-Led Conference
18. Kindergarten Student-Led Conference
19. High School Student-Led Conference
20. Schoolwide Structures for Student-Led Conferences
21. Kindergartners as Experts—Celebrations of Learning
22. Students Share Work That Matters with an Authentic Audience—Celebrations of Learning
23. Passage Presentations in Secondary Schools
24. Why Use a Standards-Based Grading System?
25. Habits of Work Prepare Students for College—Standards-Based Grading
26. Understanding Grades in a Standards-Based Grading System
27. Schoolwide Structures for Standards-Based Grading

You can also view the video clips at the following site:
www.wiley.com/go/expedlearning

To the students and staff in

EL Education schools—past and present

Foreword

For too long the national education debate has been stuck in a series of perceived paradoxes: do we need more testing or no testing at all? Is the key to school change a culture set by principals or the engagement of the students? To get dramatically different results do we need teachers to change their practices or do we need districts to change their practices? Whose fault is it and what does it take for us to get better?

Positioned at the center of this debate are a series of school models posed as opposites—more structured direct instructional models in which students are sitting in rows and mastering facts, or school as we too often see it now where students are assigned low level tasks without knowing what they are doing, why they are doing it, or what they will know when it is over.

The problem is that too much of the national debate focuses on a series of false dichotomies: that we must either choose rigor or child centered instruction, but not both; that we must either focus on curriculum design or focus on results, but not both; that we must build systems that authentically engage students or systems that deliver authentic student results, but not both.

Enter EL Education, the refreshing antidote to that debate and an organization with a long track record of building and sustaining success with students of every age and background in schools across the country. From King Middle School in Portland, Maine to the Odyssey School in Denver, EL Education has succeeded by inspiring students, supporting teachers, and engaging parents.

Rather than more or less testing, the EL Education model insists on making testing useful, focusing on weekly and even daily assessment data that help teachers understand what students know and how to design instruction to best fill the gaps that remain.

As you'll see in the following pages, EL Education leaders have done all this by being deeply committed to gathering data on student performance and using it to guide instruction and accountability. Data is used to measure student progress and alter teaching techniques to enhance the learning experience on an individual level. That's matched with regular, descriptive feedback so students know exactly where they are succeeding and where they need to focus their attention.

Long before the nation began discussing Common Core standards, EL Education was working with thousands of educators to design learning targets that expressed clear, shared understanding for what students should know and be able to do. Long before the country was talking about building a curriculum with fewer, clearer and higher standards, EL Education was building expeditions that prioritized depth over breadth, and analysis over memorization. Long before the country began a debate about how grit, work ethic, and school culture drove individual and collective success, EL Education was committed to building school cultures that intentionally developed character traits, and in pioneering ways to evaluate and develop those characteristics in every child.

When students leave a school like Denver's Odyssey School, they are prepared to enter the most rigorous traditional high school programs available. They have not only learned, they have learned *how to learn.*

In the past, the schools that were more student-centered were not results-focused. That helped perpetuate a national debate that we could either have schools with rigor and structure or with freedom and mediocrity. EL Education has defied this by building school environments with real accountability linked to cultures intentionally built around student engagement.

One of the best examples of this is the passage presentation, a high-stakes assessment that requires students to do far more than successfully pass a standardized test; it requires that they reflect on what they learned and why they learned it, apply that knowledge to other content, and answer real time questions from adult professionals about their learning process and product. A process not unlike what most students experience before a doctoral dissertation defense, this process is in place for EL Education students from the elementary level to the high school level and has helped build a culture of intense intellectual discourse, high-stakes accountability, and student-centered instruction all in the same space.

Using data, requiring accountability, giving feedback, creating daily assessments, letting students guide themselves as appropriate, celebrating learning and turning education into a journey—it all seems so simple, yet the concepts have eluded so many.

From an early belief that students should learn by doing, EL Education developed in-depth explorations of specific content that would help students focus on how to apply learning rather than how to recite it. In the years that have followed, EL Education has grown into a comprehensive model—that engages students in learning through connecting their own passion to new content, that provides explicit focus on character and culture, that sets high expectations and high levels of support for both students and teachers—and has shown the country that there is a way out of these educational paradoxes; it just requires that we look longer and deeper in the right places.

Let what follows serve as your guide to EL Education, a concept so successful but so simple that you will wonder aloud why it isn't universally available for those kids who would benefit from it most. Hopefully these pages inspire you to take some small steps to make sure that it is.

Denver, Colorado
September 2013

Mike Johnston
Colorado State Senator

Preface

Leaders of Their Own Learning is a practical, practitioner-created book. The stories, resources, strategies, and techniques described here come from the classrooms of EL Education schools across the United States. These classrooms are animated by the belief that when students and teachers are engaged in work that is challenging, adventurous, and meaningful, learning and achievement will flourish. For twenty years we have worked side by side with teachers and school leaders to create classrooms where teachers can fulfill their highest aspirations, and where students can achieve more than they think possible.

Two years ago, we made a commitment to making our approach more accessible and widely available to teachers beyond our immediate network. We saw the adoption of the Common Core State Standards and the growing national call for higher student achievement as an opportunity to reenvision teaching, learning, and assessment around a new definition of student achievement: one that marries mastery of rigorous academic content to equally important outcomes such as critical thinking, effective communication, collaboration, and the ability to reflect on one's learning, agency, and character.

We chose student-engaged assessment as the focus of our first book because these practices are the foundation for building a culture of engagement and achievement in any school. Student-engaged assessment develops student ownership of learning, which makes learning in any subject area, at any grade level, and in any kind of school richer, deeper, and more fulfilling. One young student, a sixth-grader, at Grass Valley Charter School in California, summed up the power of student-engaged assessment when she responded to a question about the usefulness of rubrics with this: "If I didn't get one, I'd create a rubric in my head, so I could set my goal and try to achieve it." When students take responsibility for their learning, they see themselves as the key actors in their own success.

We believe that teachers are innovators and creators. In that spirit, this book provides strong models of teacher and student work that can be used to develop student-engaged assessment practices and provoke conversations about what good teaching looks like. We present concrete tools—case studies, protocols, and videos—to help teachers implement these proven practices in their classrooms.

Teachers and school leaders in all kinds of schools—urban, rural, and suburban; district and charter; and at all grade levels—will be able to see themselves and their students in these pages and the accompanying videos. There are entry points to student-engaged assessment for every teacher, in every setting. With growing demand for new levels of rigor and engagement in our nation's classrooms, we have an opportunity to reimagine our profession and reconnect with the reasons we became teachers in the first place.

New York, NY
September 2013

Scott Hartl
President and CEO, EL Education

Acknowledgments

If you've ever tried to write a book in collaboration with twenty-five other people, you'll know that it's no easy task. The only thing that can make it easier is when those twenty-five people are some of the smartest and most dedicated you can find. We lucked out in that department—we found the very best. We owe a debt of gratitude to the following EL Education staff and teachers who gathered the stories from the schools that fill this book, and countless others who contributed in small but important ways. They all helped document the practices that make student-engaged assessment so transformational for students and their families:

- Stephanie Aberger
- Tony Altucher
- Mary Pat Ament
- Dale Bergerhofer
- Marcia DeJesús-Rueff
- Chris Dolgos
- Liza Eaton
- Cyndi Gueswel
- Symon Hayes
- Lucia Kaempffe
- Caitlin LeClair
- Steven Levy
- Dirk Matthias
- Jill Mirman
- Lily Newman
- Sharon Newman
- Deborah Pinto
- Suzanne Nathan Plaut
- Cindy Rice
- Meg Riordan
- Sheri Scarborough
- Corey Scholes
- Kippy Smith
- Colleen Stanevich

Special thanks to our videographer, David Grant, whose value to this project is indescribable. His technical video skills, combined with his sixteen years as an

EL Education educator, bring student-engaged assessment practices to life in a way that no one but David could achieve.

Our heartfelt thanks and admiration goes to all of the EL Education teachers and school leaders whose work has helped us codify these student-engaged assessment practices, particularly those who welcomed us into their classrooms to learn from them and their students. Finally, thank you to the William and Flora Hewlett Foundation for their financial support and visionary leadership for the Deeper Learning outcomes that can transform our schools and ensure that our students develop the skills, knowledge, and competencies they will need to succeed in college, in their careers, and as global citizens.

About the Authors

Ron Berger is chief academic officer for EL Education, overseeing resources and professional learning for schools nationally. Berger works closely with the Harvard Graduate School of Education, where he did his graduate work, and currently teaches a course that uses exemplary student work to illuminate Common Core State Standards. Prior to his work with EL Education and Harvard, Berger was a public school teacher and master carpenter in rural Massachusetts for more than twenty-five years.

Berger is an Annenberg Foundation Teacher Scholar and received the Autodesk Foundation National Teacher of the Year award. His previous books include *An Ethic of Excellence* and *A Culture of Quality.* Berger's writing and speaking center on inspiring quality and character in students, specifically through project-based learning, original scientific and historical research, service learning, and the infusion of arts. He works with the national character education movement to embed character values into the core of academic work.

Leah Rugen has worked as an educator and writer for more than twenty years. Beginning her career as a high school English teacher, she went on to be part of the founding staff at EL Education. Rugen previously worked at the Center for Collaborative Education for twelve years as writer and editor, school coach, and program director of the national Turning Points network. She is the author of several books including *Understanding Learning: Assessment in the Turning Points School* and *Creating Small Schools: A Handbook for Raising Equity and Achievement.*

Libby Woodfin is the director of publications for EL Education. Woodfin started her career as a fifth- and sixth-grade teacher, and went on to become a counselor at a large comprehensive high school before arriving at EL Education in 2008. Throughout her career Woodfin has written articles, chapters, and books about important issues in education. Her first book was *Familiar Ground: Traditions That Build School Community.*

About EL Education

EL Education

EL Education is one of the nation's leading K–12 education organizations committed to creating classrooms where teachers can fulfill their highest aspirations and where students can achieve more than they think possible. For more than twenty years, EL Education has helped new and veteran teachers—in all types of school settings—strive for a vision of student success that joins academic achievement, character, and high-quality work. Our approach is grounded in respect for teachers and school leaders as creative agents in their classrooms. We build their capacity to ignite each student's motivation, persistence, and compassion so that they become active contributors to building a better world and succeed in school, college, career, and life.

The EL Education model is characterized by the following:

- Active instructional and student-engaged assessment practices that build academic skills and students' ownership of their learning
- Rigorous academic projects connected to real-world issues that meet state and Common Core standards
- A culture of learning that builds persistence, collaboration, critical thinking, problem solving, communication, and independence in every student

EL Education offers a comprehensive suite of professional development, coaching, Common Core curriculum, publications, and online tools to support schools to be engaging environments where kids love to learn and teachers love to teach. For more information, visit www.elschools.org.

Introduction

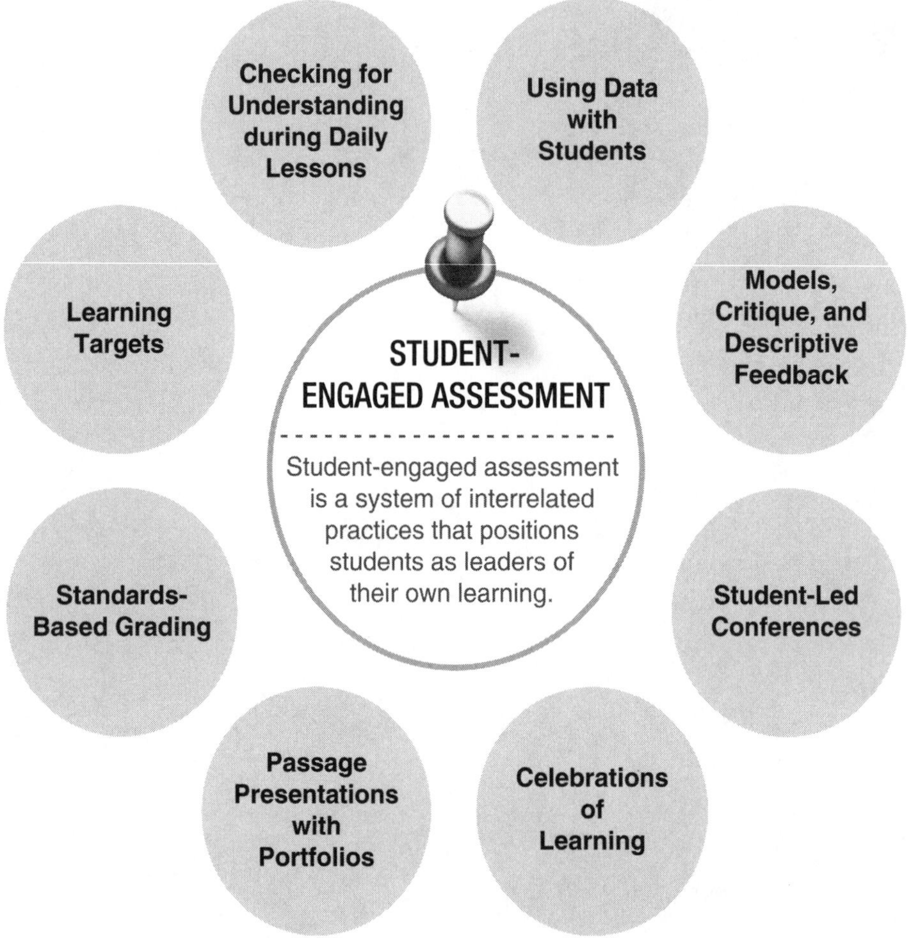

Checking for Understanding during Daily Lessons

Using Data with Students

Learning Targets

Models, Critique, and Descriptive Feedback

STUDENT-ENGAGED ASSESSMENT

Student-engaged assessment is a system of interrelated practices that positions students as leaders of their own learning.

Standards-Based Grading

Student-Led Conferences

Passage Presentations with Portfolios

Celebrations of Learning

Matthew, a shy sixth-grade student, approached my desk on a June morning looking very nervous. "I don't think I'm ready," he said. In a few hours he would be presenting his portfolio of work to a panel that included the superintendent, school board members, community members, and visiting educators. He would have a presentation partner—a friend—supporting him, but it was really up to him. He had to present and reflect on evidence of his learning in order to graduate. This was Matthew's first year in the school and he had come with some significant weaknesses in academic skills. He knew he had to address this honestly. We had done a great deal of preparation and rehearsal, but he was still terribly nervous.

All of my students had been nervous since the first day of school in September when they learned about the presentations. I worked with them to turn their apprehension into anticipation. I knew that if students felt nervous, it meant that they cared about the outcome. This kind of energy, harnessed and focused, drove them through their sixth-grade year. Knowing these presentations were coming, students worked hard all year, with high standards for the work they produced. They would have an audience for their work—was it good enough? They would be questioned by a panel—did they understand their disciplinary concepts well enough to explain them? They had strengths and challenges as learners—could they describe them well? They were on a yearlong mission to prove that they were ready and that they had work that was worthy.

Over the course of two days, every sixth-grader presented portfolios of work in academics, arts, fitness, and character. They shared final drafts and early drafts, rubrics and charts, quantitative and qualitative assessment data, writing and math samples, journals and reflections. Some of them gave live performances of readings, drama, music, or dance. They shared their achievements, challenges, and goals and gave evidence of why they were ready for promotion.

Some of the students were natural presenters. Others overcame shyness, language challenges, physical and cognitive challenges. They all succeeded. One student with cerebral palsy had a particular challenge in presenting, and needed her presentation partner to voice her reflections about her work for her and to carry documents to the panel.

Though her speech was difficult to understand, the words her partner spoke for her were hers, the work was hers, and the success was hers.

I did not get to watch Matthew's presentation that morning. I was back in the classroom teaching and helping students prepare. That evening I watched his presentation on video and I couldn't have been more proud. He opened with these words: "The first thing I would like to share with you is that this was my first year at this school. . . . It's been a challenge for me fitting in and making friends. But, I did. I came to this school with some strengths, but also some weaknesses. Some of my weaknesses were that I wasn't that strong in writing, and in math I was about two years behind grade level. But, in the first few months of school I worked really hard and I caught up to grade level. And by now I have actually passed it. As you can see here in my math work . . ."

Matthew went on to describe his work and growth with candor, insight, and pride. My wife was sitting next to me on the couch and turned to me, amazed. She asked, "Could you have done that in sixth grade?" I thought, no way. I didn't understand myself as a learner; I didn't own my learning.

—Ron Berger

Students as Leaders of Their Own Learning

The presentations mentioned in the chapter-opening vignette are just one part of a larger assessment system. This system has unique power—it puts students at the center and students in the lead. It is more than a framework for evaluation. It is a framework for motivation and a framework for achievement. When students succeed in school and life one doesn't usually assume that their success is fueled by smart assessment. But it can be. This book describes a system of assessment—student-engaged assessment—that does just that.

Student-engaged assessment involves students in understanding and investing in their own growth. It changes the primary role of assessment from evaluating and ranking students to motivating them to learn. It empowers students with the understanding of where they need to go as learners and how to get there. It builds the independence, critical thinking skills, perseverance, and self-reflective understanding students need for college and careers and that is required by the Common Core State Standards. And, because student-engaged assessment practices demand reflection, collaboration, and responsibility, they shepherd students toward becoming positive citizens and human beings.

Student-engaged assessment changes the primary role of assessment from evaluating and ranking students to motivating them to learn. It builds the independence, critical thinking skills, perseverance, and self-reflective understanding students need for college and careers and that is required by the Common Core State Standards.

Student-engaged assessment encompasses a wide array of practices that bring students into the process of assessing their growth and learning. They gain a deeper sense of their progress and ultimately become more independent learners. Through student-engaged assessment, students learn the language of standards and metacognition, set academic goals and monitor progress, identify patterns of strengths and weaknesses, become self-advocates, and assess their own work with a striking degree of honesty and accuracy.

This is assessment at its best—when students know what is expected of them and when teachers are precisely attuned to support them to meet academic standards. Yet, assessment can be more than a measure. The right set of assessment tools can also motivate students, provide models for high-quality work, lead students to discovery, serve teachers as forms of instructional feedback, contribute to a sense of classroom community, and invest school activities with a strong sense of purpose. In short, assessment not only measures growth but also has the power to stimulate it.

Student-engaged assessment practices equip teachers and students to use assessments—from frequent checks for understanding that occur multiple times throughout daily lessons to traditional end-of-unit tests—to monitor progress. Although assessment is most often seen as something done to students, the root meaning of the word *assess* is "to sit beside." When schools adopt student-engaged assessment practices, teachers and parents will find themselves often sitting beside students, discussing with them the quality of their work and thinking, and their plans for growth and improvement.

Why Student-Engaged Assessment Matters: A New Way of Thinking about What Students Can Do

The most important assessments that take place in any school building are seen by no one. They take place inside the heads of students, all day long. Students assess what they do, say, and produce, and decide what is good enough. These internal assessments govern how much they care, how hard they work, and how much they learn. They govern how kind and polite they are and how respectful and responsible. They set the standard for what is "good enough" in class. In the end, these are the assessments that really matter. All other assessments are in service of this goal—to get inside students' heads and raise the bar for effort and quality.

Student-engaged assessment is effective because it draws on these internal assessments that occur naturally for students. Unfortunately, students and teachers often don't know how to tap into this level of assessment and learn how to capitalize on it. Students frequently have widely varying internal standards for quality and aren't clear about what "good enough" looks like. Some students have internalized a sense that they don't have a value or voice in a classroom setting and that anything they do will be inferior to the work of the "smart kids." In other cases, they believe they have only one chance to do something and begin to work from a place of compliance and completion rather than working toward quality through a series of attempts.

Teachers frequently fall into the trap of simply saying, "try harder" without giving students specific targets, feedback, time to revise, and a purpose for doing quality work. What students really need are tools and support to assess and improve their own learning and the motivation to do so. Motivation is in fact the most important result of student-engaged assessment—unless students find reason and inspiration to care about learning and have hope that they can improve, excellence and high achievement will remain the domain of a select group. The following sections describe the key reasons why student-engaged assessment practices matter.

Motivating Students to Care

Nothing is more important in fostering growth in students than the degree to which they care. Recent research suggests that student perseverance, grit, and self-discipline correlate strongly with academic success (Blackwell, Trzesniewski, & Dweck, 2007; Duckworth & Seligman, 2005; Dweck, Walton, & Cohen 2011;

Good, Aronson, & Inzlicht, 2003; Oyserman, Terry, & Bybee, 2002; Walton & Cohen, 2007). This will not surprise teachers or parents—it is common sense. But these "noncognitive" strengths are entirely based on the degree to which students care about their learning and their growth. If students don't care, they are not going to work hard.

The apathy, disconnection, or lack of self-esteem that causes students to disengage in school—to stop caring—is not inherent. It is learned behavior. Kindergartners come to school excited to learn. In the course of their schooling, however, some students lose touch with their ability to thrive in a school environment. School becomes something that is done to them, something that they are not good at. They may feel they are good at sports, music, or video games, but school is just not a place where they succeed. Their test scores and grades make this clear. Student-engaged assessment puts students back in the driver's seat, in charge of their own success. It makes clear to them that hard work and practice pays off—just as it does for them in sports, music, or video games—and that the immediate, clear feedback they get in these other pursuits can also guide their academic progress.

Most important, student-engaged assessment supports students to do work that they are proud of, which motivates them to step up to challenges. As Mike McCarthy, principal of King Middle School in Portland, Maine, puts it in chapter 6, "Anytime you make the work public, set the bar high, and are transparent about the steps to make a high-quality product, kids will deliver."

Changing Mindsets

Student-engaged assessment requires and inspires students and teachers to change their mindsets about intelligence, effort, and success. As they experience success and track actual progress, their positive mindsets strengthen. They recognize the connections among their attitude, effort, practice, and increased achievement.

It doesn't mean an easy ride, as the story of a third-grader struggling with reading in chapter 3 illustrates. Her teacher, Jean Hurst, underscores the role of student-engaged assessment in changing her mindset: "Although she's still not at grade level, she's made two years of progress, and making that progress visible through the use of data has helped Jacelyn to become a more motivated and informed reader." Rather than getting stuck with a view of herself as a "poor reader," she realized that with effort and support she could and would catch up.

Student-engaged assessment helps students see the connection between effort and achievement.

Engaging Students as Leaders of Their Own Learning

As students are given the tools to understand and assess their own strengths and challenges, their ability to take ownership increases. In very concrete ways, students become leaders of their own learning—understanding learning targets, tracking their progress, using feedback to revise their work, and presenting their learning publicly—and partners with their teachers. In our video series you will see students looking directly into the camera, explaining how student-engaged assessment practices work and how they have benefited. Their comments are genuine and unrehearsed.

Teaching Reflection

Skillful reflection is at the core of becoming a self-directed learner and thus is essential for college and career readiness. Student-engaged assessment builds reflection into every step of the process, ensuring that students develop the skills to reflect deeply and concretely, beyond vague statements of preferences, strengths, and weaknesses. This process can begin in kindergarten. As kindergarten teacher Jane Dunbar describes in chapter 4, "I then ask the group, 'What would you do on the next draft if this were yours?' And 'What would you change?' I challenge them for details." Imagine the power of building this ability to reflect on drafts over years of practice.

Building a Culture of Collaboration, Trust, and Evidence

A strong schoolwide and classroom culture is both a requirement and a result of student-engaged assessment. First, students need to know that their teachers care about and respect them. In the context of a collaborative and trusting culture, student-engaged assessment practices produce tremendous results for students—their ongoing reflection on evidence of their learning leads to increased achievement and growth.

Within a school culture that respects students and teachers and explicitly focuses on their capacity to grow and improve, a different concept of evidence develops. Instead of relying almost entirely on a single source of evidence—a yearly test—to assess students and teachers, evidence is collected, cited, and used everywhere, all day and all year, to promote growth. Teachers and students collect qualitative and quantitative data and analyze those data to understand the trends of their strengths and struggles in order to help them improve.

Strengthening Home-School Connections

Student-engaged assessment engages families in their children's learning at many levels. When student progress is reported clearly and transparently, and standards are made accessible and understandable, families are reassured. They gain confidence in their relationship with the school. Nothing is more powerful for a family than witnessing their child's self-confidence and joy in learning as they present and share their work in student-led conferences, celebrations of learning, and passage presentations.

What the Research Says

Our work in student-engaged assessment draws heavily on the work of Rick Stiggins and his colleagues at the Assessment Training Institute, pioneers in the field of assessment (Stiggins, 2005; Stiggins, Arter, Chappuis, & Chappuis, 2006). Their work has brought assessment for learning strategies (formative assessment) to classrooms around the country, helping teachers and students see the power of assessment as a tool to support improvement and further learning, rather than just a way to measure learning at a fixed point in time. You will see many formative assessment strategies throughout our student-engaged assessment book; however, our approach widens the focus from the instructional strategies that are at the center of formative assessment to strategies that improve school culture, elevate leadership roles for students, engage families and communities, and deeply affect curriculum.

Formative assessments are assessments for learning that occur frequently at the outset of and during learning to enable teachers to adapt instruction and foster student improvement, such as entrance or exit tickets, whereas **summative assessments** are assessments of learning that reflect student progress at a particular point in time, such as formal essays.

There is ample evidence that formative assessment increases student achievement, improves the quality of instruction, and increases motivation. In the most prominent study, Black and Wiliam (1998) found that gains in achievement associated with formative assessment nearly doubled their rate of learning. In *Advancing Formative Assessment in Every Classroom,* Moss and Brookhart (2009) survey a range of research that supports the powerful effect of formative assessment on teacher efficacy. "In a very real way it flips a switch, shining a bright light on individual teaching decisions so that teachers can see clearly (and perhaps for the first time) the difference between the intent and the effect of their actions" (p. 10). A similar transformation occurs in the motivation of students when they are taught that intelligence is malleable and growth comes through effort (Dweck, 2006; Vispoel & Austin, 1995). Thus, formative assessment can be used to build confidence and empower student ownership over learning and growth (Yin, Shavelson, Ayala, Ruiz-Primo, Brandon, & Furtak, 2008).

Student-Engaged Assessment and the Common Core

The Common Core State Standards usher in a unique moment in US education—an opportunity to raise the bar for rigor, critical thinking, problem solving, and communication skills. The standards themselves, with their precise technical language, are not typically inspirational for students or, for that matter, teachers. However, they represent educational ideas and capacities that can be genuinely inspiring. The standards have the potential to catalyze fundamental improvement in teaching and learning across the country.

The standards will not live up to their potential, however, if teachers do not know how to transform their instruction to meet these new goals. The standards demand a different type of teaching and learning. Essential to the new Common Core classroom is a sophisticated and sharp system of assessment that continually checks for understanding. And—the standards are explicit about this—a system that involves students in critiquing, reflecting, and revising. The skills embedded in student-engaged assessment—reflection and self-assessment, use of feedback, goal-setting, revision, and presentation—are integral to meeting the rigorous demands of the Common Core State Standards.

The math and literacy standards prioritize students' ability to work independently, to problem solve, to communicate ideas with evidence, and to critique the ideas of others. They demand a system of assessment that does not put students in the role of being passive recipients of information but rather active agents in monitoring, communicating, and promoting their own growth. The strategies described in this book provide teachers with the ongoing, daily information they need to adjust lessons and provide students with effective support so that they can all meet the demands of the Common Core. Just as important, the strategies and structures help students learn to self-assess, set meaningful goals, and take ownership of the journey toward reaching standards.

Beyond Individual Practices to an Integrated System

This book is for teachers and school leaders who wish to implement a student-engaged assessment system in their schools. Although there are many possible entry points, and many practices may be implemented by a single teacher working with his or her students, the ultimate goal is to create an integrated schoolwide approach to student-engaged assessment. Each chapter offers how-to advice for teachers and school leaders interested in developing a strong and comprehensive system of student-engaged assessment that will help students meet state and Common Core standards and raise student achievement. These practices require substantial commitment from teachers and school leaders who must be willing to work collaboratively to restructure classrooms and schools.

Indeed, to fully implement a student-engaged assessment system requires a mindset that goes beyond "how-to" and represents a new way of thinking about assessment. Schools must rethink the nature of class tests and report cards, rethink

Student voice is at the heart of student-engaged assessment.

how the data from class, school, district, and state assessments can be understood and used by students and teachers together to contribute to student growth, and rethink the notion that some students will succeed in school and others will fail.

The rewards for taking on this work are extensive. The schools we work with that have fully adopted student-engaged assessment have found strong results, evidenced in high test scores, high graduation and college acceptance rates, high-quality student work and thinking, and community understanding and pride (see figure I.1). This book draws heavily on the experiences of students, teachers, and school leaders in our schools around the country. You will hear their voices throughout the book. The stories and voices are not just seasoning, however. They are the heart and soul of student-engaged assessment.

It bears repeating that unless students care about learning, they will not make significant progress. When an eighth-grade student declares, "I know I understand the learning target when I feel the confidence to say, 'I can,'" it reflects an uncommon investment and awareness of his role in learning. Jessica Wood, a sixth-grade English language arts teacher at the Springfield Renaissance School in Springfield, Massachusetts, reminds us that the purpose of student-engaged assessment is to reach each individual student: "It's not just the recalcitrant rebel kid. It is also the quiet girl in the front row. For those children, the checking for understanding strategies [and all of the other strategies and structures] give them a voice." Student-engaged assessment practices are transferable to any school environment in which educators are committed to igniting the capacity of students to take responsibility for their learning.

Figure I.1 Student Achievement in Schools Implementing Student-Engaged Assessment Practices

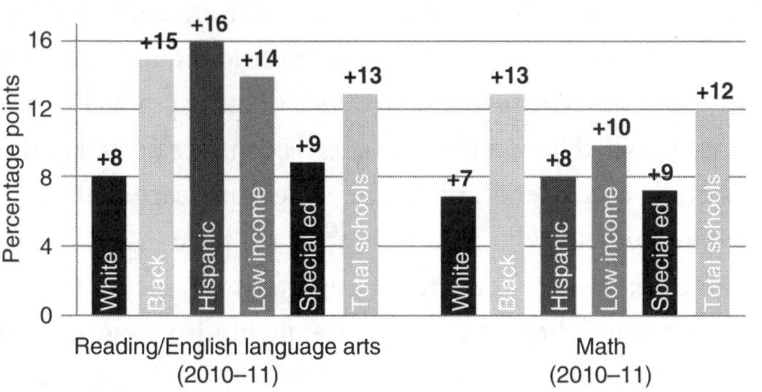

EL Education mentor schools are leaders in student-engaged assessment practices. In 2010–11, their students outscored their peers by an average of 13 percentage points in reading/English language arts and 12 percentage points in math.

About This Book: A Multimedia Toolkit for Teachers and Leaders

This book contains chapters on eight key practices that will engage students in making academic progress, improve achievement, and involve families and communities in the life of the school. Each chapter describes a practice, gives advice on how to begin, and explains what teachers and school leaders need to put it into practice in their own classrooms and schools. The chapters include descriptive text, resources, advice, and stories from schools successfully using the practice. The written text of the book is supplemented by the *Core Practices in Action* video series—found on the accompanying DVD and pointed to throughout the book—which takes key strategies and animates them in real schools with real students, to serve as models, to raise questions, and to stimulate discussion. Also accompanying the book is a suite of appendixes to support and enrich implementation of these practices, which can be found on our website: www.elschools.org/leadersoftheirownlearning.

Although all of the practices have an impact on the day-to-day teaching and learning occurring in the classroom, chapters 5 through 8 also focus on communicating learning and achievement with an outside audience. Each of the distinct communication structures represents a significant moment in time when students and teachers reflect on progress and understanding, describe achievements and challenges, and mark important transitions.

Chapter 1: Learning Targets

Learning targets are the foundation of a student-engaged assessment system. They translate state and Common Core standards into learning goals for lessons, projects, units, and courses, and are written in student-friendly language that is concrete and understandable. Because learning targets must come from teachers' deep understanding of the standards they need to teach, they are the foundation and the connective tissue of a student-engaged assessment system. All other practices refer back to them. Learning targets, which begin with the stem "I can," are posted in the classroom and tracked carefully by students and teachers. Because learning targets are written for and owned by students who are striving to say, "I can . . .," they are an essential ingredient in the *engaged* part of student-engaged assessment.

The learning targets chapter will help teachers write quality learning targets based on state and Common Core standards; develop the supporting learning targets that guide daily lessons; align standards, learning targets, and assessments; and create character learning targets that help students track their progress toward good work habits and citizenship. This chapter also supports school leaders on the key decisions and actions necessary to work toward schoolwide implementation of learning targets.

Chapter 2: Checking for Understanding during Daily Lessons

Checking for understanding embeds assessment into instructional practice. It includes all of the minute-by-minute ways that a teacher checks to make sure that students understand the content of a lesson. Checking for understanding strategies help students monitor and articulate their progress toward learning targets and guide teachers toward adjustments in instruction to ensure that all students understand the material and are able to meet state and Common Core standards. As with the other components of the student-engaged assessment system, checking for understanding strategies produce useful, immediate feedback for teachers and students.

This chapter guides teachers toward structuring lessons to maximize opportunities to check for understanding and offers numerous concrete strategies to do so, ranging from strategic questioning and observation to quick-check strategies such as go-arounds, exit tickets and human bar graphs. This chapter also supports school leaders to set manageable schoolwide priorities for implementing the practice and building a culture of strong practice.

Chapter 3: Using Data with Students

Reflective teachers and school leaders collect and analyze data to understand student achievement, assess teaching practices, and make informed decisions about instruction. However, if students are to be primary agents in their learning, they also must learn to make sense of and use data related to their performance.

This chapter focuses on classroom practices that build student capacity to assess, analyze, and use data effectively to reflect, set goals, and document growth toward mastery of state and Common Core standards. These practices help students learn to use their classwork and interim assessments as data sources that help them analyze their strengths, weaknesses, and patterns in order to improve their work. In this way, even standardized test data can become useful evidence of learning and feedback with which students can engage. School leaders and teachers will be guided in developing a culture in which students understand that intelligence is malleable and that they can improve with practice and persistence.

Chapter 4: Models, Critique, and Descriptive Feedback

When the quality of student work is weak, it's usually for a very simple reason—the students have never seen a good example of the work assigned. Whether the assignment is a persuasive essay, a geometric proof, or a history report, most students have never analyzed what a strong model of that work actually looks like. Many teachers offer verbal or written descriptions of their expectations, and sometimes rubrics, but without models of quality work, those descriptions are just words. They don't create a vision of quality in students' minds. This chapter guides teachers to use strong models of work and analyze them during critique lessons with students to collectively create a vision of quality.

We distinguish between descriptive feedback, in which a teacher or peer provides an individual with specific and helpful feedback to help him or her improve a piece of work, and critique lessons, in which a whole class uses models of strong and weak work to identify the criteria for quality work that will guide a lesson or project. Both require students to engage in discussions of what makes quality work and how they can use their knowledge, skills, and resources to improve and grow.

This chapter will help teachers and schools build cultures that are conducive to giving and receiving feedback, develop protocols for critique lessons, and provide students with the skills they need to act on feedback and to self-assess their progress toward established criteria for success. These interrelated practices are key tools in helping students master learning targets and meet state and Common Core standards.

Chapter 5: Student-Led Conferences

Student-led conferences give students a leadership role in communicating their progress to their families. They are a key strategy for engaging students deeply in assessing their own work and motivating them to improve. Student-led conferences are also highly effective at involving nearly all families in the learning process. Student-led conferences are meetings with students, families, and teachers during which students share their progress toward mastery of academic and character learning targets and state and Common Core standards. Whether at the kindergarten level or the high school level, student-led conferences are facilitated by students, who discuss and reflect on their learning and set goals for improvement.

The student-led conferences chapter guides teachers and school leaders through the key decisions necessary to set up student-led conferences, including communicating with families, defining roles for participants, and preparing students to lead quality conferences.

Chapter 6: Celebrations of Learning

Celebrations of learning are another key student-engaged assessment practice that is focused on communicating learning. Although we use the term *celebration* (and these events are indeed community celebrations), they are most importantly student exhibitions of high-quality work that impel students to work hard in class all semester. Celebrations of learning are culminating grade-level or schoolwide events during which students display and present high-quality finished work to the school community, families, and members of the wider community. Often student performances are a part of celebrations of learning. Such events provide an authentic opportunity for students to reflect on their progress and tell the story of their learning journey.

This chapter will help teachers prepare their students for celebrations of learning—including the self-reflection on progress toward learning targets, state and Common Core standards, and habits of scholarship that lead up to the event and the revisions necessary for students to display and present their highest-quality work. School leaders will be guided in setting up the structures and systems necessary to host a community-wide event that reflects joy in learning as well as academic and artistic excellence.

Chapter 7: Passage Presentations with Portfolios

Passage presentations and portfolios are two distinct but interrelated practices within a student-engaged assessment system that require students to document and communicate evidence of their learning. They are closely linked to student-led conferences, which often lay the groundwork for passage presentations. A portfolio is a collection of student work that evidences student progress toward mastery of learning targets derived from state and Common Core standards, growth in habits of scholarship, and personal goals in academics, arts, and character. Passage presentations are benchmark demonstrations of learning over multiple years that mark pivotal transitions during a student's schooling (e.g., at the conclusion of elementary, middle, or high school; at key grade levels, such as second, fifth, eighth, or tenth). During the presentations, students use their portfolios as a guide to articulate their proficiency and growth.

This chapter will guide teachers toward the productive use of portfolios as living documents that are a vital part of the classroom. Important questions such as "what goes into portfolios and what gets left out?" and "how will progress on habits of scholarship be reflected?" are addressed. This chapter will also support teachers and school leaders to set up the structures necessary to implement passage presentations that effectively include educators, families, and community members.

Chapter 8: Standards-Based Grading

In a standards-based grading system, grades communicate clearly about a student's current achievement on standards. Of all the practices within a student-engaged assessment system, it is perhaps the most complex. It is best implemented as a schoolwide structure with district support, because it represents a change in the traditional model of grading and reporting in schools. Standards-based grading is closely linked to all of the other student-engaged assessment practices. State and Common Core standards are shaped into priority learning targets—written in student-friendly language—and grades are determined through evidence-based assessments of those learning targets. Standards-based grading is grounded in several key principles: grades must accurately describe a student's progress and current level of achievement; habits of scholarship should be assessed and reported separately; grades are for communication, not motivation or punishment; grades must be specific enough in what they measure that it is clear what students need to work on to improve; and student engagement is key to the grading process.

The standards-based grading chapter will help schools set up the structures and expectations necessary to transform grading and reporting into a tool that promotes student accountability and motivation and gives families clarity on what students can do to improve. Extensive examples of faculty grading guides, grade books, and other resources will bring the practice to life.

Last year I joined student ambassadors at the Springfield Renaissance School in Springfield, Massachusetts, as they gave Governor Deval Patrick a tour of their school. For the third consecutive year, the school was poised to send 100 percent of its graduates on to college, a remarkable achievement for an urban district school. Governor Patrick was there to honor the school and learn from its success. He posed a question to a student ambassador: "Destiny, would you say you are a good student?"

Destiny paused before responding: "That's a hard question," she said. "My habits of work learning targets are excellent. My academic learning targets are a mix—I'm still struggling to meet some of them." Now the governor paused: "Learning targets?" he said. Destiny clarified: "The goals for what we need to know and be able to do." The governor smiled. "Yes. Course objectives, lesson objectives. I know those." Destiny shook her head. "No, sir. These are not the teacher's course objectives. Learning targets belong to students. These are the things that I have to demonstrate that I can do well. I need to show evidence that I can factor equations and write essays or explain a concept in history—things like that."

The governor nodded. "Interesting. And what are 'habits of work'" learning targets?" Destiny was quick to answer. "Those are the most important targets of all. They are the study skills and habits we need to succeed in college and life. You *have* to focus on them here. That's why we all go to college."

—Ron Berger

The Foundation of Student-Engaged Assessment

The process of learning shouldn't be a mystery. Learning targets provide students with tangible goals that they can understand and work toward. Rather than the teacher taking on all of the responsibility for meeting a lesson's objectives, learning targets, written in student-friendly language and frequently reflected on, transfer ownership for meeting objectives from the teacher to the student. The seemingly simple work of reframing objectives written for teachers to learning targets, written for—and owned by—students, turns assessment on its head. The student becomes the main actor in assessing and improving his or her learning.

Learning targets are goals for lessons, projects, units, and courses. They are derived from standards and used to assess growth and achievement. They are written in concrete, student-friendly language—beginning with the stem "I can"—shared with students, posted in the classroom, and tracked carefully by students and teachers during the process of learning. Students spend a good deal of time discussing and analyzing them and may be involved in modifying or creating them.

When the students in Lori Laliberte's kindergarten class at the Odyssey School in Denver learned that their "bessbugs" had died, they were sad. They had been observing and caring for the bugs as part of their study of the life cycle. The "bessbug" company agreed to send them new bugs and because one of the Common Core literacy standards for kindergartners (W.K.2) is, *Use a combination of drawing, dictating, and writing to inform informative/explanatory texts in which they name what they are writing about and supply some information about the topic,* the occasion provided an authentic opportunity to learn how to write a thank-you letter. Two learning targets guided their effort: "I can identify the main parts of a letter" and "I can explain the purpose of sending a letter." The students knew what their learning targets were from the outset of their lesson. In the accompanying video we see Laliberte's students actively working toward meeting these learning targets.

Watch video: "Using a Learning Target throughout a Lesson"

By translating standards into learning targets her students could make sense of, Laliberte engaged them as active partners in making progress. She knew they had met the target when they could say, "I can." The term *target* is significant. It emphasizes that students are aiming for something specific. Learning targets are meant to focus students in this way, directing their efforts and attention, as would a physical target. Every day, students discuss, reflect, track their progress, and assess their work in relation to learning targets. Learning targets build investment in learning by giving students the language to discuss what they know and what they need to learn. As an eighth-grader at the Odyssey School remarked, "The teacher will take time to break down the target, so we know where we're going with the learning."

Why This Practice Matters

Learning targets help students define what they are learning and why they are learning it, enabling them to monitor their progress toward the learning goal and giving them the language for and practice with metacognition. But why do these things matter? How does student ownership of learning make them better learners? How does self-monitoring increase student achievement? What's so special about metacognition? The answer lies in their power to motivate students to learn. Learning targets help stimulate that motivation.

Learning Targets Represent Clear, Manageable Goals

Among the dynamics for student motivation is the desire to take on challenges that call on a student's present capacity. In other words, students feel motivated to accomplish a task when they know it is within their reach.

Learning Targets Inherently Provide Short-Term Success

Motivation increases when students feel successful at previous attempts. Learning targets, by definition, break down abstract content standards into smaller learning tasks.

Learning Targets Let Students Know Where They Are

One of the hallmarks of student motivation is a sense of purpose. Motivated students know how the task at hand fits into the larger scheme of things. Reaching, or not quite reaching, a learning target represents critical information for students about what they know and can do, and what they still need to learn.

Common Core Connections

- The practice of writing learning targets deepens teachers' understanding of the standards and helps them prioritize the content and skills needed to meet them.
- The Common Core standards represent a big shift in how standards are manifest in K–12 classrooms. They are not simply about coverage of content; instead, they prioritize transferable skills that will enable students to be independent learners across all disciplines. Learning targets increase students' independence by bringing the standards to life, shifting ownership of meeting them from just the teacher to both the teacher and the student.

(continued)

- Character learning targets support students in developing the habits of scholarship (e.g., independence, self-direction) named in the standards and necessary to meet them.

Character learning targets, similar to academic learning targets, articulate specific expectations for students in language that promotes student understanding and ownership. Character learning targets relate to fostering a respectful community and commitment to learning.

GETTING STARTED

Writing Learning Targets

Choose a Standards-Based Lesson with Which to Get Started

Learning targets are derived from a number of sources—from Common Core, state, or local standards, school-developed habits of scholarship, or content area program materials. Some teachers work in schools where they have the autonomy to choose which standards they will address during a given time frame. Some work in schools where curriculum maps have already been developed by school-based leadership teams. Still others work in schools where curriculum decisions are made at the district level. In any case, teachers can employ learning targets in their classrooms to engage students in tracking their learning. When first getting started with learning targets, teachers should choose a lesson that meets required standards, that can be completed in one session, and that can be assessed during that time frame.

Write Learning Targets for the Lesson

It makes good sense to start small. After choosing a lesson, translate the objectives for that lesson into manageable, assessable, and student-friendly learning targets. It is important not to try to cover too much ground with the learning targets, especially when just getting started writing them. It may not be wise, for example, for a second-grade teacher to attempt to create her first learning targets for a daily lesson for the entire Common Core State Standard W.2.1: *Write opinion pieces in which they introduce the topic or book they are writing about, state an opinion, supply reasons that support the opinion, use linking words (e.g.,* because, and, also*) to connect opinion and reasons, and provide a concluding statement or*

These targets were derived from the fifth-grade Common Core writing standard, W.5.2: *Write informative/explanatory texts to examine a topic and convey ideas and information clearly.*

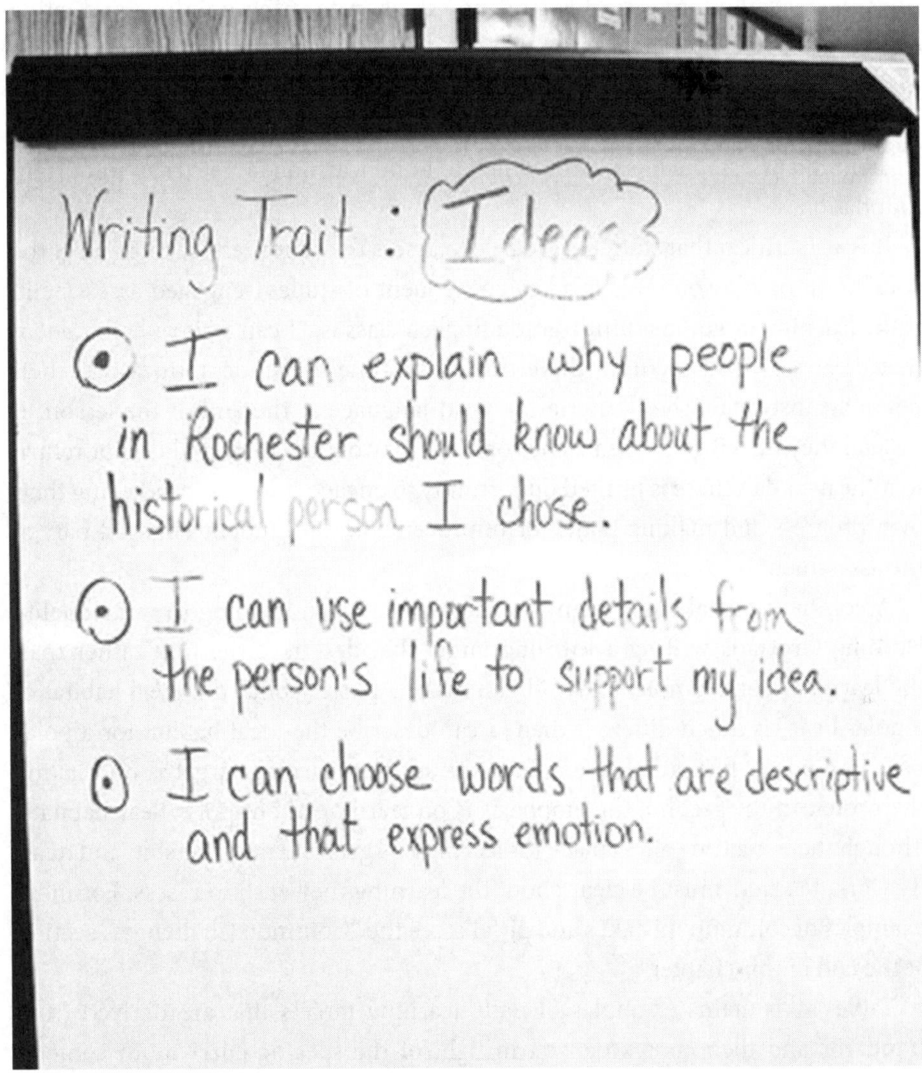

section. It would be more reasonable for her to choose one manageable and assessable component of this standard for which to create learning targets. For example, the teacher may decide that the most important place to start is for students to learn to form an opinion of a story they have read, supported by evidence. She may choose, "I can develop an opinion about my story," followed by, "I can craft one sentence that describes my opinion of my story," followed by, "I can support my opinion with one example from my story." A well-designed lesson that identifies the learning target, builds students' skills in forming opinions and citing evidence, and checks for their progress along the way and at the conclusion has a high likelihood of seeing most, if not all, students meeting the learning target during the lesson. For a teacher just getting started with learning targets, determining feasible and assessable lessons for which to build learning targets is an important foundation.

It is also critical that students are able to assess their progress during and at the conclusion of a lesson. This is a key component of student-engaged assessment. If the learning target in a ninth-grade English class is, "I can write a haiku poem that creates a vivid picture," there should be time for students to assess their poem against established criteria for vivid language at the end of the lesson. If instead they turn it in to the teacher on their way out the door and do not return to it the next day, there is limited opportunity to engage students in assessing their own progress and making plans for improvement. The student-engaged part of the assessment is lost.

A common mistake that many teachers make when learning to write quality learning targets is writing a learning target that describes the task rather than the learning. For example, to say "I can make a poster about the ideal habitat of a polar bear" is much different than "I can describe the ideal habitat for a polar bear in a poster format." The emphasis in the first learning target is on making the poster. In the second, the emphasis is on learning about polar bear habitats. Though there is a time and a place for learning targets on craftsmanship and quality work, teachers must be clear about the learning they wish to assess. For more examples of common mistakes and pitfalls, see the "Common Challenges" section at the end of this chapter.

Table 1.1 contains examples of daily learning targets that are derived from standards and then contextualized in light of the specific curriculum content. For example, the learning target "I can describe historical events that affected the Sacco and Vanzetti case using a primary source text" links to the Common Core reading standard, RI.9–10.8: *Delineate and evaluate the argument and specific claims in a text, assessing whether the reasoning is valid and the evidence is relevant and sufficient; identify false statements and fallacious reasoning.*

Table 1.1 Examples of Daily Learning Targets

Learning Targets for Younger Students	Learning Targets for Older Students
• I can describe the differences between living and nonliving things. • I can explain my reasons for sorting and classifying insects. • I can find words I want to use in books, word walls, and word cards. • I can write words that send a message.	• I can show two variable data on a scatter plot. • I can describe how photosynthesis and cellular respiration help an ecosystem maintain homeostasis. • I can describe historical events that affected the Sacco and Vanzetti case using a primary source text.

Using Learning Targets

Introduce the Learning Target(s) to Students at the Best Point in the Lesson

In most lessons, the learning targets are shared with students at the start of the lesson and then referred to throughout as teachers and students assess progress. Some teachers have students read the targets aloud, restate them to a classmate, or discuss them in small groups or as a class to ensure that they understand what they are aiming for. As students become more sophisticated with using learning targets, they may wish to critique or revise them. Teachers can choose to collaborate with students in revising them to be more clear, compelling, or measurable, and even in creating new learning targets. The process of sharing and discussing learning targets provides meaningful learning opportunities, especially for building key vocabulary. For example, in the accompanying video, we see Jon Exall's sixth-graders at the Odyssey School spend several minutes grappling with the term *primary source documents* before they start working toward the learning target "I can use primary source documents to develop introductory understanding and introductory research questions for our first immigration case study."

Watch video: "Students Unpack a Learning Target and Discuss Academic Vocabulary"

For some lessons, it is better to hold off on sharing learning targets with students until partway through the lesson. For lessons that open by engaging students with a mystery text—a provocative piece that stimulates interest and generates questions—or by enabling students to grapple with a new math concept or experiment with scientific or artistic materials, it may be best to delay revealing the learning targets so that students will not be constrained in their thinking or discoveries. After discussing the ideas that emerge, the learning targets can be introduced to frame the next steps of work.

Case Study

Finding the Right Time to Introduce a Daily Learning Target in an Algebra II Class at the Springfield Renaissance School in Springfield, Massachusetts

Just as they do every day, students in Hilary Ducharme's eleventh-grade algebra II class come into the room and get right to work grappling with new problems, which are written on the board. Today Ducharme has asked her students to FOIL a series of problems, multiplying terms within parentheses in a particular order (first, outer, inner, last). A quiet hum settles on the room. Students are working together in groups while Ducharme walks around taking attendance and checking in with individual students. As students finish, several of them walk to the board and write their solutions.

Students pull out their homework, a problem set with one of four long-term learning targets for the semester written at the top: "I can construct quadratic models to solve problems." Below that is the supporting learning target that Ducharme introduced to students the previous day: "I can find the zeroes of a quadratic function by completing the square." Students complete a reflection form about what was easy and challenging for them about the homework and then they check their "complete the square" solutions using the quadratic formula. This leads into a lively classwide debate about the pros and cons of using "complete the square" versus the quadratic formula. "I like to have them take a stand like that," Ducharme says. "It increases their engagement. Suddenly they are speaking passionately about quadratic models!"

It isn't until about thirty-five minutes into the class that Ducharme points out the new daily learning target to the students: "I can identify and factor a difference of two squares." She brings them back to the FOIL problems they had done in the first ten minutes of class. As they explore the patterns in the solutions, awareness begins to dawn on the students. They see that their solutions to those problems have put them well on their way to the conceptual understanding they need to meet the new learning target.

Ducharme is strategic about when she introduces students to the daily learning target. She doesn't think it's a good use of time to introduce the learning target before her students have had a chance to do some grappling on their own. She says, "It will be meaningless to them unless they've had some experience with it." In this case, Ducharme knew that the students should be able to see the patterns based on the rules they have already learned about quadratics. "This is the fourth year I've taught these learning targets," Ducharme says, "and by now I've had enough experience to know how to build students to those 'aha' moments."

Develop Techniques to Check for Student Understanding

In order for students to assess their progress toward meeting their learning targets, teachers must build in checkpoints along the way. For example, in the accompanying video Jason Shiroff employs several checking-for-understanding techniques as he probes his fourth- and fifth-graders' understanding of transition phrases while unpacking a learning target with them.

Watch video: "Students Unpack a Learning Target"

Even well-written learning targets will contribute little to engaging, supporting, and holding students accountable for their learning if they are not referred to and used actively during the lesson. In addition to frequent checks throughout a lesson, the end of a lesson is also an important moment for checking for understanding. A well-constructed debrief will enable students to reflect on their learning, returning to the day's learning targets to assess their progress.

There are a wide variety of techniques to check for student understanding and progress toward learning targets during the course of a lesson and at its conclusion. Among the possible strategies are the following:

- Hand signals (e.g., fist-to-five; thumbs up, down, or sideways; high, middle, or low)
- Written checks (e.g., whiteboards, exit tickets, guided practice)
- Verbal checks (e.g., cold-call questions, class go-arounds)
- Progress charts (e.g., students posting sticky notes, dots, checks, or initials)
- Peer check-ins (e.g., pair-shares, peer critique, small-group check-ins)
- Quick quizzes, written or verbal
- "Clicker" technology (e.g., computer-projected responses from all students)

See chapter 2 for more extensive discussion of these techniques.

Building in checkpoints along the way ensures that students understand the material and gives the teacher the opportunity to address learning gaps.

IN PRACTICE

Using Learning Targets over the Long Term

There are many layers to learning targets. Writing and using discrete learning targets for daily lessons is the first step in gaining facility with the practice. Employing learning targets for longer-term goals takes this work one step further, requiring that teachers consider the more sophisticated features of the practice:

- Prioritizing and contextualizing Common Core, state, and local standards
- Using long-term and supporting learning targets
- Integrating character learning targets
- Considering the rigor of learning targets
- Aligning standards, targets, and assessments

Prioritizing and Contextualizing Common Core, State, and Local Standards

It is one thing to transform the objectives for a lesson into learning targets, and quite another to do this work for all of the standards for a long-term project, unit, or course. Schools can prioritize standards by identifying the big ideas and enduring understandings they want students to master, and distinguishing between what's critical to know and be able to do and what's worth being familiar with. A schoolwide standards-based curriculum map is a solid foundation for planning and instruction and an invaluable tool for teachers. If a school does not have a curriculum map in place, teaching teams should work together to identify the standards that address the big ideas that are compelling and important for students and that can be reasonably addressed during the course of a project, unit, or course.

> "I know I understand the learning target when I feel the confidence to say 'I can.'"
>
> —*Eighth-grade student, Odyssey School, Denver*

Strategy Close Up: Using a Learning Target Concept Map

Hilary Ducharme uses vocabulary concept maps as visual representations of the learning targets for any given unit in her algebra II class at the Springfield Renaissance School in Springfield, Massachusetts. She creates the concept maps when introducing new long-term learning targets to her students as a way to foreshadow the learning. She and the students refer to the maps frequently as new learning targets, with new vocabulary, are introduced over days and weeks. Ducharme is careful that the visual arrangement of the vocabulary words also gives students information about their meaning. When students are reviewing for summative assessments, the words are a map of their learning throughout the unit. Ducharme finds the concept maps especially helpful for visual learners or students with Individual Education Plans (IEPs) who may need the extra support that the visual provides (see the vocabulary concept map).

This vocabulary concept map highlights the key vocabulary and learning targets for a unit on quadratic models.

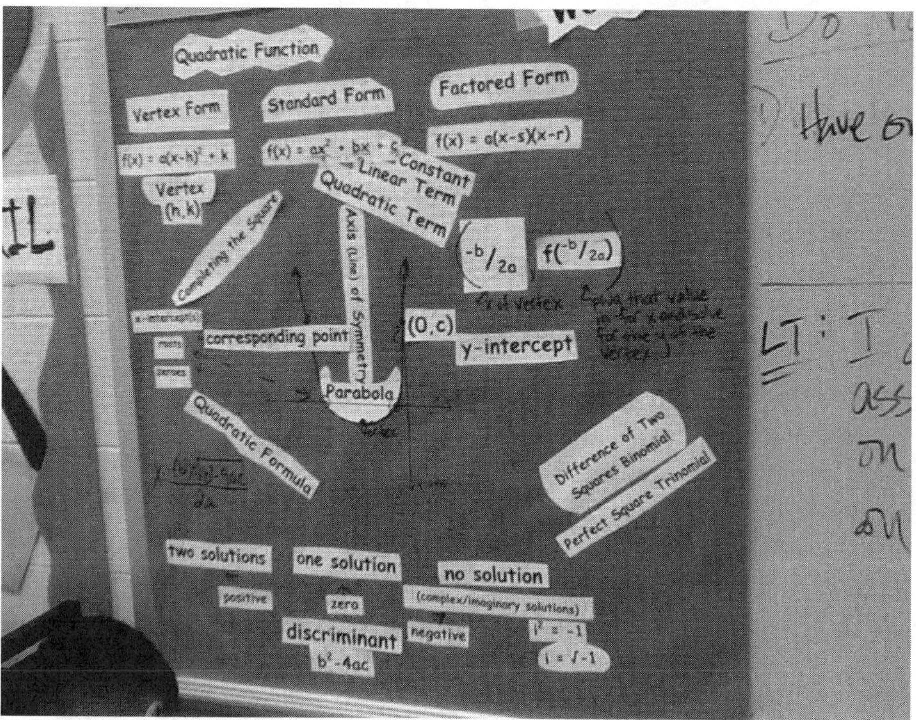

In the schools where our examples and stories are drawn from, the primary unit of study is the learning expedition. Learning expeditions are based on case studies that give broad topics a specific—often local—context. The specific context enables teachers to translate required standards on broad topics into learning targets that are meaningful to students in the context of a locally specific case study. Students are more likely to be engaged in protecting the river that runs through their neighborhood than they are in river ecosystems in general. In a school that does not have a curricular structure such as learning expeditions, choosing a locally relevant case study through which to study academic content makes the curriculum more compelling for students and increases engagement.

Learning expeditions are interdisciplinary studies, usually lasting six to twelve weeks, led by a teacher or teaching team. Learning expeditions are based on state and Common Core standards, aligned with local curriculum maps, and focused on essential content and skills. Each learning expedition includes guiding questions, kickoff experiences, case studies, projects, lessons, fieldwork, experts, service learning, and a culminating event that features high-quality student work.

To illustrate the prioritization and contextualization process, consider the "We All Live Downstream" learning expedition from the sixth grade at the Odyssey School. Students spent approximately three months studying Colorado's endangered Platte River. Using the school's curriculum map as a guide, instructional guide Liza Eaton worked with teachers to identify the key state science standards and Common Core literacy standards that they would address during the course of the learning expedition.

From there, they prioritized the most salient standards that would offer opportunities for depth and a compelling local context, and wrote long-term learning targets that guided the students throughout the expedition. They paid careful attention to a sequence of learning targets that would address the standards. For example, reading standards were drawn on more in the beginning of the learning expedition as students built background knowledge about the Platte River and river ecosystems. Writing standards entered the process more toward the end, as students prepared to present their experimental findings.

Figure 1.1 illustrates how two state science standards and one Common Core literacy standard were combined to form long-term learning target 1, one of several long-term learning targets for the learning expedition.

Figure 1.1 Prioritizing and Contextualizing Standards into Long-Term Learning Target 1 for the "We All Live Downstream" Learning Expedition

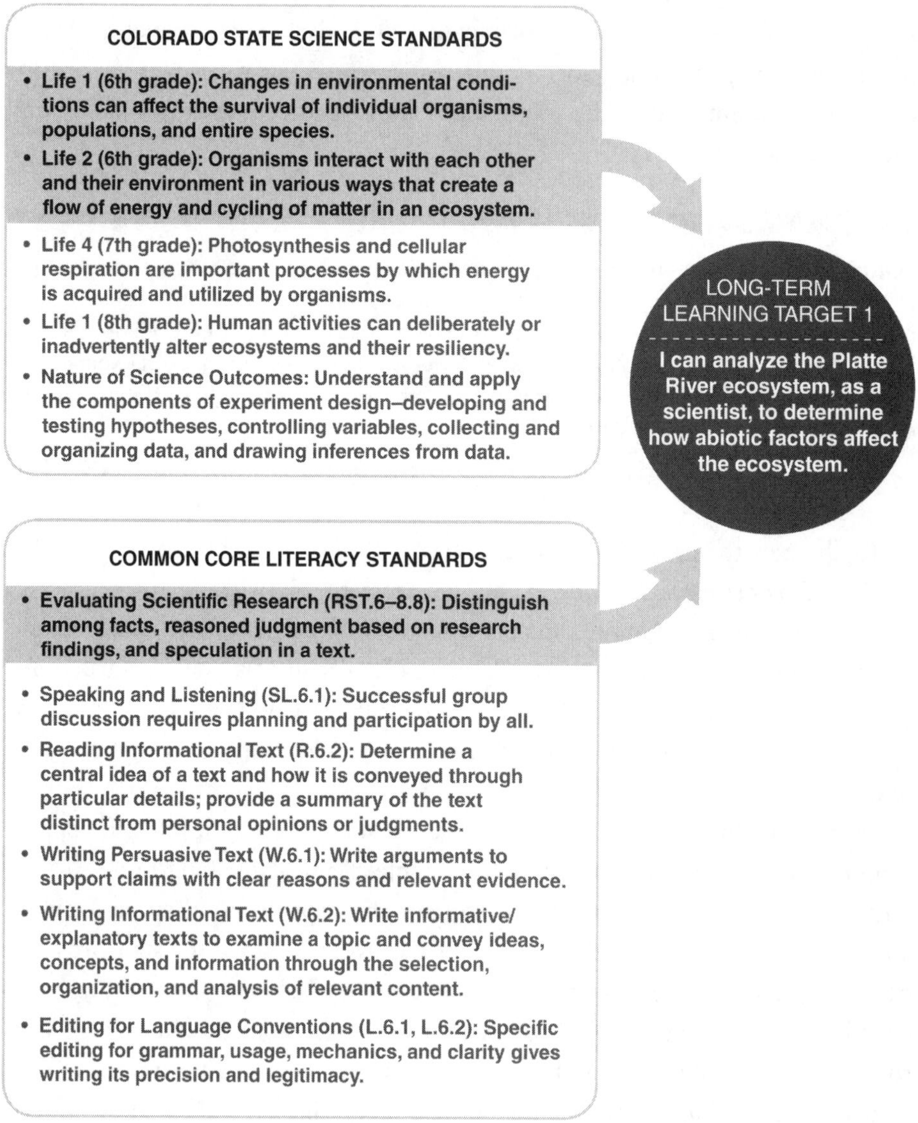

COLORADO STATE SCIENCE STANDARDS

- **Life 1 (6th grade): Changes in environmental conditions can affect the survival of individual organisms, populations, and entire species.**
- **Life 2 (6th grade): Organisms interact with each other and their environment in various ways that create a flow of energy and cycling of matter in an ecosystem.**
- Life 4 (7th grade): Photosynthesis and cellular respiration are important processes by which energy is acquired and utilized by organisms.
- Life 1 (8th grade): Human activities can deliberately or inadvertently alter ecosystems and their resiliency.
- Nature of Science Outcomes: Understand and apply the components of experiment design–developing and testing hypotheses, controlling variables, collecting and organizing data, and drawing inferences from data.

LONG-TERM LEARNING TARGET 1

I can analyze the Platte River ecosystem, as a scientist, to determine how abiotic factors affect the ecosystem.

COMMON CORE LITERACY STANDARDS

- **Evaluating Scientific Research (RST.6–8.8): Distinguish among facts, reasoned judgment based on research findings, and speculation in a text.**
- Speaking and Listening (SL.6.1): Successful group discussion requires planning and participation by all.
- Reading Informational Text (R.6.2): Determine a central idea of a text and how it is conveyed through particular details; provide a summary of the text distinct from personal opinions or judgments.
- Writing Persuasive Text (W.6.1): Write arguments to support claims with clear reasons and relevant evidence.
- Writing Informational Text (W.6.2): Write informative/explanatory texts to examine a topic and convey ideas, concepts, and information through the selection, organization, and analysis of relevant content.
- Editing for Language Conventions (L.6.1, L.6.2): Specific editing for grammar, usage, mechanics, and clarity gives writing its precision and legitimacy.

Using Long-Term and Supporting Learning Targets

Supporting learning targets are the building blocks for meeting long-term learning targets. They nest inside long-term learning targets. There are no rules about the number of supporting learning targets, but it is common for each long-term learning target to be supported by three to five supporting learning targets. Supporting learning targets are specific and easily measurable. They guide a teacher's daily lessons. At times a supporting learning target will need to be broken into even more specific daily learning targets. Alternatively, often the same supporting learning target, such as, "I can ask questions and develop testable hypotheses," will take a series of classes to address.

Long-term and supporting learning targets should never be developed by tacking "I can" onto the beginning of a Common Core or state standard. Learning targets may address just a small part of a standard or span multiple standards. The language of the learning target must make things clear to students, and standards are rarely written with this goal in mind. For example, a first-grade teacher can translate a state social studies standard that reads *Students understand the monetary value of standard U.S. coinage* into two sequential learning targets that students can more easily understand: "I can make change for a quarter in many ways" and "I can make change for a dollar in many ways."

Continuing with the "We All Live Downstream" learning expedition, we see a good example of creating supporting learning targets to guide the daily work of meeting long-term learning targets that address multiple standards. Figure 1.2 illustrates how this long-term learning target was further broken down into three supporting learning targets.

Integrating Character Learning Targets

Character learning targets are based on schoolwide expectations for habits of scholarship and norms for social behavior. If a school hasn't already identified the habits of scholarship that guide student learning—often called a *code of character*—a review of the school's mission statement can be a helpful starting place to identify character learning targets.

Table 1.2 contains the character learning targets for the sixth, seventh, and eighth grades at the Odyssey School, which guide students throughout the year. Not every character learning target can be addressed during a unit or learning expedition. It is up to the teacher(s) to select two or three key character learning

Figure 1.2 Long-Term Learning Target 1 and Supporting Learning Targets for the "We All Live Downstream" Learning Expedition

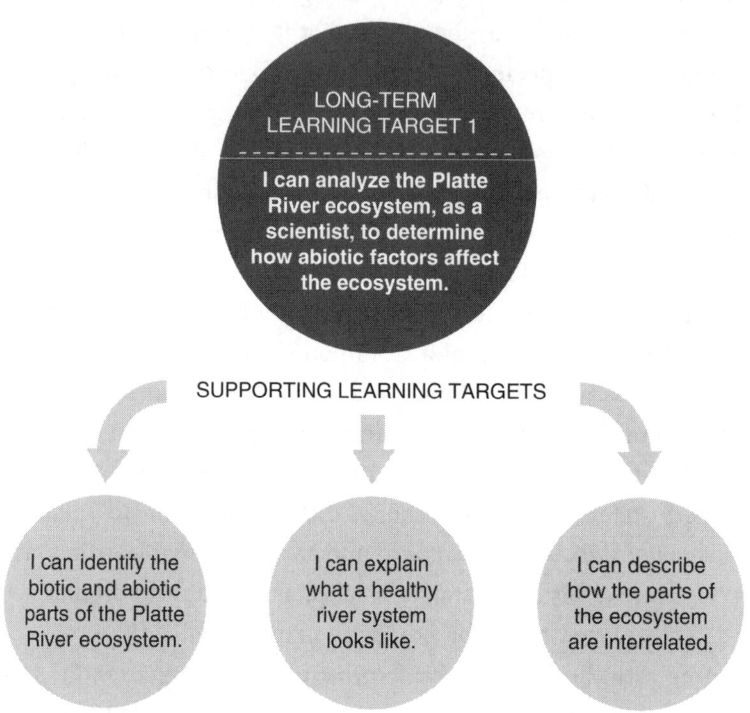

targets that are a best fit for the content or the needs of the class. For the "We All Live Downstream" learning expedition, students focused on one character learning target that addressed chronic editing errors in their written work and two that were a good fit for the collaborative lab work and fieldwork involved with their study of the Platte River ecosystem:

- *Revision:* I can use one or more effective tools or strategies to eliminate all editing errors in my final draft.
- *Collaboration and leadership:* I can identify when my contribution improved the quality of our work.
- *Service and stewardship:* I can apply what I have learned in class by taking action to improve a situation in my community or in the broader world.

Table 1.2 Sample Sixth- to Eighth-Grade Character Learning Targets

Responsibility I can begin to advocate for myself. I can maintain focus. I can complete quality work on time.	• I can demonstrate consistent use of strategies (e.g., my own notes, participation in class, before- and after-school help sessions) to fully engage in my learning. • I can complete quality classwork on time. • I can act as an intentional up-stander (i.e., stand up for others).
Revision I can use critical feedback to improve my work.	• I can demonstrate how I know my final draft is my best work. • I can demonstrate a consistent use of revision strategies. • I can use one or more effective tools or strategies to eliminate all editing errors in my final draft.
Inquiry I can use the practices, tools, and skills of an academic discipline to investigate, evaluate, form, and test theories. I can use those skills to understand specific situations and make sense of big ideas in that discipline.	• I can develop deep, probing questions and theories based on initial research and background knowledge. • I can locate diverse and quality resources that help me answer my questions and deepen my understanding. • I can evaluate and synthesize the information and evidence I find. • I can report findings in a way that helps my audience access them.
Perspective Taking I can consider multiple perspectives and their implications in terms of justice, freedom, and human rights.	• I can make use of diverse opinions to help me make sense of the world. • I can use conversation to gain understanding of others' ideas and not just as a way to voice my ideas. • I can explain how my understanding of an issue has been altered or deepened after investigating an opposing viewpoint.
Collaboration and Leadership I can engage positively with others to learn things and create work that is larger and deeper than I could create on my own.	• I can identify when our work improved because of the contribution of a peer. • I can identify when my contribution improved the quality of our work. • I can implement leadership strategies and evaluate their effectiveness. • I can walk my talk by being a good role model.
Service and Stewardship I am crew (for more on *crew,* see chapter 5). I can do things to care for my environment and my community. I can make connections between my actions and the global community.	• I can make choices that result in leaving a positive trace in the environment (classroom, school, nature). • I can apply what I have learned in class by taking action to improve a situation in my community or in the broader world. • I can demonstrate care for my buddy.

The Common Core State Standards offer descriptions of students who meet the standards and are thus ready for college or career. The descriptions closely align with the habits of scholarship identified by the Odyssey School and many other schools described in this book. In fact, actively teaching these habits is what will enable students to become the students described by the Common Core: independent learners who are able to critique the reasoning of others, value inquiry and evidence, and persevere in solving problems.

Considering the Rigor of Learning Targets

Writing learning targets is an opportunity for teachers to ramp up the rigor in their classrooms. The framework of knowledge, skill, and reasoning as three types of learning targets is a helpful starting place for analyzing what teachers expect a student to understand and do (see table 1.3). All three types of learning targets are important. Through analyzing learning target type, teachers can make informed decisions about instructional sequencing and make good estimates about how much time students will need to reach proficiency with a target. For example, knowledge learning targets in geometry that require students to memorize definitions may be reached in a single lesson, whereas learning targets requiring students to apply geometric concepts to novel problems—using reasoning—may take several days. This analysis of learning target types also equips teachers to select effective assessments.

Table 1.3 Knowledge, Skills, and Reasoning Learning Targets

	Knowledge	Skill	Reasoning
Explanation	Knowledge, facts, concepts to be learned outright or retrieved using reference materials	Use of knowledge to perform an action; demonstration is emphasized	Thinking proficiencies—using knowledge to solve a problem, make a decision, plan, and so on
Sample verbs	Explain, describe, identify, tell, name, list, define, label, match, choose, recall, recognize, select	Observe, listen, perform, conduct, read, speak, write, assemble, operate, use, demonstrate, measure, model, collect, dramatize	Analyze, compare and contrast, synthesize, classify, infer, evaluate

Source: Stiggins, Rick J.; Arter, Judith A.; Chappuis, Jan; Chappuis, Steve, *Classroom Assessment for Student Learning: Doing It Right—Using It Well,* 1st Edition, © 2006, p. 64. Adapted by permission of Pearson Education, Inc., Upper Saddle River, NJ.

However, just labeling learning targets as knowledge, skill, or reasoning can oversimplify the issue of rigor. Teachers need to also consider the complexity of students' tasks and assessments linked to learning targets. The cognitive rigor matrix in table 1.4) is a useful tool. Once teachers have learning targets and an associated task or assessment in mind, they are ready to use the matrix. The first step is to use Bloom's taxonomy to identify the type of thinking a task requires (e.g., remember, understand, apply, analyze, evaluate, create). Next, consider how deeply students need to understand the content and take into consideration how complex or abstract the content is.

Knowing where a task falls on the matrix can inform backward planning, helping teachers ensure that the learning targets will scaffold students' learning

Table 1.4 Cognitive Rigor Matrix with Sample Tasks

	Recall and Reproduction	Basic Application of Skills and Concepts	Strategic Thinking and Reasoning	Extended Thinking
Remember	Recall or locate basic facts, details, events.	N/A	N/A	N/A
Understand	Describe or explain who, what, where, when, or how.	Explain relationships, summarize, identify main ideas.	Explain, generalize, or connect ideas using supporting evidence.	Explain how concepts or ideas specifically relate to other content domains.
Apply	Use language structure or word relationships to determine meaning.	Obtain and interpret information using text features.	Apply a concept in a new context.	Select or devise an approach among many alternatives to research a novel problem.
Analyze	Identify whether information is contained in a graph, table, and so on.	Distinguish between relevant and irrelevant information.	Analyze interrelationships among concepts, issues, or problems.	Analyze complex or abstract themes or perspectives.
Evaluate	N/A	N/A	Justify or critique conclusions drawn.	Apply understanding in a novel way, with justification.
Create	Brainstorm ideas about a topic.	Generate hypotheses based on observations or prior knowledge.	Develop a complex model for a given situation.	Articulate a new voice, new knowledge, or perspective.

Source: Adapted from © 2009 Karin K. Hess: *Hess' Cognitive Rigor Matrix.*

appropriately. Using the matrix also pushes teachers to consider tasks that fall in the "Extended Thinking" column, emphasizing real-world application, cross-discipline connections, problem solving, and creative thinking—all important aspects of deeper learning through the Common Core.

Aligning Standards, Learning Targets, and Assessments

Learning targets inform a cycle of curriculum development, instruction, and assessment. Clear learning targets derived from state and Common Core standards can help teachers make decisions about what to teach and how to assess learning. Teachers should identify assessments for each set of long-term and supporting learning targets, taking care to select assessment methods that are appropriate for the type of learning target a student is working toward. For example, an extended written response may not be appropriate for a teacher to assess the learning target "I can collect specific accurate data in metric units." A performance assessment, however, may be just right for this skills-oriented learning target. Table 1.5 shows possible assessments based on the type of learning target.

Table 1.5 Selecting Assessment Methods Based on Type of Learning Target

	Selected Response	Extended Written Response	Performance Assessment	Personal Communication
Knowledge	**Good match**—for assessing mastery of elements of knowledge	**Good match**—for evaluating understanding of relationships among elements of knowledge	**Not a good match**—too time consuming to cover everything	**Match**—can ask questions, evaluate answers, and infer mastery, but a time-consuming option
Skills	**Not a good match**—can assess mastery of prerequisite knowledge, but do not tell the evaluator that the student can use the skill itself		**Good match**—can observe and evaluate skills as they are being performed	**Good match**—when skill is oral communication proficiency
Reasoning	**Match**—only for assessing understanding of some patterns of reasoning	**Good match**—written descriptions of complex problem solutions provide a window into reasoning proficiency	**Good match**—can watch students solve some problems and infer reasoning proficiency	**Good match**—can ask students to think aloud or can ask follow-up questions to probe reasoning

Source: Stiggins, Rick J., *Student-Involved Assessment for Learning*, 4th Edition, © 2005. Adapted by permission of Pearson Education, Inc., Upper Saddle River, NJ.

Critical Moves for Deepening Student Engagement

Writing good learning targets takes time and care, but it is only the beginning. The practice really gains traction when students internalize the value of learning targets and use them to assess their progress. In the accompanying video, seventh- and eighth-grade students at the Odyssey School discuss their classroom learning targets as a part of everyday life in their classrooms. As a result of using learning targets in every class every day, they have a strong sense of responsibility and accountability for their learning.

Watch video: "Students Discuss the Power of Learning Targets"

"As a professional, I am making a determination of what is most important and measuring student success based on a body of evidence. I design assessments that demonstrate mastery of content and collect evidence that helps me to determine whether or not the student has met the target. The evidence also points to where students may need additional support or extension. All the work along the way informs me about whether or not the students are understanding or may need reteaching or coaching."

—Aurora Kushner, tenth-grade biology teacher, Springfield Renaissance School, Springfield, Massachusetts

If the teacher—and not the students—owns the learning targets, it doesn't matter how well they are crafted and worded; they won't have power. Students need to be drawn into analyzing and unpacking the learning targets, building a clear vision of where they need to go. If the learning targets do not create a clear and resonant goal for students, they may need to be fine-tuned or reworded collaboratively with students to make them plain. Once students are experienced with using learning targets, they and their teachers can collaboratively build learning targets that address standards and goals effectively. Although it may seem daunting at first, getting started with learning targets can be approached through a series of manageable activities. Table 1.6 describes the who, what, and why of using learning targets to increase student engagement.

Table 1.6 The Who, What, and Why of Learning Targets

What Do Teachers Do?	What Do Students Do?	What's the Result?
Craft learning targets for lessons aligned to state and Common Core standards. Determine the best point in a lesson to introduce the learning target—at the beginning of the lesson or later (to promote discovery or grappling with new concepts). Discuss and unpack the learning targets with students.	Engage with the learning target—explain it in their own words with a partner or small group; discuss specific vocabulary; ask clarifying questions; and explore how they will demonstrate that they've met the target.	Lessons have purpose and direction and students are more engaged. Students can articulate a clear vision of the learning.
Refer to learning targets throughout the lesson and align activities to support students in meeting them.	Articulate how each activity is helping them move closer to achieving the learning target.	Students are engaged in the lesson because the purpose of their work is clear.
Check for whole-class understanding.	Self-assess where they are in relation to a specific learning target using quick checks, such as fist-to-five. Support other students in assessing and meeting learning targets.	Teachers and students can make informed decisions about next instructional moves (e.g., offering or attending an additional guided-practice session before moving into independent practice).
Check for individual understanding and use data to make decisions about next instructional steps.	Turn in written checks for understanding (e.g., exit tickets, reflection journals, quick quizzes) that demonstrate where they are in relation to one or more learning targets.	Teachers can make informed decisions about next instructional steps related to individual students (e.g., oral or written feedback, differentiated materials, and instruction in the next lesson).
Connect daily and supporting learning targets to long-term learning targets and engage students in understanding the state and Common Core standards they are working toward.	Understand how daily lessons will help them meet long-term learning targets. Support peers in understanding the learning targets and standards.	Students can see how daily lessons are part of a larger plan to meet standards.
Institute use of learning target trackers.	Track and record their progress toward long-term and supporting learning targets and make an effort to understand what they need to do to improve.	Teachers and students can see more progress toward standards. They recognize gaps in understanding and take steps to address them.

Table 1.6 Continued

What Do Teachers Do?	What Do Students Do?	What's the Result?
Integrate character learning targets and academic learning targets.	Understand how the habits and skills embedded in character learning targets support academic progress.	Academic and character growth are linked.
Ensure the rigor of learning targets with a balance of knowledge, reasoning, and skills targets and attention to the complexity of tasks and assessments.	Develop a range of capacities, from skill building to higher-order thinking.	Students are appropriately challenged by the right kinds of learning targets at the right time.
Align standards, learning targets, and assessments. Create the summative assessments that will evaluate whether students have met the targets.	Understand how they will be assessed from the beginning of a learning experience. Prepare to do their best in meeting the targets.	Learning targets aligned with formative and summative assessments enable effective communication about what students are learning.

SCHOOLWIDE IMPLEMENTATION

The practice of using learning targets is a foundation for all student-engaged assessment practices and a vehicle for deepening teaching and learning across a school. It takes skillful and collaborative leadership to facilitate probing discussions, examine data, decide on content and priorities, and build the key structures that support the full implementation of learning targets. It will take time for teachers to develop consistently strong learning targets that are at the right level of cognitive demand for students, that are aligned to standards and assessments, and that are actively used by students. Leaders can offer support with professional development and good communication.

Learning targets have the potential to tie into almost every important school structure: student-led conferences, passage presentations, standards-based report cards, celebrations of learning, graduation ceremonies, professional development plans, and school improvement plans. The more they are used throughout a school, the more power they will have. We have highlighted some of the key leadership actions that will support smooth implementation of learning targets throughout a school.

Lay the Groundwork

- Use professional literature and professional development to train staff on the benefits of learning targets to engage students in making progress toward standards.

- Analyze state and Common Core standards in faculty teams. Understanding the standards deeply is a prerequisite for developing curriculum maps with accompanying learning targets.
- Work with the school leadership team to create curriculum maps across all grades and content areas, clarifying what standards are assessed at each grade level. Collaborate with and seek input from teachers.
- Create schoolwide habits of scholarship and clarify appropriate character learning targets for each grade level. Determine how progress toward these targets will be tracked and communicated in a way that supports, engages, and holds all students accountable.

Build Teacher Capacity

- Create a long-range professional development plan that engages staff in examining their practice writing and using learning targets.
- Ensure that teachers have time and support, through ongoing professional development structures, to craft long-term and supporting learning targets from standards and match assessments to learning targets before each chunk of instruction begins.
- Model learning targets in the professional working culture of the school (e.g., professional development sessions).

Communicate with Stakeholders

- Establish the schoolwide practices that ensure that learning targets are communicated and understood by everyone. This encompasses small, daily practices such as posting learning targets and discussing them at the beginning of a class, as well as larger schoolwide practices such as aligning grades and report cards with learning targets.
- Communicate with parents about what learning targets are and where they can expect to see them (e.g., on assignments or report cards, at student-led conferences).
- Exhibit students' work and explicitly link this work to learning targets. Label work so that family and community members walking through the school understand what is on display and what learning targets were met. Work can be accompanied by rubrics to explain the criteria for the product.

Well-organized displays illustrate the progression of student work over time, leading to work that clearly demonstrates mastery of learning targets.

Support Teachers to Deepen Their Practice

- Collaboratively critique assessments during professional development and provide feedback to ensure that learning targets drive instruction and act as the framework for assessments.
- Provide time for diary mapping—retrospectively documenting what content and skills teachers actually assessed. Content and skills maps require refinement once they are created, and diary mapping provides a reality check against the ideal. The process also enables teachers and leaders to analyze assessment data from state tests, cross-referencing achievement with what was emphasized at the classroom level.
- Observe and discuss teacher and student use of learning targets by analyzing student work and video clips during professional development or holding school-based classroom labs.

Case Study

Getting Results with Learning Targets at the Odyssey School in Denver

When staff at the Odyssey School began their work on assessment several years ago, they thought it was going to be a yearlong focus. They quickly realized that assessment needed to be a multiyear focus. For Liza Eaton, teacher and instructional guide, a key turning point was when she realized the power of student involvement in the process. "I started realizing it wasn't just about me and my planning. I had been writing the targets on the board, but we weren't necessarily using them. Then I developed a self-assessment tool and in using it, kids started to understand where they were in relation to the target." As the process of using learning targets with students expanded, the school began to see achievement results. "That year our state test scores went up a ton, and they stayed up. Suddenly we realized the power of our assessment work. Not just through what we saw in our classrooms, but in numbers."

At Odyssey, getting the structures established took some time and has been central to their progress. There is schoolwide professional development from 1:45 to 4:00 every Friday, during which the staff focuses on a schoolwide goal and topics that support that goal (e.g., how to make a good standard-target-assessment plan and how to support students in self-reflecting with accuracy). A newer structure supports teachers with an hour of instructional coaching every week, and schoolwide labs create opportunities for peer observation with a particular instructional focus. It's clear that refining their assessment practices has been a professional learning journey with twists and turns. As Eaton says, "From the outset it seems easy and linear, but then you get into it and discover it's messy and hard. If the students are not getting to the target, and that's a pattern, then you have to teach differently. On the other hand, there are immediate results that you see in your classroom."

WHAT TO EXPECT

This book on student-engaged assessment begins with the practice of learning targets because this is an essential first step in making students full partners in their own education. Mastering the practice is an act of translation. As anyone who has been a translator understands, the act of translation is no mere job of substituting one word for another. Effective translation requires a deep understanding of the original idea, including its nuances and contexts. A translator must have a firm foot in two worlds. A teacher who writes effective learning targets is such a translator, with deep knowledge of the standards *and* with the ability to identify how to express them in just the right terms for his or her students.

This is a paradigm shift. For teachers new to writing and using learning targets this practice requires that they frame lessons, units, and semesters by what students will learn, rather than by what teachers will teach. For many teachers, this represents a different way of thinking about the enterprise of teaching and about the learning that goes on in the classroom. Many teachers may not be familiar with the role of a translator.

Writing and using learning targets usually starts at the classroom level. Teachers experiment with designing learning targets to guide daily lessons, paying attention to word choice. Teachers will discover, through trial and error, how to best translate standards and curriculum into meaningful learning targets for their students. They will witness the power of learning targets to engage students in their own learning, and will look for ways to expand their use in the classroom. They will understand the value of learning targets as road markers for their curriculum. Ultimately, teachers will translate state and Common Core standards into long-term learning targets and nest supporting learning targets within them. Even more important, through the consistent practice of understanding, meeting, and reflecting on learning goals, students will have developed habits of scholarship associated with school success. As teachers gain comfort with this practice, they can use learning targets to help their students develop the skills, work habits, and character traits needed for success in school and beyond.

Once school leaders and teachers gain experience with and see the benefits of learning targets, their use will likely spread throughout the school. Students benefit from this kind of consistent and predictable framing of learning throughout their school experience. It is empowering for them to understand where they are headed and what they are expected to learn in every classroom, every day.

We have identified some of the benchmarks that teachers and school leaders can expect at the beginning, intermediate, and advanced phases of implementing learning targets.

Beginning

- Teachers write learning targets for daily lessons.
- Learning targets are visibly posted in the classroom and introduced to students at the best point during the lesson—teachers unpack the learning target, identifying key vocabulary and criteria for success.
- Teachers plan their instruction to ensure that all students can meet the learning targets.
- Students are able to articulate what they are learning.
- Families have more information about what concepts and skills their children are learning.

Intermediate

- Faculty members have rich conversations about state and Common Core standards and what learning targets will help students demonstrate proficiency on standards.
- Long-term learning targets frame curriculum units, and supporting learning targets guide daily lessons.
- Students come to expect learning targets to guide their lessons and long-term units of study. They are invested in analyzing and understanding them.

- Teachers create effective plans that align standards, targets, and assessments. Learning targets are clearly derived from standards, and assessment methods match learning target types.
- Teachers use checking-for-understanding strategies to monitor students' progress toward learning targets.
- Character learning targets are used to assess habits of scholarship.
- Teachers balance knowledge, reasoning, and skills learning targets.
- Students can articulate to their families what they are learning and what they need to do to make progress.

Advanced

- Students adeptly track their progress and make decisions alongside the teacher about next steps. They own the learning and the assessment process. They are invested in understanding standards and modifying or creating new learning targets to best help them meet them.
- Teachers assess students on long-term and character learning targets within a schoolwide standards-based grading system.
- Teachers write learning targets attending to the cognitive rigor of the intended student learning.
- Parents, students, and teachers have detailed conversations—referencing character and academic learning targets—about students' strengths and areas for improvement. Students often lead these conversations in student-led conferences.
- Teachers and schools continually align standards, learning targets, and assessments.

COMMON CHALLENGES

Learning Targets That Are Owned by the Teacher, but Not by the Students

Build student ownership. Many teachers succeed in creating and posting learning targets; some schools even require this practice. But posting learning targets and reading them aloud are not enough. Teachers and students should discuss the learning targets to ensure that students fully embrace and understand them and can collaborate with the teacher in tracking them.

Learning Targets versus Doing Targets

Focus on learning. As mentioned previously, learning targets should describe what students will learn as a result of a lesson, learning expedition, or unit of study, not what they will do as the task—"I can use metaphor to convey a complex emotion," not "I can complete or fill out my note catcher."

Learning Targets That Are Too Complex

Watch your language. Aim for clarity when crafting learning targets. Those that pack in too much information may confuse students or make a teacher second-guess the intended learning and assessment. Watch out for learning targets that contain the following: two verbs (e.g., "I can identify and analyze"); compound content (e.g., "I can describe the ecosystems of coral reefs and forests"); broad scope of content (e.g., "I can evaluate continuity and change over the course of US history").

Learning Targets That Are Too Big or Too Small

Get the scope right. Often it can be challenging to create long-term and supporting learning targets that efficiently pace life in the classroom and stimulate rich learning. Long-term learning targets should be tied directly to standards, and each may take one to two weeks to address completely. Nested within each long-term learning target, supporting learning targets (typically three to five) guide the daily lessons that support students to meet standards. Careful planning and practice will help teachers craft learning targets that don't try to cover too much or that are overly narrow.

Learning Targets That Are Not Used on a Daily Basis

Use it or lose it. Learning targets must be displayed, referred to, owned by the students, and worked toward in a meaningful way. Learning targets that exist only on paper don't support students' engagement, motivation, and learning.

Learning Targets That Require All Lower-Level Thinking and Skills

Mix it up. Learning targets should reflect different levels of thinking, from the foundational knowledge level (e.g., name, identify, describe) to higher-order skills (e.g., analyze, compare and contrast, and evaluate). Check to see that sets of learning targets ramp up the rigor in the classroom.

Learning Targets That Are Not Linked to a Powerful Context for Learning

Make them meaningful. Learning targets are most powerful when they guide learning experiences that are engaging for students and are part of a compelling curriculum that requires critical thinking and problem solving.

Learning Targets That Are Mismatched to Assessments

Check the alignment. The method of assessment should match the learning target. A target that asks a student to analyze would be assessed not with a multiple-choice quiz, but rather with a written response or verbal teacher-student conference. Well-matched assessments are both effective and efficient.

Learning Targets That Miss the Heart of the Common Core State Standards

Get to the heart of the matter. If learning targets and assessments touch on standards but don't address them fully, sharply, and deeply, teachers will miss an opportunity to help their students develop the critical thinking skills emphasized by the Common Core State Standards. Teachers must read and discuss the standards carefully to create effective learning targets.

Learning Targets That Are Different for Different Groups of Students

Ensure rigor and equity. Learning targets should remain consistent for all students, whereas the instruction employed to help students meet them is differentiated to meet the needs of a diverse range of learners (with the possible exception of students working toward an IEP-based diploma that calls for curriculum modifications or for those participating in other alternative pathways).

Chapter 2

Checking for Understanding during Daily Lessons

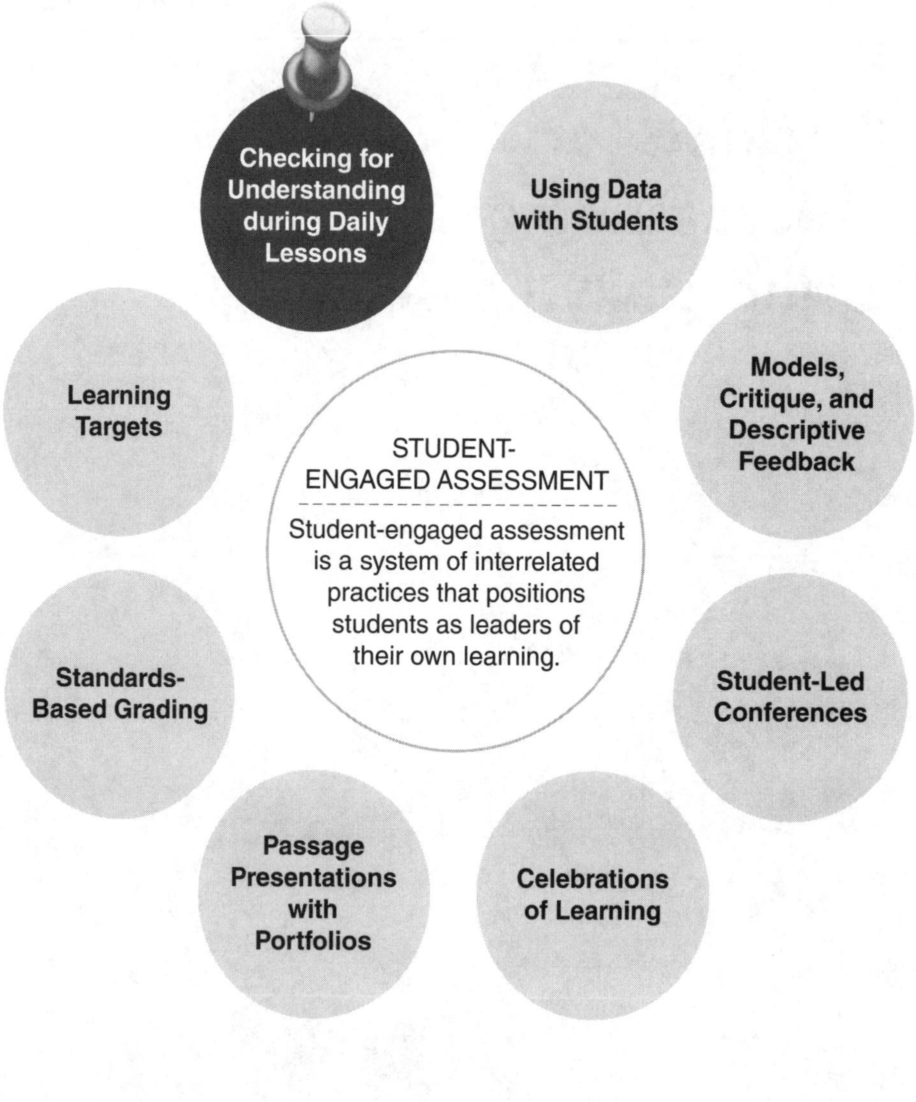

Checking for Understanding during Daily Lessons

Using Data with Students

Learning Targets

STUDENT-ENGAGED ASSESSMENT

Student-engaged assessment is a system of interrelated practices that positions students as leaders of their own learning.

Models, Critique, and Descriptive Feedback

Standards-Based Grading

Student-Led Conferences

Passage Presentations with Portfolios

Celebrations of Learning

When I was in second grade, my teacher was a patient older woman who wore large plastic glasses covered with fake diamonds. She would stand at the blackboard, her glasses dangling from a gold chain, and write and solve math problems as she talked at the board. The boys who sat around me paid no attention, because they were always building small cars out of rectangular pink erasers, staples, and thumbtacks. Occasionally she would turn to the class, lift her glasses to see us, and check for understanding: "Everyone understand?" she would ask. A few of us would nod and she would return to writing.

Recently when I was visiting an elementary school in Virginia, I observed a second-grade math lesson that was an interesting counterpoint. The teacher used a simple but remarkable checking-for-understanding technique called "red light, green light." Every student had three index cards on his or her desk, with a red, yellow, or green circle on each card. During the flow of the lesson, one card was on top, visible to the teacher looking out over the class: green if the student self-identified as clearly understanding the material, yellow if understanding was hazy, and red if the student was really confused.

As the teacher explained new material and facilitated student discussion, I watched students continually switching their cards as they grew more or less clear, and I watched the teacher scanning the class to look for patterns of understanding. She went quickly when the trend was green; when things began to turn yellow and red she slowed down and clarified. As students worked independently, she focused her support where there were pockets of red cards. The students were highly engaged, intent on assessing in real time their own comprehension of concepts.

The beauty of this system was that it did not require stopping instruction or discussion to check understanding. The teacher could see the flow of understanding at all times and worked to address gaps in real time. There appeared to be no self-consciousness impeding honesty. The process of continually updating their top card as the lesson progressed kept students engaged and carefully tuned to their level of understanding.

—Ron Berger

A Daily Practice for Teachers and Students

Andrew Hossack's fifth-grade ELA class at Tapestry Charter School in Buffalo, New York, is a lively dance, tightly choreographed to balance student work time, assessing progress, and targeted instruction to meet diverse student needs. The class is developing tools to write narrative stories and today they are studying the sequence of events in literature. The learning target for the day is, "I can write summary sentences for a story along a narrative arc," which is derived from the Common Core writing standard, W.5.3, *Write narratives to develop real or imagined experiences or events using effective technique, descriptive details, and clear event sequences.*

For Hossack, the learning target guides the lesson. To ensure all students know where they are going and what success looks like, students not only review the learning target but they also explain and describe it using their own words and examples. "That first check for understanding is really important because it reminds me that I can't move at the same speed for all students. I can stop for a second more and review the narrative arc to make sure everyone understands the learning target before we move on," says Hossack. For him, however, this is not enough. Throughout the lesson, he uses a variety of techniques, such as "cold calling," strategic observation as he listens in to pair-shares, strategic questioning, and exit tickets to assess the understanding of all of his students and their progress toward meeting the learning target.

The checking-for-understanding techniques described in this chapter are the missing link for teachers such as Hossack, who are not sure if their students are understanding the intended learning. They are oral, written, and visual techniques that are implemented in a variety of configurations of student groupings—large and small group, individual, and peer. These techniques include all of the minute-by-minute ways a teacher assesses and students self-assess the content and major concepts of a lesson. Checking for understanding encompasses both teacher and student actions. Student engagement and ownership is a central part of the process. As students grow accustomed to these practices, they learn to monitor their own progress, support their reasoning with evidence, and ultimately become more independent learners.

Checking for understanding during daily lessons encompasses a wide range of techniques—formal and informal, oral and written, verbal and nonverbal—used by teachers and students to track what students understand and can do throughout a lesson. As a result of this ongoing assessment, teachers and students make adjustments to what they are doing to ensure that gaps in understanding are addressed and that students who have mastered concepts may comfortably move on to another learning task.

Checking-for-understanding strategies include the following:

- Writing and reflection
- Student discussion protocols
- Quick checks
- Strategic observation and listening
- Debriefs

Linked to all aspects of student-engaged assessment, checking for understanding is a key part of supporting students to build lifelong skills of self-assessment. Helping students understand where they currently are in the learning process and where they are going is what enables them to grow and is more important than getting it "right." It is also no simple task. It requires a classroom culture of trust, safety, and collaboration, and a student mindset that learning comes from effort, that making mistakes is a key part of how everyone learns, and that everyone has different learning needs.

This chapter is focused on checking that students understand content and concepts and that they can apply them with fluency. The focus here is on the techniques that teachers and students can use during daily lessons that enable teachers to adapt instruction quickly and respond to student needs in real time, and that students can use to self-assess their progress and take responsibility for their learning. These checking-for understanding techniques fall into five categories:

- Writing and reflection
- Student discussion protocols
- Quick checks
- Strategic observation and listening
- Debriefs

There are many other forms of checking for understanding, such as tests, essays, interviews, and performance assessments, that may be essential to assess understanding with more depth; however, they often don't enable teachers to react quickly to gaps in their students' understanding. This chapter focuses exclusively on techniques that can be used during the flow of lessons to adjust instruction and plan next steps.

Although it is important to start small and set clear priorities, simply adopting a checking-for-understanding technique or two won't lead to improved results. Part of what makes the task complex is that "understanding"—beyond simple recall of facts and information—is hard to pin down. What does it mean to truly

Checking for understanding during daily lessons enables teachers to respond quickly to students' needs.

"understand" a concept in math or history? How do you know if students actually understand what they are working on? How do students know if they understand if they don't have the opportunity for reflection?

"Understanding is a matter of being able to do a variety of thought-demanding things with a topic—like explaining, finding evidence and examples, generalizing, applying, analogizing, and representing the topic in a new way" (Perkins & Blythe, 1994, p. 5). The best way to check for understanding is through transfer, in which students apply their learning to novel situations. In other words, if students know it, they can use it in new and different contexts. In general, transfer is something a teacher will incorporate into a performance assessment or other summative assessment, but smaller checks for this kind of understanding are possible even at the daily lesson level. Teachers must always strive to create the types of questions and tasks that will help students figure out if they actually "get it."

When discussing a learning target or task, it is powerful for teachers to include students in considering how they will know if they really "get it." Ask them, "How will you know if you understand this well? What might you be able to do or show to demonstrate understanding?" For example, if students are working on fractions problems, they may suggest that they should all be able to solve a small, diverse set of sample problems; perhaps they create those problems together. Although this is almost identical to a teacher-created mini-quiz, it has significantly different meaning when it is a student creation and, as such, imbued with shared ownership and investment in success.

Why This Practice Matters

On an intuitive level, teachers know it is important that students understand a concept before moving forward in the instruction. Some teachers might scan the room, looking for signs of comprehending faces, or ask generally, "Got it?" Unfortunately, knowing that one needs to check for understanding is not the same as doing it. Checking for understanding is an essential component of good classroom instruction, showing teachers where students are mastering concepts or faltering, letting students see on a regular basis what they are getting or not getting, and providing in this way a kind of staircase to achievement. This practice comes from the hard-won wisdom among teachers that just because we teach it, doesn't mean that students are learning it.

Thoughtfully implementing the checking-for-understanding techniques described in this chapter will support teachers to find out in real time whether or not students have comprehended a concept or lesson and if they are ready to move on. The following sections describe some of the key benefits of this practice.

> "In our school it's really important that students can track their own learning and understanding because it's going to be so important when they go to college. We are a college-bound school."
>
> *—Vanessa Cramer, ninth-grade science teacher, Springfield Renaissance School, Springfield, Massachusetts*

Provides Immediate Information about Progress toward Standard or Learning Target Mastery

Teachers will know right away whether the instructional approach is working or if they need to make adjustments. Instead of finding out after a quiz or mid-unit evaluation, a teacher will know more precisely where students require additional instruction or practice.

Supports Students toward Meeting Rigorous Goals
Checking for understanding on a daily basis and after the introduction of key content guides students toward subject mastery by breaking down large goals into smaller targets and tasks.

Builds Capacity for Reflection
Regularly checking for understanding develops the habit of mind that students will stop and evaluate their progress as they are learning.

Prepares Students for College and Career
Checking-for-understanding techniques are invaluable tools for tackling work of increasing complexity. As students learn to use these strategies independently, they will internalize the habits of self-evaluation, practice, and transfer—skills essential for college and workplace success.

Common Core Connections

- Alongside the clear student-friendly goals that learning targets provide, checking-for-understanding techniques enable students and teachers to monitor progress toward standards.
- Checking-for-understanding techniques help students develop the self-awareness needed to be independent, confident learners who take ownership of their progress toward meeting standards.

GETTING STARTED

Laying the Groundwork

Implementing checking-for-understanding techniques may seem simple at first glance. However, if these techniques are to have the desired effect, which is to ensure that students are learning what teachers think they are learning (i.e., meeting the standards) and that they are actively engaged in self-assessment, classroom culture and lesson design must be approached with forethought and intention.

Build a Classroom Culture of Trust and Collaboration

> "I always know the place I'm headed [the learning target], but to make sure everyone's on that train I have to check for understanding all the time."
>
> *—Jessica Wood, sixth-grade ELA teacher, Springfield Renaissance School, Springfield, Massachusetts*

A classroom culture of trust, safety, challenge, and joy is the cornerstone of engaged and effective learning. Culture and community building at the classroom and schoolwide levels are the foundation for every aspect of improved teaching and learning and particularly important when checking for understanding. Students must feel safe to communicate honestly about their progress. A series of actions set in motion by the leadership and faculty members of the school builds strong school and classroom culture:

- Treat students as partners in the learning process. Engage them in understanding and shaping learning targets, classroom rules and norms, project ideas, and every other aspect of learning.
- Show students the rationale for curriculum and instruction and be transparent about the standards and important decisions.
- Get to know students as individuals and continually assess and adjust practice according to their readiness for certain content or tasks, and trends in their interests and learning profiles (e.g., balance challenging all students with complex texts with supporting them to independently read texts of their choosing).
- Create school- and classwide norms that encourage everyone to persevere with challenging tasks and justify their thinking with evidence.
- Model collaboration. Students need to see the adults in the school community working together, giving feedback, and being open about their questions and mistakes.

Classroom cultures that grow from these actions enable students to understand their learning goals and teachers to be responsive to the learning needs of all students. Such classrooms need a climate of courtesy and respect, built from safety, clarity, and trust, not simply compliance and control. Implementing checking-for-understanding techniques requires that teachers are particularly intentional about creating this climate. Students must trust that if they expose their challenges and vulnerabilities,

A positive classroom culture is an essential building block for all student-engaged assessment practices.

teachers and peers will treat them with respect, and their mistakes will be seen as an opportunity to learn.

> "Being really transparent with students helps. Most of them have experienced 'gotcha' in prior classrooms [when they were caught unprepared]. Explain 'here is what I'm trying to do and here are the reasons why.'"
>
> *—Jessica Wood, sixth-grade ELA teacher, Springfield Renaissance School, Springfield, Massachusetts*

One place to start is by helping students adopt a growth mindset. Described in the work of Carol Dweck (2006), a growth mindset is defined by the belief that human brains develop intelligence with study and effort. By contrast, a fixed mindset is defined by the belief that intelligence is set by native ability. Research by Dweck and her team suggests that students with a fixed mindset often feel that hard work is a sign of weakness—that skill should come easily—and are hesitant to take academic risks, because doing so might make them appear weak. These mindsets are not permanent—when students are shown, for example, that they can "grow their math brain" by struggling with hard problems, they work harder at math problems and improve their skills. A growth mindset changes the belief that some will succeed academically and some will not. Believing that intelligence can grow helps all students to be honest in sharing their questions and confusions as they work to gain skill and understanding. Dweck's research suggests that small interventions aimed at building a growth mindset can result in profound changes in student attitude and performance. All teachers would be well served to study her work and learn more about mindsets.

Teachers can set expectations for checking for understanding by modeling and practicing different techniques with students. Teachers should talk about the purpose of each technique so that students know why it is important for them to be honest in their self-assessment. Having the opportunity to practice will help them see how the techniques affect their teacher's instruction and ultimately their understanding of the material.

Structure Lessons to Support Frequent Checks for Understanding

A key element of implementing checking-for-understanding techniques is designing lessons that allow time for students to demonstrate their understanding. They need the opportunity to think and do. If a teacher gives a lecture and asks students questions about it, the evidence she gathers will be limited. A deeper level of student understanding, including the ability to apply knowledge to a new situation or problem—transfer—will only be evident by engaging students in a task. Certain kinds of lessons, such as the workshop model, the five Es (engage, explore, explain, extend, evaluate), and protocol-based lessons, among others, provide meaningful opportunities for students to grapple with new material and apply their learning, and for teachers to assess understanding. In the accompanying video, teacher Jessica Wood uses the workshop model to provide plenty of student work time and then employs a variety of techniques to check for understanding.

Watch video: "Instructional Strategies That Support Learning—Checking for Understanding"

No matter what lesson structure is selected, a rich task must be at the center in order to give students the opportunity to learn new content and show what they know. Ground the lesson in the learning target and ensure that students understand it well enough to know where they are headed. Design tasks that are matched to learning targets with supports in place to build students' capacity to reach them. Teachers should ask themselves, Where are students going? How does this task move them toward the learning target? How is this task set up to engage students so I can gather information about what they are learning?

> "The important thing is that students in your classroom know that they can be asked to share their ideas at any time. Creating a strong sense of urgency and pace to your lesson helps keep students engaged. It provides excitement and an edge to things that keeps them on their toes."
>
> *—Christian Zwahlen, seventh-grade ELA teacher, World of Inquiry School, Rochester, New York*

Tasks should be structured so that all students think and participate. A variety of discussion protocols, recording forms, and other participation techniques ensure that teachers hear from all students and track their learning and understanding. For example, instead of asking the class if everyone understands, and being satisfied with a few responses, a protocol in which every student must explain a concept to a peer or fill out an exit ticket ensures involvement by all students. (For more examples of protocols and strategies to promote participation, see *Total Participation Techniques* by Himmele and Himmele, 2011.)

Preplan Strategic Questions to Monitor Student Learning

Good questions are central to almost every technique teachers use to check for student understanding. Developing good questions in advance and planning for their use during a lesson is critical to gathering the right information about student learning. Teachers need to think about what questions they will ask to drive at learning targets and stimulate and assess powerful thinking. They also need to consider how questions will be asked so that all learners are engaged in thinking and supporting their ideas with evidence. Figure 2.1 illustrates strategic questioning strategies to check for understanding along with accompanying examples.

Figure 2.1 Preplanning Strategic Questions

Strategy: Design questions to provide a clear vision of the learning target(s).

Use questions to clarify the meaning and connections between learning targets (long-term and supporting), to connect prior lessons, establish criteria for success, and track learning along the way.

Examples

A first-grade teacher designs questions to check his students' understanding of the learning target, "I can mentally find ten more for any two-digit number."[1]

- What does it mean to do something mentally?
- Give an example of a two-digit number. What is the difference between a two-digit number and a one-digit number?
- Which number is bigger, 40 or 9? How do you know? 4 and 0 are less than nine; what makes 40 bigger than nine?
- What did you picture or visualize in your head to help you figure out what 10 more is of a number?
- How will you know if you found 10 more?

Strategy: Scaffold questions from basic to complex.

Plan questions that start at the knowledge and comprehension levels and move quickly to reasoning and critical thinking. This helps students practice thinking skills, make connections between ideas, align and evaluate evidence, synthesize information, and apply learning to new situations. These questions are generative, eliciting multiple correct answers.

Examples

A teacher designs questions to elicit prior knowledge and a series of probing follow-up questions related to the learning target "I can describe the characteristics of living and nonliving things."

- What is a living thing and how do you know?

After initial learning experiences . . .

- What is one characteristic of a living thing and how does it help that organism?

As learning moves to analysis and evaluation . . .

- How are the characteristics of living things different than those of nonliving things? How do characteristics of living things help them survive?
- Is this bouquet of flowers (or other example) living or nonliving? What evidence could you use to prove it?

(continued)

Figure 2.1 Continued

Strategy: Ask questions that are text dependent.

In order to check for understanding and comprehension of complex texts, ask questions that are text dependent rather than drawn from the students' personal opinions or past experiences. This questioning strategy compels students to read carefully and cite evidence, which in turn raises the quality of student thinking. Carefully crafted questions serve as a scaffold to "lift" students to the text and build higher-order thinking skills and new perspectives.

Examples

An eighth-grade teacher chooses a complex text about Aztec culture then designs text-dependent questions to check for understanding related to the learning target, "I can cite specific textual evidence to describe the relationship between Aztec culture and their physical environment."[2] For each question, the teacher prompts the students to draw specific evidence from the text and defend their answers:

- Where did the Aztec people live?
- What geographical features defined the Aztec landscape?

As learning moves to analysis and evaluation . . .

- How did geography of the land affect their way of life?
- What does the city's layout reveal about their values?
- What conclusions can you draw from the demise of the Aztec civilization?
- What are the implications of these developments for other societies?

Strategy: Clarify expectations.

Use questions to clarify criteria for success and help students check their own understanding to determine their next steps.

Examples

A sixth-grade teacher designs questions to clarify expectations for the learning target "I can conduct research to prove or disprove my hypothesis."[3]

- What will collaborative research look and sound like today as we look for sources?
- What would a good report on the water cycle look like? What will you include to show you really understand it?
- What do you think about your classmate's idea about how to use pictures to tell the story?
- What changes could be made to meet the criteria for evidence on the rubric? How could you make this work even better?

Notes: [1] Based on Common Core math standard, NBT.C.5: *Given a two-digit number, mentally find 10 more or 10 less than the number, without having to count; explain the reasoning used.*

[2] Based on Common Core literacy standard, RH.6–8.1: *Cite specific textual evidence to support analysis of primary and secondary sources.*

[3] Based on Common Core literacy standard, RST.6–8.3: *Follow precisely a multistep procedure when carrying out experiments, taking measurements, or performing technical tasks.*

Table 2.1 Writing and Reflection Techniques

Techniques	Descriptions
Interactive writing	Together a group of students and teacher develop a short piece of writing (e.g., a friendly letter, a poem, a set of sentences to illustrate vocabulary).
Read-write-pair-share	Students read or watch something, write a short response, and share their written responses with a partner. A teacher circulating the room and listening in on the conversations can pull out key ideas to bring back to the whole class as well as surface any misconceptions that need to be clarified.
Summary writing	Students summarize what they have learned. This technique gives them valuable practice in condensing information and provides the teacher with a window into student learning.
Note catchers	Students record facts, observations, and insights on a note-catcher template as they work.
Journals	Students keep a journal to capture their ongoing reflections, observations, and responses to prompts.
Admission and exit tickets	As an opening or closing activity to a class, students write a reflection on their learning in the class that day or the previous day in response to a specific prompt. The teacher collects the writing, gathering a source of data on student understanding to help shape subsequent lessons.

Writing and Reflection Techniques

A wide repertoire of checking-for-understanding techniques enables teachers to capture the full range of student needs, keep their instruction engaging and focused, and get a complete picture of student understanding. During a lesson, choosing the right technique at the right time is key. There are many ways to use writing as a way for students to articulate and reflect on their developing understanding of a topic. Such writing techniques are best described as *writing to learn* rather than *learning to write.* In general they are short, informal assignments and are completed and checked quickly. If they are graded at all, the grade is based on the content not the quality of the writing (Fisher & Frey, 2007). Table 2.1 contains several such techniques.

Snapshot: Exit Tickets in a Sixth-Grade Math Class

Ali Morgan uses exit tickets to check for understanding in her sixth-grade math class at the Odyssey School in Denver. The exit tickets—which often consist of the learning target and a problem or follow-up question related to it—enable Morgan to quickly assess the students' learning and their ability to justify their reasoning with precision. The exit

(continued)

tickets also give students an opportunity to self-assess and reflect on their learning and needs through questions such as, "How did you grow in your understanding of the target today?" and "What do you need to know in order to master this target?" Morgan uses these exit tickets to determine trends that may inform the next day's lesson or to indicate that students are ready to move on to new targets.

Sample Exit Ticket Questions

Learning target: I can find the greatest common factors of two whole numbers (up to 100).

- What is the greatest common factor of 36 and 54? How do you know?
- What did you learn about finding the greatest common factor today?

Student Discussion Protocols

There is a wide variety of structured formats for student discussion and interaction (see table 2.2). Some are long and may take a whole class period (e.g., the Socratic seminar) and some are brief. These protocols can help engage all students and also provide teachers with valuable information about understanding as they observe and listen. (For more protocol ideas, check out the National School Reform Faculty website at www.nsrfharmony.org.).

Table 2.2 Student Discussion Protocols

Techniques	Descriptions
Back-to-back and face-to-face protocol	Partners stand back to back and wait for the teacher to ask a question or give a prompt. After listening to the prompt and thinking, they wait for the teacher to signal "face-to-face" and each take turns speaking and listening. This can be repeated with different partners as many times as is helpful. During the debrief, students share something new they learned or a new question they have.
Carousel brainstorm	Students are divided into small groups. Different questions are posted on newsprint at separate stations around the room. Each group, using a different color marker, spends a set amount of time at each station, brainstorming and recording responses to each question.
Write-pair-switch	Students begin by working alone on a written prompt. In the second step, they share what they have written with the student sitting next to them. In the final step, partners are changed and everyone shares with the person sitting in front or behind them.
Think-pair-share	In response to a question or prompt, students think individually for a set amount of time. When cued, students turn to a neighbor and each shares his or her thinking, also for a limited amount of time. The pair then shares with the large group.

Students use the technique write-pair-switch to check each other's understanding.

Quick Checks

The techniques in table 2.3 are all quick to implement and many involve physical movement and interaction. They are used for a variety of purposes—from checks of factual knowledge, to monitoring confusion, to deeper probes of understanding and opinion. It is important to consider purpose when selecting a strategy. For example, you would not choose a one-word go-around if your goal was to probe for deeper understanding of a question.

> "'Explain this to me' sounds so simple, but it is so useful. If they can verbalize it, then they've got it. And if someone can't explain it clearly, that is useful as well. I'll know I need to go over it again."
>
> —*Kara Miller, seventh-grade inclusion teacher, World of Inquiry School, Rochester, New York*

Table 2.3 Quick Checks

Factual or Brief-Response Checks	
Go-around	When a one- or two-word answer can show understanding or readiness for a task, teachers ask students to respond to a standard prompt one at a time, in rapid succession around the room.
Whiteboards	Students have small whiteboards at their desks or tables and write their ideas, thinking, or answers down and hold up their boards for teacher and peer scanning.
Do now	A brief problem, task, or activity that immediately engages students in the learning target for the day. It enables the circulating teacher to monitor students' readiness to move on and their grasp of necessary background knowledge.
Clicker technology	Though it requires the proper equipment (or appropriate app), clicker technology can be an exciting tool. Using hand-held devices or computers, students can anonymously respond to questions or problems posed by the teacher. Data can be quickly compiled and projected onto a screen illustrating a whole class's understanding of a topic without exposing individual students.
Monitoring Confusion or Readiness	
Explain it back	Ask students to repeat or summarize instructions or content to the group or a partner in their own words to check for misconceptions.
Table tags	Place paper signs or table tents in three areas with colors, symbols, or descriptors that indicate possible student levels of understanding or readiness for a task or target. Students sit in the area that best describes them, moving to a new area when relevant.
Thumb-ometer or fist-to-five	To show degree of agreement, readiness for tasks, or comfort with a learning target or concept, students can quickly show their thinking by putting their thumbs up, to the side, or down. Or, students can hold up a hand with a fist for zero, or disagree, or one to five fingers for higher levels of confidence or agreement.
Glass, bugs, mud	After students try a task or review a learning target or assignment, they identify their understanding or readiness for application using the windshield metaphor for clear vision: glass—totally clear; bugs—a little fuzzy; mud—I can barely see.
Status Checks	
Sticky bars	Create a chart that describes levels of understanding, progress, or mastery. Have students write their names or use an identifying symbol on a sticky note and place their notes on the appropriate place on the chart.
Learning lineups	Identify one end of the room with a descriptor such as *novice* or *beginning* and the other end as *expert* or *exemplary.* Students place themselves on this continuum based on where they are with a task or learning target. Invite them to explain their thinking to the whole class or the people near them.

Table 2.3 Continued

Status Checks	
Human bar graph	Identify a range of levels of understanding or mastery (e.g., beginning, developing, accomplished, or confused, I'm okay, I am rocking!) as labels for three to four adjacent lines. Students then form a human bar graph by standing in the line that best represents their current level of understanding.
Scatterplot graph	Similar to the human bar graph, but in a scatterplot graph students place themselves wherever they feel fits best based on the question being asked. They do not need to limit themselves to lining up in a particular category.
Probing Deeper Understanding and Reflection	
Hot seat	The teacher places key reflection or probing questions on random seats throughout the room. When prompted, students check their seats and answer the questions. Students who do not have a hot seat question are asked to agree or disagree with the response and explain their thinking.
Admission and exit tickets	Any relevant questions, prompts, or graphic displays of student thinking can be captured on a small sheet of paper and scanned by the teacher or other students to determine a student's readiness for the next step or to assess learning from a lesson. Teachers may use slips as a ticket to enter a discussion, protocol, or as a ticket to leave.
Presentation assessments	Whenever students present, they must determine a method to check their peers' understanding of the material they have presented. This helps to internalize checking for understanding as something that students can and should initiate with their peers.

Strategic Observation and Listening

Observation and listening are powerful ways to check for understanding. Teachers circulate while students are working and engaged in structured small-group discussions to observe learning in action and listen in on student conversations, as well as to confer. At times, teachers use a checklist to track evidence as they circulate. Checklists are typically linked to a supporting learning target to help teachers focus their observation and listening on the academic target at hand; however, teachers can also track evidence toward character learning targets. For example, for a series of lessons focused on making inferences supported by details, a teacher could circulate with a clipboard or tablet in hand with a checklist like the following to track assessment information. The checklist not only keeps teachers focused on a particular learning target while circulating and conferring but it also helps them track how many and which students they have observed or conferred with, make decisions about differentiation, and determine next steps for instruction.

Learning Target: I Can Make Inferences Supported by Details from the Text

Date	Student	On Track	Needs Support	Notes
1.21	Sarah	X		
1.21	Jazmin	X		
1.21	Alberto		X	Infers with accuracy; needs help citing supporting details
1.22	Ben	X		Able to support other students
1.22	Dominic		X	Trying to cite details, but match with inference is off
1.22	Alicia	X		

Strategy Close Up: Cold Call, No Opt Out, and Think Time

Cold call, no opt out (Fisher & Frey, 2007; Lemov, 2010), and think time are all instructional techniques that work hand-in-hand with the checking-for-understanding techniques described here.

"I do a lot of cold call. Depending on the chemistry of your class—if you have a quiet group or one with a few strong voices—it's important to do a think-pair-share and ask them to reflect and write first before calling on them and having a class discussion. This approach gives students confidence and more thoughtful responses. You can get kids to share who might not otherwise."

—Christian Zwahlen, seventh-grade ELA teacher, World of Inquiry School, Rochester, New York

Cold Call

This technique counteracts the instinct most teachers have to call on the most eager students. After posing a question, the teacher draws students' names randomly from a deck of cards, a jar of popsicle sticks, or any other manner of creative ways to represent every student's name. Cold call compels teachers to be more equitable in questioning. Cold call should not be used as "gotcha" strategy to catch students unprepared. In fact, teachers can employ various think time techniques (see "Think Time" section on p. 73) to support students to answer questions. Some teachers use a variation called *warm call:* students are given a chance to warm up their brains through reviewing a text or problems, writing thoughts, or conferring with a neighbor before anyone gets called on. The rest of the strategy is the same—students are called on by random draw.

No Opt Out

This technique requires that all students respond accurately and completely to a question. If a student gives an incomplete or incorrect response, another student is called on until a correct or complete answer is given. The teacher then returns to the student who gave an incorrect response so that he or she can restate the correct response or put the correct response in his or her own words. It is important that this be framed as a chance to try again to find success, rather than as a punishment for getting the answer wrong. If the answer is a simple fact, the technique is quick; if the answer involves explaining a concept, it is important to be patient and supportive as students work to articulate ideas in their own words, rather than simply parrot a statement. Other students may be invited to help.

No opt out should not limit a teacher in helping students who respond with weak answers. The following strategies, from *Quality Questioning* by Walsh and Sattes (2005), support students in developing strong responses:

Cue: Use symbols, words, or phrases to help students recall.

Clue: Use overt reminders such as, "Remember when . . ."

Probe: Look for reasoning behind an incorrect response or ask for clarity when the response is incomplete.

Rephrase: Pose the same question in different words.

In the accompanying video, students at the Springfield Renaissance School reflect on what they like about cold call and no opt out.

Think Time

Questions should be followed by appropriate think time to promote understanding by all students. Teachers can structure think time of about three to five seconds in a variety of ways:

- After a teacher question
- After a student question, before other students respond
- During student responses—students are given plenty of time to articulate their responses

Note taking, illustration, and written conversations are all variations on think time that help all students engage with questions. Examples include the following:

- Students pause to illustrate a response to a question.
- Students synthesize their thinking in response to questions with an individual or group headline—short, compelling phrases that capture their thinking, such as a news report.
- Students track their own questions during a mini-lesson.

- Students pose questions to each other and respond to teacher questions in chalk talks and written conversations with a peer or small group.

Watch video: "Kids Like Cold Call and No Opt Out—Checking for Understanding"

Debriefs

An effective debrief is the last chance during a daily lesson for a teacher to check for understanding, help students synthesize learning, and promote reflection so that students can monitor their own progress. It is an essential component of each lesson. During a debrief, teachers should return to the learning target(s) and elicit student reflection, probing for students to provide evidence for their own and class progress. In the accompanying video, Vanessa Cramer, a ninth-grade science teacher at the Springfield Renaissance School, uses the debrief to remind students of the learning target, call out things she observed during the lesson related to that learning target, and let them know where they are headed next. She uses cold call to have students reflect on their personal accomplishment in class that day.

Watch video: "Strategies for Monitoring Progress—Checking for Understanding"

During the debrief and throughout instruction time, teachers can promote ownership of thinking and learning by guiding students to analyze their thinking patterns, the logic of their reasoning, and their ability to apply their learning to novel situations. Probing questions may include the following:

- Why do you think this?
- How do you know?
- What evidence supports your thinking?
- How has your thinking changed and what changed your ideas?
- How might your thinking change if . . .?

The debrief is also an important opportunity to identify—or have students identify—goals for improvement and to celebrate individual, small-group, or whole-class success. When students give affirmations and helpful critique to themselves, their peers, and the group about the learning process during a debrief, they build a metacognitive understanding of their learning process and the academic mindsets they will need for success in college and careers.

Many teachers feel they would like to include debriefs at the conclusion of their lessons, but with time so tight in the day and so much to cover, they can't fit in a ten-minute debrief in a fifty-minute lesson or even a ninety-minute lesson. This is a poor trade-off. Better to spend forty or eighty minutes learning together and ten minutes making sure that learning is well understood and etched into students' brains than to work right up to the end of the lesson and have the learning evaporate when students leave the room.

Case Study

Promoting Student Ownership and Engagement in a Math Classroom at Codman Academy in Boston

Karen Crounse's eleventh-grade math students are engaged in a long-term learning expedition called "Traveling through Space." They are trying to figure out how to find the height of a rocket as it travels. They start by using trigonometric ratios to find the height of a local church, using the same formulas and reasoning necessary to find the height of the rocket. As Crounse explains, "I believe that kids understand math when it's taught through investigations, when they discover the patterns."

In this problem-solving approach to teaching math, checking for understanding is key for Crounse. "I always give a 'do now' that builds on the previous day's class. I walk around so I can check each student's understanding. By having them write things down, I can see where they're having problems and what the errors in their thinking are. Most of the class work is done in groups, but the 'do now' is individual. I want to know what each individual got out of the previous class."

"In every 'do now' I make it a point to check in with students who struggle with the material or who were absent. I address *everyone's* questions, but I go to those students first. Walking around I might notice they are writing about math terms, but not using the correct vocabulary. When I debrief the 'do now' I make sure I bring out the correct vocabulary. [This level of precision] is very important for summarizing the data we collect."

In addition to checking individual work, Crounse is passionate about the value of having students work collaboratively. "By having students work in groups, they can help

(continued)

each other while I walk around and check their understanding." Through collaboration, students have the opportunity to critique each other's reasoning, justify their thinking, and represent their learning so that others can understand it.

"I record what the groups tell me at the board without worrying about whether it is correct. I know we will get to checking it later. It engages everyone to examine it critically and decide whether it makes sense with the patterns we're seeing." In this way, students are checking their own reasoning as they examine the accuracy and understanding evident in their peers' work. "Doing these kinds of discovery activities in math means every student is engaged. It is not possible to hide." See Crounse's class in action in the accompanying video.

Watch video: "Promoting Student Ownership and Engagement in Math—Checking for Understanding"

IN PRACTICE

Engage in Targeted Instruction to Address Gaps in Understanding

Over time, especially when there are strong professional collaborative structures in place, teachers deepen their expertise with checking for understanding. They learn to layer the techniques, choosing the right one for a particular purpose. Most important, they learn to adjust their instruction in response to information gathered from checking-for-understanding techniques in the moment-to-moment flow of a lesson and in longer-range planning. Teachers who embrace this practice link checking for understanding to the right differentiation strategies, a critical step in improving achievement for all students.

Differentiation is a philosophical belief and an instructional approach through which teachers proactively plan to meet students' varied needs based on ongoing assessment. Teachers use flexible groupings of students and design respectful tasks that enable different approaches to the same goals.

What does a teacher do when she discovers that only about half of her class is getting it? Those students are ready to move on, but the remainder represents

Figure 2.2 Adjusting Instruction Based on Gaps in Understanding

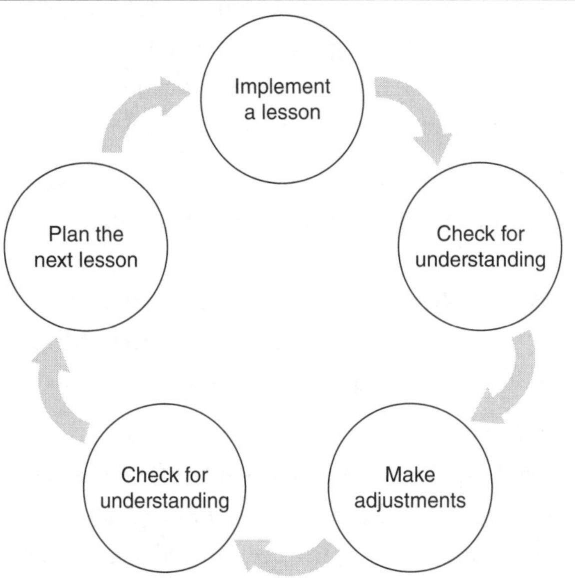

a mix of students who are on the verge of clarity and others who are totally lost. The point of checking for understanding is to enable teachers to catch when students are not understanding the material and to use that information to adjust instruction. Figure 2.2 demonstrates a typical cycle for a teacher adjusting instruction based on frequent checks for understanding.

> "Checking for understanding is challenging for students with learning disabilities. Language can be an obstacle. You need extra time, but it makes them work through the process of understanding. It's what will make it stick."
>
> —*Kara Miller, seventh-grade inclusion teacher, World of Inquiry School, Rochester, New York*

What follows are possible scenarios in which teachers respond to varying levels of understanding ascertained through some of the techniques discussed in the "Getting Started" section:

- Exit tickets reveal a large gap between those students with a firm grasp of the material and those with only a tenuous grasp, with a large number of students in the middle. The teacher plans the next day's lesson with students in differentiated groups that she can rotate through during student work time.

- The human bar graph reveals a fairly even split of the class, with those who get it and those who don't. The teacher immediately creates small groups with two students from the beginning group and two from the accomplished group joined together and gives them discussion prompts geared at bringing the beginning group up to at least developing understanding.
- During read-write-pair-share the teacher observes conversations that reveal conceptual misunderstandings. She refers to her preplanned questions, which she has organized to accommodate anticipated gaps in understanding, and carefully chooses questions that will elicit clarifying discussions. She "catches" the class to ask these questions. When it is clear that the discussion has clarified misconceptions, she "releases" them back to their partner work.
- During a writers' workshop focused on revision, with the learning target "I can revise my draft for sequence or descriptive details," the teacher hands back rough drafts with descriptive feedback based on a rubric. He offers two mini-lessons, one on organization and one on descriptive detail. Based on the feedback on their drafts, students select the mini-lesson that will best help them meet the learning target.

Teachers may choose to work with small groups to address understanding gaps.

It is important that teachers preplan their lessons to enable opportunities to check for understanding and that the particular techniques are prepared ahead of time. Table 2.4 shows some of the possible checking-for-understanding techniques a teacher might use during a workshop lesson.

Strategy Close Up: Catch and Release or Release and Catch

The catch-and-release technique is used after the teacher has introduced a new skill or concept and releases students to practice on their own. When necessary, she catches the group again to reteach or reexplain a concept and students are then released to practice or apply the concept again.

Conversely, the release-and-catch technique gives students the opportunity to problem solve and make meaning prior to a mini-lesson or guided practice. This technique gives students a chance to grapple with challenging concepts or texts individually before the teacher catches them to correct misconceptions or answer questions with guided practice or a mini-lesson. Giving students the opportunity to grapple with material independently first is key to meeting Common Core standards.

With both of these techniques it is important that teachers catch students for short periods of time, keeping teacher talk time to a minimum so that students can spend the majority of the time thinking and doing.

Teach Students to Monitor Progress and Set Goals

Teaching students how to set goals and making goal setting and self-assessment a daily practice will develop student ownership of their learning. Students in Vanessa Cramer's ninth-grade science class at the Springfield Renaissance School use learning target trackers on a daily basis and write reflections on their learning following every summative assessment. These reflections then become critical components of each student's preparation for their student-led conference (see chapter 5 for more on this topic). See Cramer's class in action in the previously referenced video "Strategies for Monitoring Progress—Checking for Understanding."

The process of formulating goals helps students translate learning targets into personal terms and requires that they check their own understanding. To be effective, goals should be specific and doable (challenging enough to advance learning but not so challenging as to overwhelm or frustrate). They should align with

Table 2.4 Opportunities to Check for Understanding during a Workshop Lesson

Components of the Lesson	Possible Checking-for-Understanding Strategies
Engage (Introduction) Students develop curiosity and a need to know linked to the purpose of the lesson.	• Explain it back—restate the learning target
Grapple (Introduction) Students build self-reliance, confidence, and perseverance through grappling with a complex text, problem, or writing skill or concept.	• Strategic observation and listening • Thumb-ometer or fist-to-five—to assess readiness for the lesson
Discuss Students hone their ability to justify their thinking, make coherent arguments based on text evidence, considering the ideas of others. They are metacognitive about their own approaches to math, reading, and writing.	• Strategic observation and listening—as students discuss, listen to note patterns of thinking, great ideas, and misconceptions to incorporate during the mini-lesson
Focus (Guided Practice) Teachers gradually release responsibility and create a safe space for students to practice the task with support.	• Strategic observation and listening—as students practice, the teacher determines needs for small- or whole-group instruction • Write-pair-switch—students practice and then share with a partner • Glass-bugs-mud—to assess readiness for independent work
Focus (Mini-Lesson) The teacher provides explicit instruction, focusing on a particular skill or concept and responding to good student ideas, gaps in understanding, and misconceptions. (*Note:* In some cases, the teacher will choose not to conduct a mini-lesson.)	• Cold call—ask students to restate the steps involved in the lesson • Think-pair-share—generate and share criteria for quality for their work during the lesson • Table tags—students indicate their understanding of the material in the mini-lesson and expectations for their work
Apply (Application) All students have the opportunity to practice the particular skill or concept.	• Strategic observation and listening—look at students' work as they create it and have focused conversations with students to address gaps in understanding • Preplanned strategic questions—ask questions tied to the learning target to assess student progress
Synthesize (Share and Debrief) Students return to the learning target, synthesize learning, and assess whether or not they have met the target. Teacher and students address misconceptions and generalize conceptual understanding.	• Preplanned strategic questions—to assess students' ability to transfer learning to new applications • Exit tickets—to assess gaps in understanding and plan for the next lesson

learning targets and be broken down into smaller chunks if necessary (Moss & Brookhart, 2009). (For more on goal setting, see chapter 3.)

Even more important than teachers monitoring understanding is empowering students with the tools to monitor it themselves. When students build the habit of catching themselves in the middle of reading a text or working on a math problem, recognizing that they are confused, and rereading to find the source of their confusion, they have taken the most important step. They may resolve it independently or seek help from a peer, teacher, text, or online source. The key is the commitment to the ongoing practice of tracking understanding as they work.

Keep the Right Balance between Consistency and a Variety of Strategies

As the following case study of Jessica Wood's classroom illustrates, it is challenging to keep the right balance between consistent use of a few effective strategies and the variety needed to ensure students' needs are met. Starting small with a few manageable priorities and creating consistency across a team or school are important ways to lay the groundwork for effective checking for understanding. As practice and expertise deepens, it is also important to mix it up—to ensure that students stay engaged and interested and to ensure that different learning needs are met. For example, some students may do their best thinking in quiet reflection through writing, whereas others respond better when they can turn and talk to a peer. Knowing students well enables teachers to match strategy, purpose, and student needs.

Case Study

Building a Checking-for-Understanding Repertoire at the Springfield Renaissance School in Springfield, Massachusetts

Jessica Wood, a sixth-grade English language arts teacher at the Springfield Renaissance School has spent the past several years building her repertoire of checking-for-understanding techniques. "I started with a couple of strategies, built by necessity, and then learned more explicitly what to do as time went on. For example cold call is

(continued)

something we teachers do instinctively, but it's hard to keep track of who you have called on and who you haven't." Wood uses a box of cards with students' names on them—she pulls a name from the box and then puts that card aside to avoid calling on students more than once. She was drawn quickly into the practice. "As any teacher will tell you, if something is practical, you use it the next day."

"A lot seems really obvious, and my initial trepidation was wondering if the kids would respond well. I was surprised to discover that kids really are pretty open. When we do thumbs up, it's close to their chest and no one is really looking. They were more open and honest than I expected. After they are trained in how and why to use the strategies, most students are pretty accurate in their self-assessment."

Delving into Instruction and Differentiation

The greater complexity came with figuring out what to do next. "When you get into catch and release and repeating lessons and differentiating, it's much harder. Okay, so you've discerned a group of kids is not up to speed, how do you go back and reteach and differentiate?"

"One thing I found challenging after a while was that I felt I just had a few techniques and wanted to switch it up. I wanted to have enough variety to really get at all kids' levels of understanding. It's all about preparation, to have the time to put together the cards, learn a new technique, etc." The professional environment and culture of the school made a big difference to Wood's learning curve: "having a coach who really knows the practices, together with the fact my school takes it very seriously, has been invaluable." (For more on the Springfield Renaissance School's whole-school approach to checking for understanding, see the "Schoolwide Implementation" section of this chapter.)

Knowing Which Strategy to Use When

As Wood developed her repertoire of strategies, she considered their purpose and most effective use. "I use cold call and no opt out questions more for content areas that kids have had sufficient time with already, so they're ready to dig in and think more about it. A lot of kids have anxiety and processing difficulty. The strategies work if kids have had time to study up on the topic and it's really a review. I wouldn't use it with new content."

"'Thumbs' is only useful in a traditional seating arrangement. When they're facing each other, they are too curious. True-false is a helpful strategy, but only with processing time. To use think-pair-share, the seating arrangements are very important. If I am entering a unit with lots of sharing, I have to be really thoughtful about who's on the left and who's on the right."

Keeping the End in Mind

For Wood, the real value of checking-for-understanding techniques lies in the way they enable you to help students who might otherwise fall through the cracks. "It's not just the recalcitrant rebel kid. It is also the quiet girl in the front row. For those children, the checking-for-understanding strategies give them a voice to say they need other tools. They don't know how to ask. If you set up your classroom where you only check for understanding in one way, it's going to favor a certain type of learner."

The time and effort she has spent seem well worth it to Wood: "It's an exercise in trust. Even though you have an end goal in mind, if you can be flexible in how you get there it's so much more effective. Monitoring how kids are doing at every step really does work. I find that kids' needs fall into clumps [of similar needs]. So it's not that you have to come up with twenty-five different plans, but rather identify groups of needs." Helping her students develop ownership of their learning is a central focus for Wood: "If kids can't assess where they are and think meta-cognitively, how can they be critical thinkers?" See Wood's class in action in the previously referenced video "Instructional Strategies That Support Learning—Checking for Understanding."

Critical Moves for Deepening Student Engagement

As with all of the practices in this book, checking for understanding during daily lessons involves students as key actors in the assessment process. The practice enables teachers to make adjustments in real time and encourages students to be constantly engaged in the lesson and aware of their levels of understanding. Table 2.5 describes the who, what, and why of the key checking-for-understanding actions that lead students to greater engagement with learning.

Table 2.5 The Who, What, and Why of Checking for Understanding

What Do Teachers Do?	What Do Students Do?	What's the Result?
Create quality learning targets and assessments and ensure that students understand what is expected of them.	Make an effort to understand the learning targets and connect them with the purpose of each lesson and learning activity.	Students have greater engagement and ownership of learning. They understand the purpose of their work.
Build a classroom culture of trust and collaboration.	Students communicate honestly about what they understand and what they don't.	Students can identify when they are struggling. Teachers can address gaps in understanding.
Preplan strategic questions to assess understanding throughout the lesson.	Support thinking and ideas with evidence.	Teachers can target questions to ensure they are driving at the learning target.

(continued)

Table 2.5 Continued

What Do Teachers Do?	What Do Students Do?	What's the Result?
Build lesson plans that support students in meeting learning targets, emphasize student participation, and include ongoing checks for understanding throughout.	Monitor their own understanding throughout a lesson and advocate for support as needed; support peers with their understanding.	Teachers quickly catch students who may be struggling. Students stay on track with learning targets and can continue to close the gap between where they are and where they need to be.
Check for whole-class understanding using a variety of techniques and make adjustments to instruction as necessary. Ensure that all students are included.	Self-assess progress in relation to a specific learning target.	Teachers and students can make informed decisions about next moves (e.g., offering or attending an additional guided-practice session before moving into independent practice).
Check for individual understanding using a variety of techniques and use data to make decisions about next instructional steps to meet the needs of all students.	Participate in class and turn in work (e.g., exit tickets, reflection journals, quizzes) that demonstrates progress in relation to one or more learning targets.	Teachers are able to make informed decisions about next instructional steps related to individual students (e.g., oral or written feedback, differentiated materials, and instruction in next lesson).
Teach students to set goals based on self-assessment of progress toward learning targets. Model good goals and make use of goal-setting guides to assist students.	Set goals for class time and ongoing projects. Use checking-for-understanding strategies to self-assess.	Students develop more independence in self-assessment and deeper understanding of learning targets.
Over time build a repertoire of checking-for-understanding techniques to engage students with varied learning styles in self-assessment. Increasingly emphasize student ownership and capacity to self-assess.	Become more proficient at self-assessing their level of understanding as the variety of strategies employed by the teacher expands to meet their learning needs.	Students become increasingly aware and metacognitive about where they are in the learning process, and can use this information to guide their work. More students meet learning targets and do not fall behind as teachers can adapt instruction to meet the general and individual needs of the students. Students trust that their honest self-assessment will help them progress.

SCHOOLWIDE IMPLEMENTATION

Checking for understanding, as the bridge between teaching and learning, is an essential part of a schoolwide student-engaged assessment system. School leaders will need to devote time for professional development and classroom observations to support teachers in moving beyond a superficial approach to checking for understanding. It is important to help teachers use the techniques described in this chapter as a source of data about their students' progress so that they can adapt instruction and support learning.

Similarly, leaders can support teachers to see these techniques as a strategy for student engagement, encouraging students to internalize the habit of self-assessing their own understanding throughout the day. At the juncture between instruction and assessment, leaders need to carefully plan how to engage, support, and hold faculty accountable for the practice as it is implemented. We have highlighted some of the key leadership actions that will support smooth implementation of checking-for-understanding techniques throughout a school.

Lay the Groundwork

- Leaders must share and express a common vision of quality and develop schoolwide goals. Launch with schoolwide professional development to look at models and share the research behind the practice, the rationale, and strategies for success.
- Build background knowledge—leaders and teachers must deeply understand checking-for-understanding techniques and their potential impact.
- Provide time and professional development for teachers to know their state and Common Core standards and the impact that checking for understanding will have on helping students meet them.
- Set specific goals for deepening the work tied to measurable student outcomes.

Build Teacher Capacity

- Select a set of priority practices and work collaboratively with faculty members to develop a common practice rubric and criteria for success.

"Embed some common checking-for-understanding methods in every classroom at the start of the school year and spend more time on that initially. When you try to do everything at once, it's too overwhelming. Better to focus on three to four priorities."

—Stephen R. Mahoney, principal, Springfield Renaissance School, Springfield, Massachusetts

- Differentiate support for teachers. Look at data with them to examine the impact of checking-for-understanding techniques in their classrooms. Discuss any adjustments in instruction that occur as a result of the checking for understanding. Evaluate results in relation to student achievement and support teachers to expand their repertoire.
- Prioritize instructional leadership and develop a coaching cycle with teachers.
- Align resources to support the practice, including supplies, access to professional literature, and professional development offerings.

Support Teachers to Deepen Their Practice

- Support all teachers to meet criteria for implementing checking-for-understanding techniques. Incorporate criteria for quality into professional development and link to individual coaching plans for all teachers to provide individualized ongoing support for implementation.
- Monitor progress and make adjustments. Use regular learning walks, data collection, and feedback. The leadership team should analyze results and adapt professional development and coaching plans to meet schoolwide needs. Table 2.6 illustrates a tool for this purpose adapted from one created by the Springfield Renaissance School.
- Collaboratively analyze results and impact on student achievement with faculty members.
- Develop models of quality and a peer observation structure so that teachers can model practices for all faculty members to learn from. Promote increased coaching opportunities, a culture of peer support and professionalism, and a mindset of ongoing improvement.

Table 2.6 Sample Classroom Observation Checklist

	Exemplary	Meets Expectation	Approaching Expectation	Not Meeting Expectation	Not Applicable
Learning targets: The daily learning target is connected to a supporting learning target. Students discuss the target at the beginning of the lesson, during, and at the end (with debrief).					Note why practice was skipped.
Do now: A short assignment relevant to course learning targets gets kids on task. Students can handle the work independently and produce tangible evidence of understanding.					Note why practice was skipped.
Guided practice: Teachers gradually release responsibility, creating a safe space for students to practice the task with support, and give students experience with success.					Note why practice was skipped.
Catch and release as needed: Teacher "catches" students by pulling class together to check on progress, share strategies, correct common misunderstandings, or address frequent questions or issues.					Note why practice was skipped.
Cold call: Cold call is used with cards and keeps all students alert and engaged. Students are familiar with the routine, and it is used in a positive way to check for understanding.					Note why practice was skipped.
No opt out: All incorrect or incomplete student responses are followed with coaching, cold calling peers, or providing correct information until those students provide corrected and accurate responses.					Note why practice was skipped.
Debrief: Return to the learning target, synthesize learning, and assess whether or not students have met the target. Address misconceptions and generalize conceptual understanding.					Note why practice was skipped.
Homework: Homework is designed to improve student mastery of learning targets. It is accessible to all learners and includes a product to assess student effort and understanding.					Note why practice was skipped.

Case Study

Setting Schoolwide Priorities for the Use of Checking-for-Understanding Techniques at the Springfield Renaissance School in Springfield, Massachusetts

The Springfield Renaissance School staff spent their first several years developing the systems, structures, and classroom culture to know their students well. Once a strong sense of community was established, they shifted focus to checking for understanding as a schoolwide instructional practice that would take them to the next level.

According to principal Stephen Mahoney, "The practice keeps teachers and kids accountable for learning. The regularity of it breeds familiarity and confidence. The kids know what to expect in every classroom. You set a tone and set of expectations, and as a teacher you get immediate feedback on whether what you are doing is working."

Creating a Set of Manageable Schoolwide Priorities

The staff chose five strategies as their focal point:

- Posting and using the learning target
- Guided practice
- Catch and release
- No opt out and cold call
- Debrief at the end of class

The instructional leadership team—the principal, two assistant principals, and two full-time instructional coaches—observe three classrooms every week. They stay for a whole class (in order to observe all of the strategies) and use a common checklist to gather data on which strategies are used (see table 2.6). Mahoney then shares compiled data about practices they have observed in classrooms with the whole faculty in his Monday memo. "Our goal is that practices will be observed 80 percent of the time. In the memo we say, for example, 'Here's what we observed this week—100 percent of classrooms observed had learning targets posted. Fifty percent did cold call and no opt out. Eighty percent ran a debrief.' The data are also used in coaching conversations, evaluation meetings, and in shaping professional development. It is definitely an ongoing learning process." See an interview with principal Mahoney in the accompanying video.

Watch video: "Schoolwide Structures for Checking for Understanding"

WHAT TO EXPECT

Teachers should be able to implement the majority of the checking-for-understanding techniques described in this chapter immediately. Many are easy to learn and use. As sixth-grade teacher Jessica Wood reminds us, "If something is practical, you use it the next day." However, Wood also reminds us of the importance of moving beyond rote implementation of a few techniques to a strategic approach that employs a wide variety of writing and reflection prompts, discussion protocols, quick checks, strategic observation and listening, and debriefs. With practice, teachers will gain confidence knowing what technique to use—and when—in order to accurately monitor student progress. They will use the information students give them about their understanding to adjust instruction and meet students' needs. Most importantly, students will begin to take ownership of the process. They will view checking for understanding as an essential part of the learning process—their honest self-assessments will help them meet their learning goals.

When entire schools embrace the kinds of checking-for-understanding techniques described here, the benefits for students grow exponentially. From class to class students gain skills to monitor their progress toward learning targets. They will increasingly gain independence and ownership of the process. Schoolwide implementation will also enable school leaders to observe classrooms feeling assured that they know what kind of progress students are making toward learning targets. They will better support their teachers' professional growth and learning.

We have identified some of the benchmarks that teachers and school leaders can expect at the beginning, intermediate, and advanced phases of implementing checking-for-understanding techniques.

Beginning

- Teachers put time and energy into establishing a classroom culture of trust and respect and one in which students believe they can improve with effort.
- When planning lessons, teachers simultaneously preplan the questions they will ask students to assess their understanding throughout the lesson.
- Teachers structure lessons to ensure that students have time to apply concepts and skills so that both students and teachers can accurately monitor understanding.
- Teachers implement a manageable set of techniques to monitor understanding at the beginning, middle, and end of lessons.

Intermediate

- Teachers begin to expand their repertoire of techniques.

- Teachers consistently use checking-for-understanding techniques throughout their lessons.
- Teachers strategically align checking-for-understanding techniques to the assessment purpose.
- Students can describe their progress toward learning targets and tasks at varying points in a lesson and assess what they need in order to meet their goals.
- Based on information gleaned from checking for understanding, teachers are able to implement a variety of differentiation strategies aligned to learning targets and matched to student need.

Advanced

- Schoolwide expectations for common checking-for-understanding techniques and professional development are established.
- All teachers receive coaching on checking-for-understanding techniques.
- Checking-for-understanding techniques are observed across classrooms with increasing regularity and frequency.
- Professional development and coaching is differentiated to meet individual teachers' strengths and needs.
- Teachers throughout the school target instruction to address gaps in student understanding and develop enrichment strategies for students whose checks for understanding reveal early mastery.

COMMON CHALLENGES

A Lack of Rich and Rigorous Lesson Content

Make it matter. Ensure each lesson asks students to learn meaningful content and perform rich, challenging tasks based on Common Core and state standards. Otherwise, there won't be much "understanding" to check.

Weak Classroom Culture

Build a strong foundation. Checking for understanding will fail to take root and will become just another technique if there is not a classroom culture to nurture it. There must be a climate of safety and trust in the classroom where students share their struggles and work together to help each other. Students must be celebrated for hard work, honesty, compassion, collaboration, and their commitment to revision and growth.

Lack of a Growth Mindset

Everyone can get smarter. Make sure that students understand that their brains actually get stronger and smarter by grappling with hard work. If they believe that there are the "smart kids" and the "dumb kids," they will hide their confusions, and their progress will be limited.

An Overemphasis on the Teacher's Role

Hear from students. Involve and teach students to take an active part. Effective checking for understanding involves communication—whether verbal or nonverbal—between teacher and student. Teaching students to be reflective about their understanding and setting goals accordingly empowers them to meet those goals. Students should actively and regularly consider and discuss what understanding looks like. They should work together to make sure the whole class "gets it."

Falling into an Obedience Model

It's not about compliance and control. The goal of using any checking-for-understanding technique is to figure out what students are learning and how instruction should be adjusted. Paying attention, raising hands, and speaking when called on can be a means, but they are not the end.

Inconsistencies from Class to Class

Be consistent schoolwide. The power of checking for understanding increases dramatically when it is implemented across a school or grade level. Students notice and benefit when teachers use common strategies and speak the same language.

Overreliance on Self-Report Techniques without Checks

Be strategic. There needs to be a balance between students checking their own understanding and the teacher checking the students' understanding. Without the first, students will never become independent learners, but without the second, it's possible that students will have an inaccurate sense of what they understand. Know what techniques give you the information you need at the right time.

Lack of Variation in Methods Used to Check for Understanding

Change it up. Although it is good to start with a few key techniques, broadening your repertoire will support deeper engagement and clearer achievement information. Different strategies produce different kinds of evidence and match different learning styles.

Letting the Debrief Fall off the Map

Closure is important. Reflection solidifies learning and clarifies important needs and new questions. Make sure the scheduled debrief happens. Preplan strategic questions that tie to the target and construct debriefs that emphasize time for reflection and student self-assessment.

Lack of Follow-Up on Gaps in Understanding

Act on gaps in understanding. Checking for understanding must lead to differentiation and adapted instruction. Effective teachers adapt their instruction and curriculum plans to make sure that every student is learning. A focus on professional development for differentiated instruction should be connected with the focus on checking for understanding.

Chapter 3

Using Data with Students

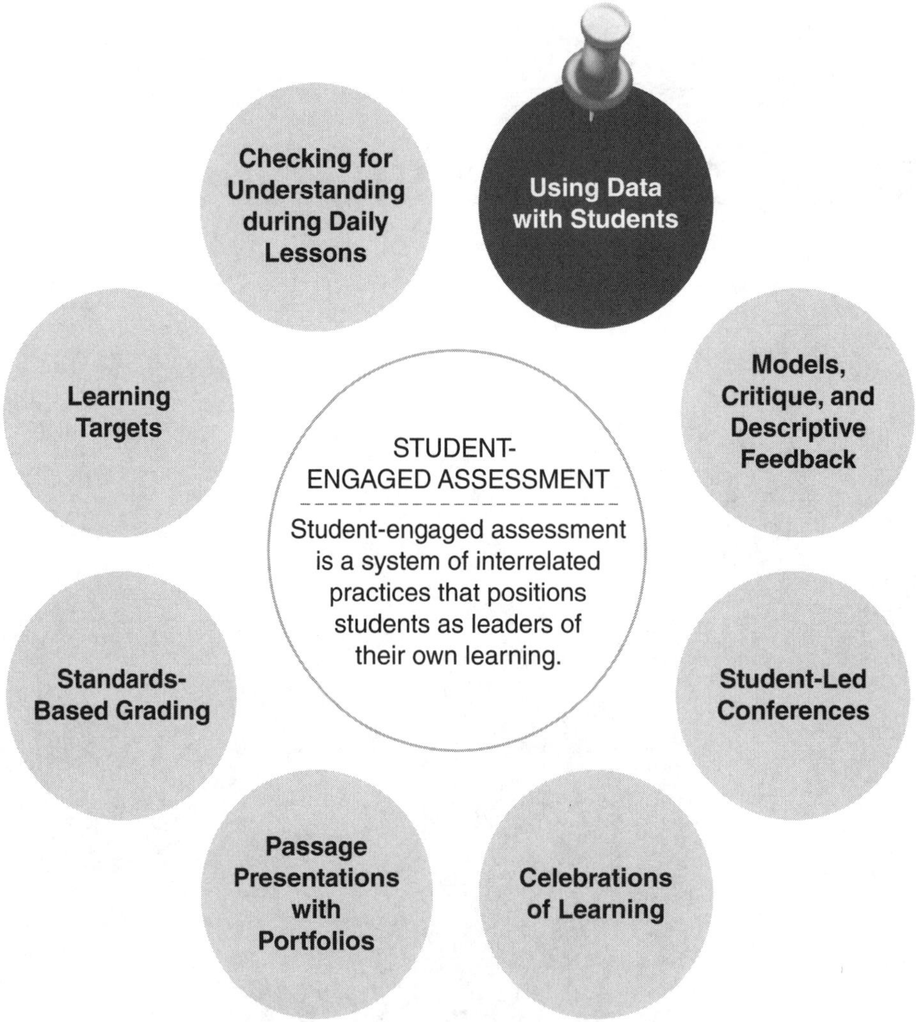

Checking for Understanding during Daily Lessons

Using Data with Students

Models, Critique, and Descriptive Feedback

Learning Targets

STUDENT-ENGAGED ASSESSMENT

Student-engaged assessment is a system of interrelated practices that positions students as leaders of their own learning.

Standards-Based Grading

Student-Led Conferences

Passage Presentations with Portfolios

Celebrations of Learning

For more than a dozen years I taught students who would describe their ability in math by their test average: "I'm a good math student" (i.e., my test scores are high); "I'm an okay math student" (i.e., my test scores are middling). Despite all of my work trying to help them develop a growth mindset in mathematics—pointing out that their ability is not fixed—and trying to help them understand how different they performed across various aspects of mathematics, they only seemed to remember concrete test numbers: "I got an 89 percent and an 84 percent on my last two tests. I'm doing pretty well." This was a good testament to the memorable power of quantitative data, but it was certainly not helping their mindset or growth as students.

Then I borrowed a strategy from a colleague and everything changed. We began using a data tracking form with categories of error types. Students analyzed tests and assignments and assigned each error to a category (e.g., copying error, computation error, using the wrong operation) and noted it on the form. Because the nature of their errors wasn't always clear, students worked together to understand what went wrong. They became intrigued by the patterns of their errors. Over time they had a great deal of test and assignment data to draw on. They created charts with distribution patterns of errors and of changes in performance over time. They shared and analyzed these charts with classmates during math sessions.

When these students presented their math at student-led conferences, everything was different. They described the terrain of their strengths, challenges, and growth and the latitude and longitude of who they were as math learners. It wasn't uncommon to hear statements like these:

- "I am good at understanding ratios and percentages, but I still make computational errors sometimes in percentage work."
- "My weakness in division turned out to be mostly in lining up numbers; graph paper has almost solved that, as you can see from my data."
- "In positive and negative integers, I was confused by the concepts until February 5th, when it started to make sense as you can see here . . ."

We strive to be data driven or data informed in education these days, but typically we limit our vision of who can productively use data:

school leaders, coaches, and teachers. Students are left out. When students are equipped to analyze data for their own learning, whether from large-scale summative assessments or daily formative assessments, the power of data as an engine for growth is centered where it has the greatest potential to improve learning—with students.

—Ron Berger

Increasing Engagement and Achievement

At Genesee Community Charter School in Rochester, New York, third-grade teacher Jean Hurst leans in and listens intently as her student, Jacelyn, reads aloud. Hurst is listening for greater fluency in Jacelyn's oral reading, a skill they have been working on for several weeks. As she listens, she hears greater cadence and confidence in Jacelyn's voice. Hurst is careful to note miscues and the length of time it takes Jacelyn to read the passage. They start their follow-up discussion by reviewing Jacelyn's previous goals and successes and reviewing a chart that shows the growth in her reading level. They focus in on fluency and the word substitutions Hurst heard as Jacelyn read aloud. "Let's take a look at this word," says Hurst. "Read it back to me." Jacelyn struggles at first, but calls out the word *proclaims.* Hurst shares that when she read it aloud, she read it as *announces.* "We call that a substitution. Do you think you know what happened as you were reading?" Hurst asks. Jacelyn thinks a little more and shares, "Well, I wasn't sure what the word was but I knew it had to mean something like *says* or *announces* because of where it was in the sentence."

Hurst and Jacelyn discuss how her substitution enabled her to make sense of what she was reading without slowing down her overall rate. Hurst shares with Jacelyn her Developmental Reading Assessment (DRA) fluency score, and they compare it to older data. It is apparent that her fluency score is improving.

Jacelyn is reflective about her growth as a struggling reader: "It's kind of how there are all kinds of runners. Some are fast and some are slow, but we all need to cross the finish line. Well, I just need to move faster than everyone else to get where I need to be." The use of data has helped her (with the guidance of her teacher) to set goals that have moved her from a late kindergarten level in September to an early third-grade level by the end of the year. As Hurst points out, "Although she's still not at grade level, she's made two years of progress and making that progress visible through the use of data has helped Jacelyn to become a more motivated and informed reader."

Using data with students encompasses classroom practices that build students' capacity to access, analyze, and use data effectively to reflect, set goals, and document growth. Using data with students encompasses the following activities:

- Students use their classwork as a source for data, analyzing strengths, weaknesses, and patterns to improve their work.
- Students regularly analyze evidence of their own progress. They track their progress on assessments and assignments, analyze their errors for patterns, and describe what they see in the data about their current level of performance.
- Students use data to set goals and reflect on their progress over time and incorporate data analysis into student-led conferences.

Teachers and school leaders everywhere collect and analyze data to make informed decisions about instruction that will support all students in meeting state and Common Core standards. However, in many schools, the power of data to improve student achievement is not fully leveraged because students are left out of the process. The most powerful determinants of student growth are the mind-sets and learning strategies that students themselves bring to their work—how much they care about working hard and learning, how convinced they are that hard work leads to growth, and how capably they have built strategies to focus, organize, remember, and navigate challenges.

When students themselves identify, analyze, and use data from their learning, they become active agents in their own growth. They set personal goals informed by data they understand, and they own those goals. The framework of student-engaged assessment provides a range of opportunities to involve students in using data to improve their learning. As the story about Jacelyn illustrates, using data with students has the potential to build reflective and confident learners with key dispositions of college and career readiness.

Why This Practice Matters

Using data with students means much more than sharing test results with students a few times a year. The practice is most effective as an ongoing part of a classroom culture in which students are always collecting and analyzing information in order to improve. *Data driven* has become a ubiquitous phrase in schools today. Typically it refers to using the results of standardized tests—yearly state assessments and interim district assessments—to inform the focus and pacing of classroom instruction. If we limit our use of data to this purpose, however, we are missing the great potential of gathering data related to a wider range of evidence of learning (e.g., individual patterns in writing and math assignments, homework habits, reading stamina). Data of this kind can be collected and analyzed with students and by students and can be used to help them set and achieve goals for improved learning. The following purposes for using data with students point to the power of the practice to engage and support all students.

Empowering Students to Accurately Assess Their Current Level of Proficiency in Order to Set Challenging and Effective Goals

In order to establish and reach aspirational goals, students must first be aware of their starting point. Too often, in the name of protecting children's self-esteem, we avoid explicit discussions of standards and where students stand in relation to them. Rather than boosting confidence, such "protection" actually prevents students from advancing and blocks their understanding of what it takes to succeed. Providing students with the opportunity to identify their own strengths and weaknesses through data analysis gives them a powerful tool for learning. It moves conversations about progress from abstract, generic goals (e.g., try harder, study more) to student-determined, targeted goals (e.g., increase my reading level by 1.5 years, master 80 percent or more of my learning targets, ensure that 100 percent of my homework is fully completed and submitted) and provides them with skills to track those goals. Of course, making data transparent requires a safe classroom culture, a topic that will be explored further later in this chapter.

Transforming Student Mindsets from a Belief That Intelligence Is Fixed to a Belief in the Power of Their Own Potential to Grow through Effort

In order to meet challenging goals, students must believe that the goals are within their capacity to achieve (Dweck, 2006). Many students who have previously been unsuccessful in school acquire a fixed mindset, rather than a growth mindset (i.e., some kids are good at math, others in art or reading). They see intelligence as something you are born with rather than something that can be developed through hard work. Strategic use of data in the classroom provides an opportunity to overcome this mindset of limitation. It gives students the chance to document their learning over time and have concrete evidence that they know more and can do more than they could previously. And, it develops the connection between hard work and achievement, replacing the idea that "some kids are smart" with "if I work hard, I'll get better."

Making Progress toward Standards and Making Grading Transparent

Too often what it means to achieve or reach a standard stays shrouded in mystery. Students and their families may have no idea why they receive a certain grade or why they continue to struggle with learning a particular content area. Using data with students is one way to shine a light on learning. It helps students see actual evidence of what they know and can do. It also helps shift their thinking from all or nothing—I met my goal or I did not meet my goal—to a more complex understanding focused on growth over time (e.g., I've successfully mastered 75 percent of this content since my initial assessment; to reach my goal of 90 percent or more I need to work on . . .).

Making Students More Responsible for Their Own Learning

Data inquiry and analysis is a fitting and rich component to many schools' professional development cycles. Yet, it is often removed from the classroom and something that happens about rather than with students. Bringing data analysis into the classroom is one more example of transforming what is traditionally reserved for adults into an opportunity for student leadership. Although investigating data takes different forms at different developmental stages, even the youngest students can and should be given opportunities to explore data related to their academic and character growth.

Common Misconceptions about Data

Many of us have preconceived ideas about data. For that reason, it's important that we clear up a few misconceptions.

Misconception 1: Using Data Is Only about Basic Skills and Information

Although an appropriate starting point for many teachers may be to record and share data about basic skills and knowledge (e.g., identify the seven continents,

Learning to analyze and track data about individual and class performance helps students take responsibility for their learning.

distinguish between parts of speech, name the parts of a cell), students can and should use data to uncover and understand many kinds of student achievement. These include critical thinking, clear communication, content knowledge, increased engagement, character, and the production of high-quality work. For example, when students have opportunities to track their own patterns of work and behavior (e.g., when they are focused and engaged, when they get confused, or when they have behavior challenges), they gain the power to improve their own learning strategies.

Misconception 2: Use of Data Is Only about Test Preparation

Higher scores on state, national, and school-created assessments can be one goal of data use, but shouldn't be the sole focus. Rather, the goal should be to embed data into classroom routines and a wide range of student-centered instructional practices to improve student achievement and engagement.

Misconception 3: Data Collection Is Limited to Quantitative Data

Although it is wise to begin student-engaged data practices with things that are easy to count (e.g., mistakes in math assignments, minutes spent on independent reading), there is also a great deal of qualitative data that can help student growth. Rubrics, which are composed of qualitative descriptions of student work, are filled with this kind of data. Many recording forms, such as journals, note catchers, and entrance and exit tickets can be powerful data sources to track the why and how of student thinking. These kinds of forms are opportunities for students to back up their ideas with evidence, an essential skill for meeting Common Core standards.

Common Core Connections

- Engaging students with data analysis enhances their ability to make evidence-based claims, a skill that permeates the standards.
- Using data reflectively (e.g., engaging in error or success analyses) helps student meet the Common Core's more rigorous (and often complex) standards. Noting trends focuses students' attention on how to improve.
- Understanding data about one's own progress toward meeting standards is a key to developing the independence and self-direction emphasized by the Common Core. If data tracking about progress remains solely in the possession of the teacher, students are deprived of the opportunity to actively work toward standards. Their partnership in the process increases their engagement and motivation along with the likelihood they will meet with success.

GETTING STARTED

Creating a Culture of Safety for Data Investigation

There are many different ways that teachers, teams, and whole schools can use data with students. It is important to start by developing a classroom culture that supports students to assess their progress, and to take small steps that enable them to build their skills analyzing data.

It can be intimidating to look at data of one's own performance and analyze strengths and weaknesses. A critical first step is to develop a classroom culture where it is safe to make mistakes and where a guiding belief is that effort leads to learning. Creating such a classroom culture is a foundation of all student-engaged assessment practices. It begins with building a growth mindset and creating strong group norms and being careful to model them and follow up on their use.

Students should not be in competition with each other. Data use in the classroom should not result in a zero-sum game in which one student's "win" necessitates another student's "loss." Rather, students should compete against themselves to achieve their own goals at a sufficient level of challenge. Student data use should also stay focused on students learning how to compare their work and progress against clear standards. It is not about identifying the top 10 percent of students. Students will want to know where they stand in relation to their peers, but it is important to bring them back to their own progress and goals. Understanding that everyone has a unique learning profile made up of strengths and weaknesses is a key part of building a safe data culture.

Building structures for students to collect, analyze, and share data about habits of scholarship (e.g., participation in class, persistence with revision) is an important part of creating a healthy data culture. This kind of data collection should not be presented as a short-term strategy to "fix" their problems. It is a long-term—we hope lifelong—disposition and skill that will empower them to better understand their personal behavioral and learning patterns. Moreover, understanding how data about habits of scholarship connects to data about academic achievement builds critical-thinking skills in students—this metacognition is a college- and career-ready skill that can affect positive change in students' lives. For example, a student who knows that she consistently locates only 20 percent of the grammatical errors in her essays is more likely to seek out a peer editor or a tutor at the campus writing center when she attempts to revise her college papers.

Snapshot: Introducing Students to Data with "Mini-Me"

Before students can understand how to use data to inform their own academic goals, they must first learn about data and how to collect, sort, analyze, and represent data in its various forms. In Amanda Locke's seventh-grade math and science class at Four Rivers Charter Public School in Greenfield, Massachusetts, students are introduced to data collection and analysis by participating in an activity called *mini-me* (adapted from a similar activity at King Middle School in Portland, Maine). Students collect data on themselves (e.g., age, height, weight, eye color) and create mini-scale drawings, write mini-narratives, and look for whole-class patterns across all of the mini-me projects of their classmates. Students learn the difference between qualitative and quantitative data and the vocabulary of data (e.g., mean, median, mode, outlier).

"It really helps them see the pieces, parts, and groups and how all these data fit together," says Locke, who helps the students craft a survey to get at what makes the group similar as well as what makes each individual unique. From the data they collect, students create frequency charts, stem-and-leaf plots, and other visualizations that make data patterns more apparent. Although it may seem like "just math" to the students, Locke is creating the intellectual infrastructure her class will need to use data about their own academic performance. The skills they learn through the mini-me project help them make sense of how their teachers are reporting their performance within a standards-based grading system, something most of them are unfamiliar with.

Foster a Growth Mindset in Students

Just as adults in the school must buy in to the use of data to inform instruction and move students forward, students also need to be shown the power of data. For too long, data have been used to define students with little chance to move beyond the label they've "earned." As cognitive scientists have discovered, biology is not destiny, and intelligence is in fact malleable. Making students aware of this provides them with the opportunity to not only acknowledge that growth is possible but also that creating goals based on data puts them in the driver's seat.

Using data with students begins with assessing current levels of performance and determining what level of performance will demonstrate that the goal has been reached. Establishing a clear target or goal ensures that data use will help to build the "I want to succeed" ethic and growth mindset in students. Far too many students (and teachers) believe that certain people are born "smart" and others are not. Teachers can help to dispel this myth through the intentional use of data.

Explicitly Teach Students about Data

Define data and describe the ways in which data can be used to increase performance. Given the prevalence of data analysis, there are many accessible examples from popular culture that show how data are used to increase performance. An examination of the sports page shows how understanding data is a matter-of-fact part of the culture. Statistics and other data are collected on athletes and coaches and players pore over box scores, game tapes, and other evidence to identify patterns in the data that will enable athletes to set goals and improve. Retailers collect data to track sales and determine marketing strategies. Scientists and doctors collaborate to analyze data from clinical trials to assess the efficacy of new medicines.

A mathematical profile like this is a good way to get students in the practice of collecting data about their performance.

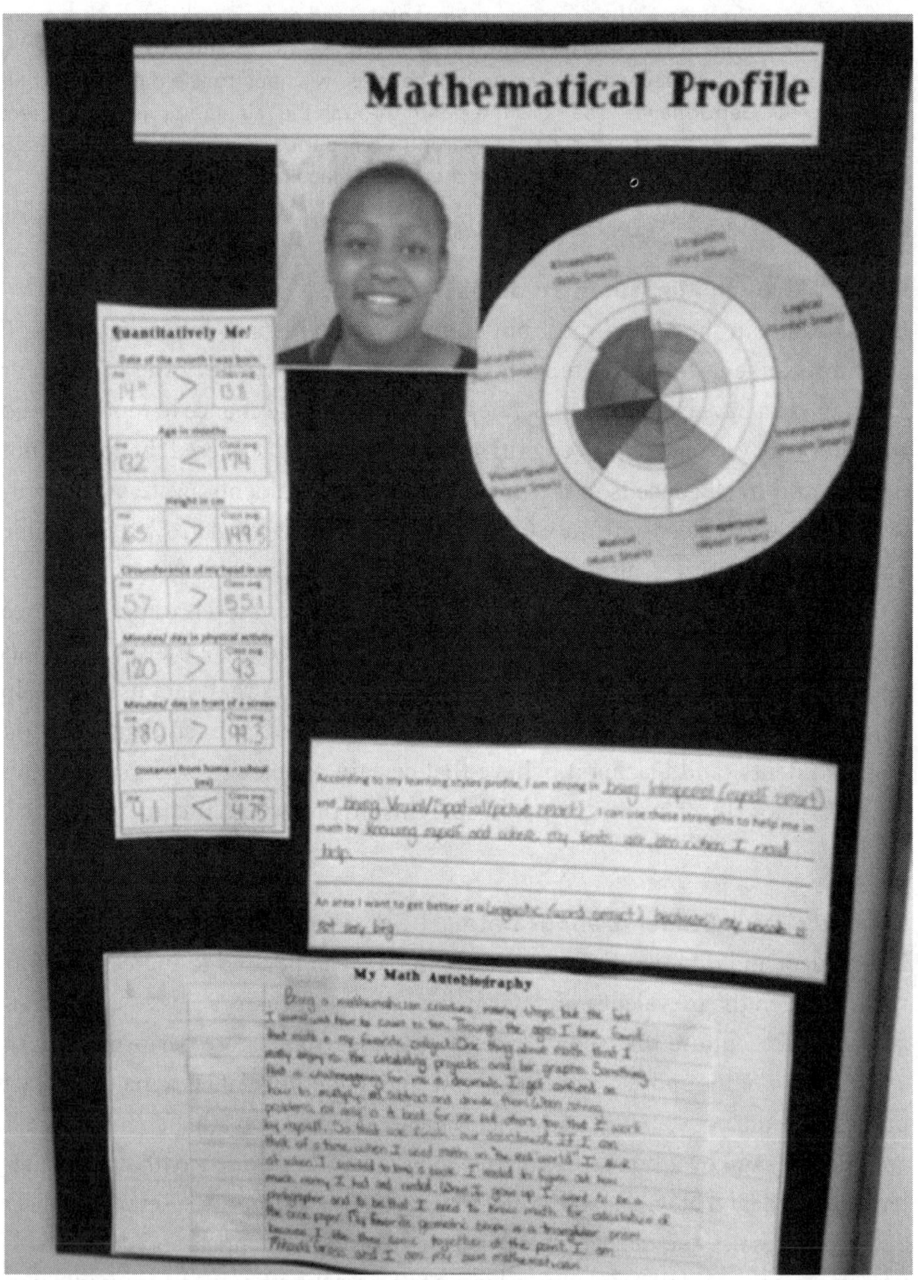

Look for everyday, authentic opportunities to see how examining data can make a difference in our lives (e.g., number of students tardy, pieces of trash on the cafeteria floor, amount of paper recycled).

Use Collective Data: Everyone Must Scale the Mountain

Starting with a collective classwide goal for data analysis fosters a spirit of collaboration—students shift their mindsets from working toward their own goals to working to ensure that all of their classmates are also successful. A third-grade class may identify a goal for proficiency in their multiplication tables—everyone completing a set number of random problems in a limited time—and work as a team to see if they can reach it. Ninth-grade students may recognize that their transitions need to be more efficient and set a class goal that all students will be in their seats before the bell rings at the start of class. Each of these goals sets challenges for the whole group but require individual accountability. It is a low-stakes way to introduce data use in a classroom, but it bears repeating that although individuals are accountable for the goal, their individual scores should not be made public.

Ensure Early Wins

For skeptical or wary students it is critical that early work with data yields results. Student investment comes when they see the return and observe meaningful growth. Although there are many ambitious ways to use data, in a novice classroom it is important to achieve the early win. Choose a data source in which you know students can show rapid improvement. Publicly celebrate the win before establishing more ambitious and long-term goals.

Focusing the Data Inquiry

Integrating student use of data into classroom routines is a long-term process. It is important to start small. Rather than flooding the classroom with data, teachers should design a focused data routine that can be expanded and supplemented over time. Figure 3.1 represents a typical data-inquiry cycle in the classroom. Teachers will need to develop an approach that best suits their students' needs. Choosing what data to investigate is one of the key questions facing teachers invested in using data with students. Not all data are equally suited to inquiry with students.

Figure 3.1 Data-Inquiry Cycle

The following guidelines will help teachers ensure that the data they use with students are useful:

- Keep standards at the forefront—data collection should be in service of meeting standards.
- Begin with quantifiable data—for teachers new to this practice, a simple maxim applies: find something to count. What you count should be something you care about improving (e.g., how many students can solve multistep word problems, the percentage of students turning in lab reports with all criteria complete). Qualitative data sources, such as journals or reflection forms from student portfolios, may be used more frequently as teachers gain confidence with these practices.
- Choose a recurrent data source—effective data investigation involves comparison between where students start and where they are at different intervals, so it's important to choose a data source that can be measured multiple times.

- Make the data matter—ensure that what you count is worthy of being counted. Students should be asked to collect and analyze data that will help them to set and achieve goals. For example, data mined from students' habits of scholarship (such as percentage of homework assignments completed) can be useful to change study habits, whereas data points gathered from ongoing numeracy drills can prove to students that their practice is making a difference. Helping students make the connection between these data points is powerful self-knowledge and a key to building critical thinking skills. In the accompanying video, sixth-grade students review data from their Developmental Reading Assessments and use the information to check in on their goals.

Watch video: "Goal Setting for Achievement in Reading—Using Data with Students"

Case Study

Using Data with Students to Build Geography Skills at Washington Heights Expeditionary Learning School (WHEELS) in New York City

Sixth-grade social studies teacher Stephanie Aberger was concerned about her new students' lack of basic geography skills. Almost all of them were performing on average two grade levels below where they should have been. She was also concerned that many seemed to lack basic concepts about the world necessary for the study of history. She needed to find a way to prepare students for the rest of their social studies experience at WHEELS. Aberger decided to use the following data-inquiry process with the class:

- Where are we now?—preassessment, diagnostic of current performance
- Where are we going?—goal setting (determined by teacher or in conjunction with students and informed by grade-level standards)
- Measurement through data—monitoring the gap between current performance and the goal
- Reflecting on growth and establishing a new goal

She started by collecting data to address the following diagnostic questions: What geographic skills do students have? What do they know about world geography and historical events?

(continued)

Next, she shared the data (diagnostic results) with students. She made the data anonymous by aggregating results by class and grade level. Students then set individual and class goals for improvement.

The third step in the process involved a series of assessments. Planning for quick, data-driven wins, the teacher made deliberate choices of skills and lesson design to ensure mastery for all and organized assessments by learning target. The class engaged in an atlas challenge every two weeks, and she shared the results publicly (e.g., 82 percent of the class can correctly identify, spell, and provide key information about Pakistan, but only 58 percent can do the same for Ecuador). The students' long-term goal was to identify, correctly spell, and provide key facts about forty countries. In the end, 95 percent of the eighty students met the goal. They were then ready to set more challenging goals related to the history of those countries.

Communicate with Families

The goal of using data with students is to have students identify their own strengths and needs, create attainable goals based on standards and learning targets, draft specific action plans, and—with teacher and parent support—achieve the goals. It is important to take time to bring parents up to speed regarding the data-inquiry process. Letters to families, conferences, and more formal presentations are all vehicles for educating parents about what the data-inquiry cycle is and what the key forms of data are for tracking student learning.

In many schools, reports on data come out at student-led conferences and portfolio presentations (see chapters 5 and 7 for more information). With the consistent and purposeful use of data, students and their families should know at any given point in time how a student is faring. Although students' reflections and perceptions of their progress based on data are not always communicated on formal progress reports, there should be a seamless connection between students' self-assessment and standards-based grades (see chapter 8 for more information). Data kept by students and data kept by teachers should be consistent. Teachers can check their grade books against student learning target trackers, work folders, or

> "Involve parents in the follow-through of the goals. Give them something specific to do, whether it's flash card drills, learning sight words, or listening as their child reads aloud. Parents want to feel a part of the process."
>
> *—Jean Hurst, third-grade teacher, Genesee Community Charter School, Rochester, New York*

other assemblages of student work for accuracy and reliability. This coherence will enable students and families to experience the connection between grades and the students' own understanding of their progress.

IN PRACTICE

Developing the Systems to Support and Deepen Using Data with Students

For any new routine to flourish in the classroom, teachers must create good systems to collect and store student data. Whether using simple forms, work folders, or computer-generated spreadsheets, teachers must provide a vehicle for students to collect data and make the time and space for them to make sense of this information. No matter the system, the outcomes are the same—students are prepared to become reflective learners, they can identify strengths and challenges, and they can set goals that enable them to meet standards.

Forms

Teacher-created forms can serve as data collection tools for students. Ongoing and predictable use of forms—such as learning target trackers, item or error analysis sheets, reflection sheets, and rubrics—helps students get in the practice of collecting data about their progress. Over time, they internalize the importance of having a record and become careful observers of patterns and trends. Forms help them organize their work and talk about their progress at student-led conferences or passage presentations. Figure 3.2 shows error analysis forms for math and writing and a preschool letter identification tracker. Figure 3.3 shows a learning

> "We try to be transparent in naming how the learning target is valuable in terms of the students' progress with skills and knowledge, and habits of scholarship. For example, the Common Core mathematical practice standards emphasize persevering in solving challenging math problems (MP1). Students can use a learning target tracker to identify growth not only in their capacity to use different strategies and make connections to other problems they have seen and solved before, but [also] to their character in overcoming challenges and seeking solutions."
>
> —*Chris Dolgos, sixth-grade teacher, Genesee Community Charter School, Rochester, New York*

Figure 3.2 Sample Forms for Tracking Data

Math Test Error Self Analysis

Name______________________________
Date_______________

Test Topic____

Number of times you've taken this test (or a different version)___________
Number of problems on the test______ Number Correct______
Percent Correct______

Error Analysis
Type A: Careless error (just a stupid mistake; you know the facts and operations)
Type B: Graphic error (copied the problem wrong, read your writing wrong, lined up columns poorly, etc.)
Type C: Confused by how to do the operation
Type D: Confused by how to do the operation
Type E: Wrong operation used
Type F: Clueless (no idea how to start or what operation to use)

List each problem number you got wrong and assign an error code letter to each:

Total Errors of each type:
A:______ **B:**______ **C:**______ **D:**______ **E:**______ **F:**______

What patterns do you notice? What does this test show you?

How careful do you feel you were on this test? (circle one):
Super Careful *Very Careful* *Careful* *Not Careful* *Awful*

How pleased were you by your performance? (circle one):
Very *Pretty Much* *Somewhat* *Not Much* *Ugg!*

EL Education 2009

Written Work Error Self Analysis

Data Collection of Mechanical and Grammatical Errors from the First Page of the Work

Name:______________________________ Date:____________

Number of Compositions Analyzed____________
Time Period (first and last dates of compositions)____________
Total Errors – Mean____________
Total Errors – Median____________

Total Errors in Each Category

Layout
Neatness ____
Margins ____
Heading ____
Spacing ____
Title ____

Organization
Paragraphs ____
Opening ____
Clarity ____
Sentence Order ____

Grammar
Full Sentences ____
Run-On Sentences ____
Tense ____
Subject-Verb Agreement ____
Subject-Object Pronouns ____
Extra Words (Like, etc.) ____

Punctuation
Periods ____
Capitals ____
Commas ____
Apostrophes ____
Quotations ____
Colons, Semicolons ____

Spelling
Total Spelling ____
Proper Nouns ____
There, Their, They're ____
Too, to, two ____
Words with ie, ei ____
Plurals ____
Conjunctions ____
Careless (Easy Words) ____

EL Education 2009

I can identify the lower case letters.

Name: Boston

letters	Progress check in Date: 9/30/11	Progress check in Date:	Progress check in Date:	Progress check in Date:	Progress check in Date:	Progress check in Date:
a						
b						
c						
d						
e						
f						
g						
h						
i						
j						
k						
l						
m						
n						
o						
p						
q						
r						
s						
t						
u						
v						
w						
x						
y						
z						

Preschool

Forms like these can help students of all grade levels work toward Common Core language standards regarding conventions of standard English and the math practice standard regarding attending to precision.

Figure 3.3 Sample Learning Target Tracker

SEMESTER 2 ~ **LT #3 Tracking (about 5 weeks)**

NAME: _______________ SECTION: ___________

Course Learning Target #3: I can construct quadratic models and solve problems.

	Sub-Learning Targets	Assessment Date(s)	Assessment Name(s):	Assessment Score(s):	Assessment Weight:
A	I can distinguish a parabola from other equations and graphs. (F-IF)				
B	I can graph quadratic functions naming: intercepts; intervals; where the function is increasing, decreasing, positive, or negative; maximums and minimums; symmetries; end behavior; and periodicity. (F-IF)				
C	I can write vertex form or factored form from the graph of a parabola.				
D	I can convert between vertex, factored, and standard forms of a quadratic equation.				
E	I can find the zeroes of a quadratic function by factoring and applying the zero product property. (A-APR)				
F	I can find the zeroes of a quadratic function by applying the quadratic formula. (N-CN)				
G	I can use the discriminant of the quadratic formula to determine the number of real or complex solutions. (N-CN)				
H	I can find the zeroes of a quadratic function by completing the square. (N-CN)				
I	I can represent complex arithmetic on the complex plane. **HONORS**				
J	I can complete the square to prove the quadratic formula.				
K	I can develop a complete and comprehensive field guide entry for quadratic functions.				
L	I can compare quadratic models to linear and exponential models.				
M	I can use quadratic models to solve problems.				
N	I can transform a quadratic function by translation, reflection, rotation, and dilation, and write the equation of the transformation. (F-BF)				

target tracker for an algebra II class. Forms should meet the needs of learners at all developmental stages.

Snapshot: Using Data to Master English Writing Conventions

Mariella, a sixth-grade student in Ron Berger's class at Shutesbury Elementary School in Shutesbury, Massachusetts, pulled her writing portfolio from the shelf while preparing for her final portfolio presentation—a graduation requirement at the school. Mariella was fluent in Spanish, but English was new to her, having just arrived in this country, and her writing in English reflected a nascent understanding of conventions. She tended to describe her proficiency with written English very broadly (e.g., "My grammar and spelling are bad"). This was neither helpful for her nor informative to the panel that would be assessing her portfolio.

Fortunately, she had data that could add more precision. She pulled out her folder of personal experience compositions (one- to two-page papers on simple topics, such as "favorite books" or "memories from birthdays"). She had written these compositions at regular intervals during the year, and Berger had marked all errors in conventions on each composition. On getting each one back, Mariella categorized the errors (with some help), and recorded those data on a form that she kept with her folder (see figure 3.2). She had excellent records on the total number of errors in grammar and spelling in each composition and the specific types of errors she made. She created data charts that made this visually clear.

When Mariella presented her portfolio to a panel of educators, the school board, and community members, she was able to speak with detail and insight about her process of learning written English, showing her growth with written conventions and syntax over the year. She could speak with confidence and evidence about what things she had mastered and what things remained challenges for her. She was able to report with some pride that her percentage of growth—as evidenced by her data charts—was the highest in the class.

Work Folders and Portfolios

For teachers not quite ready to tackle digital tools, work folders and portfolios are great analog formats. This is clearly demonstrated in Mariella's snapshot. The work folder ideally contains learning target trackers and other relevant forms and all work and assessments from a student. Work folders give students an opportunity to sort and resort work and look for patterns of growth, citing evidence from the work itself. When using data with students, managing the system of collecting and storing work can be overwhelming. It is important that teachers dedicate some time each month to putting completed work into these folders and then scheduling times for students to work with the data. In the accompanying video, we see Genesee Community Charter School sixth-grade teachers Chris Dolgos and Shannon Hillman working with students as they sort through their work folders and reflect on their data.

Watch video: "Students Own Their Progress—Using Data with Students"

Work folders can be arranged for each subject area and housed in hanging folders in a filing cabinet, or ideally, in a crate or bin easily accessible to students. Creating the mechanisms and culture of using work folders, similar to any data system, will take time. The important thing is to make the time,

Portfolios are a great way for students to keep track of their data.

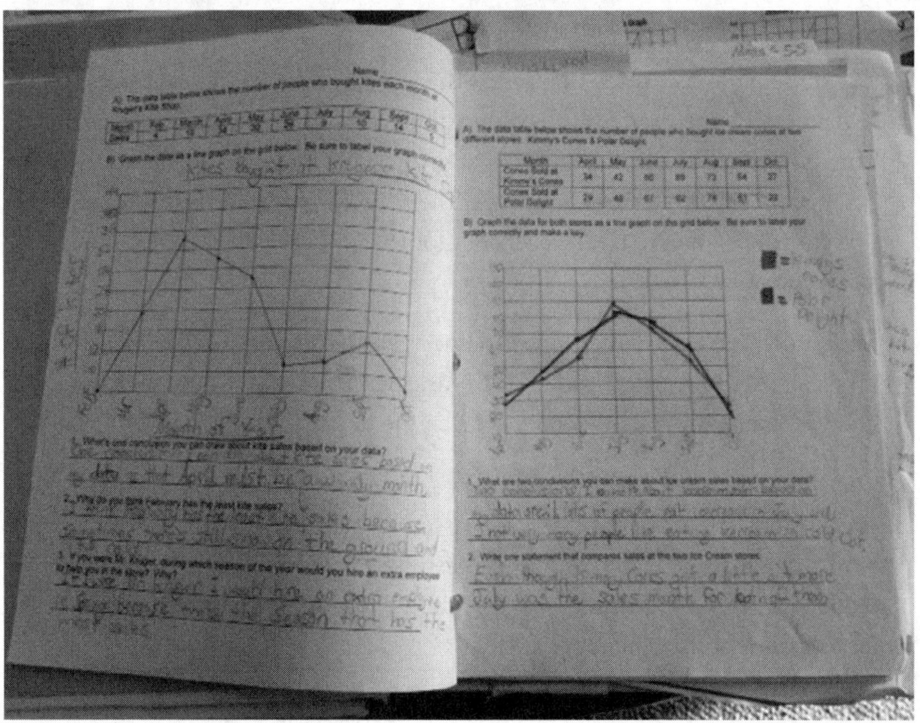

so students invest in tracking and reporting their progress toward learning targets.

Work folders can also be used as the basis for portfolios, in which students collect and reflect on more focused selections of work. Looking for patterns in their errors, trends in how their work demonstrates progress toward standards, and evidence of mastery are key facets of a strong portfolio practice.

Using Digital Tools

Excel is a useful tool for students to use to collect and synthesize data. Figure 3.4 shows an Excel spreadsheet created by a sixth-grade student at Robert E. Clark Middle School in Bonner Springs, Kansas, to track reading fluency and comprehension over the length of a semester. In this example, the sixth-grade student, who is well below grade level in reading fluency, is working on the fifth-grade Common Core foundational skills standard, RF.5.4: *Read with sufficient accuracy and fluency to support comprehension.*

Procedure

1. The student draws a black line across the tracking form from week one to week seventeen for the grade-level average fluency score, provided by the teacher. This trajectory illustrates the typical growth an average sixth-grade student shows over the course of a semester. The student repeats this task with a blue line from week one to week seventeen for the grade-level average comprehension score.

2. The student takes the week-one test and identifies his starting point. He sets a target to reach for the semester and works with the teacher to determine specific tasks and strategies needed to reach the target.

3. The student takes a reading test every two weeks to assess fluency and comprehension. The student's fluency is assessed based on the words-per-minute read. The student's comprehension is assessed based on the teacher asking the student to retell the reading passage and the teacher tracking specific vocabulary words that the student recalled.

4. After each test the student records his score on the Excel tracking form.

Figure 3.4 Tracking Progress with Excel Software

Key

X=Black Line=Grade level fluency score

*=Red Line=My fluencey score

#=Blue Line=Grade level comprehension score

^=Green Line=My comprehension score

Oral Reading Fluency and Comprehension Graph

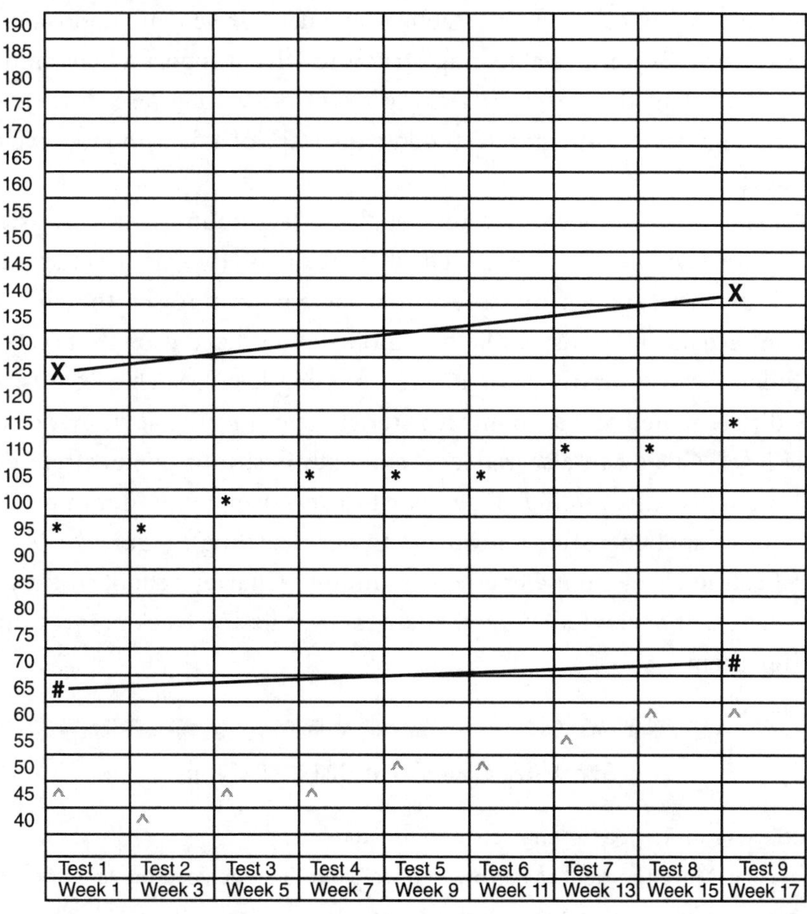

My reading fluency score at the beginning was: 95

Comprehension was: 45

My goal is to be at: 115 By: Week 17

Specific things I'm going to do to improve my reading and comprehension:

1. Read for 20 uninterupted minutes every night.
2. Daily vocabulary lesson with language specialist.

Building Students' Capacity to Set Effective Goals

One of the trickier parts of using data with students is having them establish their own goals. Students may be tempted to set their goals either too low (thereby guaranteeing achievement) or too high (unrealistic and not based on available data). Teachers should serve as coaches in determining goals, particularly early on, in establishing a data-driven and data-safe classroom culture. Beyond establishing structures that support a safe culture, it is also important that teachers seeking to introduce data use in their classrooms design lessons that teach students the steps of a data-inquiry cycle (see figure 3.1).

Students can establish rigorous goals based upon their own starting point. For example, "I've mastered 70 percent of the math standards but I think my mastery can increase to 85 percent or more by the end of the year." Alternatively, goals can be based on standardized growth targets (e.g., all students will grow 1.5 years in their reading level). Such a goal is inherently differentiated and accounts for students performing at, above, or below grade level. Goals can also reflect a student's desire to demonstrate deeper thinking skills (e.g., mining all daily exit tickets over a one-month period for evidence of applying prior knowledge to new learning). Figure 3.5 is a sample reflection sheet from Genesee Community Charter School in Rochester, New York, that helps students articulate their goals and track progress toward meeting them.

Strategy Close Up: SMART Goals

SMART goals make goal setting concrete for students.

S = specific. Make the goal as narrow as possible to help achieve the learning target.

M = measurable. Is the goal quantifiable? Can you count it somehow?

A = attainable. Can the goal be attained in the time frame allotted?

R = realistic. Teachers can help reframe goals to contextualize them in terms of a personal challenge (no low-hanging fruit).

T = timely. Students may need help prioritizing goals (for example, knowing multiplication facts should precede division of fractions).

Figure 3.5 Sample Goal-Setting Worksheet

Name ______________________ Week Ending: ________________

Weekly Reflection

A target I am working on this week is:

A goal I have around this target is: ____

____

____

I think I have made little/some/great progress towards my goal and the learning target because:

____

____

____

ON TIME
Home Learning
Return Rate: %

I am/am not missing any work.
(Missing assignments are listed below.)

____

____

Teacher Initials: __________ Parent Signature: ______________________

Comments? ____

____

____

Case Study

Using Classroom and MAP[1] Data to Assess Progress and Set Goals at Genesee Community Charter School in Rochester, New York

Several times a month, teachers Shannon Hillman and Chris Dolgos provide time for their students to review their work folders, which house assessments, recent quizzes, and projects. Students then create six-week status reports that give them, along with their parents and teachers, a clear picture of how they are progressing toward learning targets. Students share their status reports during their student-led conferences and defend their analysis of the data with their families. The status report provides a framework for the conference—students can identify areas of progress, celebrate successes, and set goals to work toward.

As students are creating their status reports, Dolgos and Hillman meet with them individually, sharing the scores from the most recent Measures of Academic Progress (MAP) assessment. Using these adaptive, computerized tests, which are based on Common Core State Standards, the teachers can produce reports that identify specific domains connected to the learning targets students are working toward. "Students can see from the MAP data that they are on track, or the data might demonstrate that the goal they thought was 'on target' was really way off," says Dolgos. "Ultimately, we want students to craft goals that will help them meet or exceed the learning target. Quite often, standardized test data is worthless in this regard because [the information] isn't timely enough. The MAP data helps us design effective instruction and helps students recognize where to go next."

Dolgos and Hillman celebrate students' gains, but they also challenge them to elaborate on their goals and prove with data that their goals are the right ones. "Using data with students isn't meant to be a mind-numbing exercise in plotting points on a graph," says Hillman. "The data represent an intellectual and emotional investment in learning from the kids, and it is important that we as adults acknowledge their commitment to progress." Because students are fully engaged in understanding what the data tell them about their progress and setting appropriate goals, they progress at a faster rate than if the teachers were the only ones tracking and analyzing their data.

[1] *Measures of Academic Progress*, published by Northwest Evaluation Association.

Critical Moves for Deepening Student Engagement

Using data with students requires careful scaffolding if students are to be fully engaged in the process. Students must be guided to think about, work with, and make sense of data about their performance so that they can set goals that will help them make progress. This can happen only within a classroom environment that is safe and supportive. Teachers must approach the work with the varying developmental needs of students in mind. Table 3.1 illustrates the who, what, and why of using data with students to increase engagement and achievement.

Table 3.1 The Who, What, and Why of Using Data with Students

What Do Teachers Do?	What Do Students Do?	What's the Result?
Create learning targets and aligned assessments—based on state and Common Core standards. Use learning targets to guide selection and analysis of data.	Explain the learning target in their own words, connect it back to the lesson and the work, and understand what success will look like.	Students and teachers have a shared vision of success.
Establish a culture of safety for looking at data, build excitement in the power of data, and develop students' data literacy. Establish class norms and the value of helping everyone meet his or her goals.	Make an effort to understand and practice the norms. Be helpful in supporting the goals of fellow students.	A foundation of safety is created for using data to improve student learning.
List relevant learning targets on classwork, admission and exit tickets, homework, and assessments.	Read and interpret learning targets and apply skills and knowledge from lessons to homework and classwork.	Teachers provide transparency and students understand what is expected of them.
Design lessons that explicitly demonstrate how to self-reflect on work (e.g., postassessment reflections, item analysis, correction procedures).	Reflect on work and identify areas of strength and areas of potential growth as they relate to the learning target.	Students begin to see patterns in their work—they can identify strengths to capitalize on and areas in need of improvement.
Create learning target trackers for students that mirror elements of the grade book.	Honestly review their work, name level of proficiency, and date the entry.	Students can see progress over time.
Model how to look for patterns in the collected data, including written work, math problems, and outcomes from standardized tests. Teach students to use forms or digital tools to keep track of their data.	Analyze data to assess current level of performance.	Students quantify their work and are ready to set goals.
Instruct students on setting SMART goals.	Create goals based on data and an action plan.	Students own the process of goal setting and are accountable to their action plan.

(continued)

Table 3.1 Continued

What Do Teachers Do?	What Do Students Do?	What's the Result?
Create multiple quality assessments (including those that mirror high-stakes tests) to determine student progress toward long-term targets.	Students show what they know and can do at multiple points in time, in multiple ways.	Students have several opportunities to show what they know while collecting several pieces of evidence toward the learning target.
Set up a system for collecting evidence, teach students how to use it, and make it accessible to the students.	Review work folders on a regular basis, identifying work that moves them toward mastery of learning targets as well as areas of need.	Students have access to the same body of work that teachers use in collecting and analyzing data.
Provide classroom time for students to work with data, reflect on goals and outcomes, and synthesize their work.	Identify the progress they have made over time and represent growth visually (e.g., charts, graphs).	Students have documentation of their progress, ready to be shared as part of student-led conferences, passage presentations, or other venues for sharing and celebrating progress.

SCHOOLWIDE IMPLEMENTATION

Using data with students will gain the most power when it is firmly embedded in a whole-school system of student-engaged assessment and a professional culture of data-based inquiry. The more familiar and comfortable teachers are with using data, the more they will be able to support students in using it. Leaders play a central role in helping teachers bring practices that previously may have only been used by the faculty members into the classroom for use by students. Helping teachers see the power of data to engage students in setting goals and making progress is key. We have highlighted some of the key leadership actions that will support smooth implementation of a practice of using data with students throughout a school.

Lay the Groundwork

- Build a common vision for the practice. Connect a strong faculty data culture to the power of using data with students. Build background knowledge among faculty members and highlight the potential impact on students' achievement and engagement.

- Align data practice with all facets of student-engaged assessment: learning targets; models, critique, and descriptive feedback; checking for understanding; student-led conferences; celebrations of learning; passage presentations; and standards-based grading.
- Connect the faculty data conversation with a vision of quality and schoolwide goals for improvement.
- Know state and Common Core standards deeply. Provide curriculum maps with prioritized standards or support teachers and teams to prioritize their grade-level standards so that student data use is in service of meeting them.

Build Teacher Capacity

- Create a safe professional culture of evidence for collecting and analyzing data. Be sure that data are used as a "flashlight" for uncovering trends, rather than a "club" for punishing staff.
- Ensure that all teachers have strong data skills. Build excitement in collecting, analyzing, and presenting data in different forms.
- Let teachers discover data trends themselves—don't tell them what the data say. When teachers uncover problems themselves they are more likely to own them and address them, rather than fight them. And, ensure that teachers use the same approach with students—let the students discover trends in their data.
- Select a focus for faculty members to examine data and ensure that the data is in usable form. For example, faculty members could look together at the data from a specific strand of an interim assessment such as the MAP test (e.g., number sense, algebraic thinking) to examine gaps across grade levels. Reports can be generated by class and faculty members can identify potential areas for reteaching or enrichment.
- Select a set of priority practices for using data in the classroom with students and work collaboratively with faculty to develop a common practice rubric and criteria.
- Support all teachers to meet criteria for implementing strategies for using data with students. Provide ongoing professional development and coaching, make professional literature available, and provide individualized support for implementation.

"The key is remembering that the data is connected to real kids."

—Sheela Webster, principal, World of Inquiry School, Rochester, New York

- Prioritize instructional leadership and develop a coaching cycle with teachers.
- Use findings from data conversations—with faculty members and in the classroom (with students)—to inform instructional goals, professional development, and coaching.

Communicate with Stakeholders

- Establish schoolwide expectations for data tracking so that families become accustomed to the use of data during student-led conferences and passage presentations.

School leaders should create a schedule for ongoing data conversations among faculty.

- Ensure that the use of student data during student-led conferences and passage presentations is well understood by families by communicating with them about the data-inquiry process at the school.
- Encourage families to help students meet their data-driven goals.
- Establish procedures and language to describe and report on the school's data-inquiry process to district leaders or charter boards.

Support Teachers to Deepen Their Practice

- Set up structures with faculty members to continually analyze results and the impact of the practice on student achievement.
- Set specific goals for deepening the work tied to measurable student outcomes.
- Support the expansion of each teacher's classroom practice by differentiating teacher support.
- Identify models of best practice within the school and set up a peer observation structure for faculty members.
- Promote increased coaching opportunities, a culture of peer support and professionalism, and a mindset of ongoing improvement.

Case Study

Translating Strong Faculty Data Practice to Strong Student Data Practice at World of Inquiry School in Rochester, New York

The World of Inquiry School faculty members committed themselves to working more closely with data when it became clear to them that their students were not making enough progress in reading. When they started, they had tons of data, but none in usable form. Principal Sheela Webster, who was an English language arts specialist at the time, recalls, "we started by putting it in binders, but that was unproductive because we spent too much time shuffling through paper. When you're inundated with data it becomes overwhelming."

In addition to making the amount of data more manageable, Webster realized that they also needed a way to make it less personal to teachers. "We wanted to find a way to have conversations about data without pointing fingers or placing blame." They decided to sort the data by grade level, rather than by classroom, and by categories specific to

(continued)

students' reading ability: highest intervention, high intervention, moderate intervention, low intervention, and extension. They depersonalized the data for teachers, but they personalized the connection to individual students.

Creating Data Walls

Focused on literacy, they had to determine the most important data from the DRA to distill and use for conversations about supporting students. This led to the creation of data walls. They created an index card with each child's name on it and relevant information including grade level and reading scores. The cards were color-coded by reading level (e.g., red for highest intervention, blue for extension). Each child's card was placed on a grade-level data wall and weekly grade-level team meetings focused on understanding why each child was at a particular level and what he or she needed to advance. "We administer the DRA three times a year, so we're able to track the child's progress in a tangible manner. Someone in red in January may have moved to green by April. We ask who made progress, who is backsliding, and try to understand the reasons why." Getting comfortable working with data in this way as a faculty was key—how comfortable a teacher is using data with students seems to depend on how comfortable she is using data herself. See Principal Webster discussing these strategies in the accompanying video, "Schoolwide Structures for Using Data."

Bringing It into the Classroom

"The translation into the classroom is what's critical. We have made progress, but it is continual reflective work. Once we could get to a place of meaningful conversations—the trick is turning it to effective instructional practice," Webster commented. "Many teachers will take the data and see patterns—such as struggles with fluency—and begin to ask 'What are strategies we can incorporate during literacy blocks?'"

Following one such team meeting, third-grade teacher Aly Ricci brought the data back to her classroom to analyze with her students. She shared with her students what she and her colleagues had discussed: "We talked about what we found out by looking at your data and we graphed the difference between your first score and your second score. But it's not about the score is it? What is it about?" A boy raised his hand "to show if you improved or you didn't so you will know how to focus." Ricci agreed and explained that the students were going to have a chance to look at their scores and compare them, making a bar graph. She was both open with them about the challenges and protective of their feelings. "These are two tests," she said. "They don't tell your whole story." She wanted the students to feel comfortable but also have ownership of their strengths and needs. "We will look at this and we'll use it to make it better," she told the class.

As the students work on their graphs, Ricci circulates and offers suggestions, encouraging students to help each other. As they were close to completing the graphs, she stopped and pointed out a set of questions they were going to respond to as a next step. "Graphing your data is fun and cool and it gives you some information, but the real important part is reflecting on it."

- What do you notice about your data?
- How do you feel about your data and what are your worries?
- What is your plan for improvement?

Students shared their initial plans for improvement: "I'm going to underline more words"; "I'm going to read more in the summer." Ricci enhanced the students' plans through her teaching of specific strategies. "I decided to use my next two readers' workshop sessions to focus on four stories from the baseline that they struggled with the most." During these readers' workshops, she continually brought the conversation back to what they had seen in the data and how they could use strategies to improve. The accompanying video, "Grade-Level Data Meeting with Third-Grade Teachers—Using Data with Students," illustrates the connection between the team meeting with its collaborative insights and sharing the data with students.

Watch video: "Schoolwide Structures for Using Data"

Watch video: "Grade-Level Data Meeting with Third-Grade Teachers—Using Data with Students"

WHAT TO EXPECT

As with any new routine, using data with students will develop in classrooms along a continuum. Although it is very common for schools to analyze student achievement data (and to use it to tailor instruction), it is less common to bring that practice into the classroom and engage students in the process. Giving students the skills to understand data about their progress and set goals that will help them improve is a critical component of a student-engaged assessment system. Devoting time to developing students' skills to work with data will be well worth it, evidenced in their increased investment in making progress toward their learning goals.

During the early phase of this work, teachers must gain comfort and experience using and speaking the language of data, setting up classroom cultures that are safe for students to explore and reflect on data, and establishing good structures for students to collect data. As the routines take hold and students gain comfort, teachers and students become partners in analyzing patterns, setting goals, and monitoring growth. The relationship of this practice to the other components of student-engaged assessment is seamless, and parents become more involved with the data through structures such as student-led conferences or passage presentations when students naturally use data as evidence of their strengths and struggles.

We have identified some of the benchmarks that teachers and school leaders can expect at the beginning, intermediate, and advanced phases of using data with students.

Beginning

- School leaders and teachers collect and analyze student achievement data as well as data on progress toward state and Common Core standards, habits of work, and student engagement. Often a robust faculty practice of data collection and analysis leads to bringing data practices into the classroom to use with students.
- Teachers set up a data-safe classroom culture in which students have a growth mindset. They strive to personally improve, but don't compete against each other.
- Students learn the language of data.
- Teachers build student confidence using data, giving them early wins with skills or behaviors that they can measure and improve. Often this is a collective effort.
- Teachers establish a system for collecting student work (e.g., in work folders).

Intermediate

- Teachers use a data-inquiry cycle to ensure that students are meeting state and Common Core standards. They continually assess student progress and adjust instruction. Students are included and involved in understanding their data and setting goals.
- Teachers develop tools, such as learning target trackers or error analysis forms, to assist students in collecting data. Whenever appropriate students are taught to use digital tools for data collection.
- Teachers and students share the responsibility for identifying what data to gather and analyze.

- A strong culture of safety and collaboration is in evidence.
- Results of data analysis not only support student pride and strength but also highlight areas of need that provide opportunities for reflection and goal setting.
- Students set goals based on individual or group work and have an established system and routine in place to track their progress. Students have access to the data about their progress.
- Student work folders or portfolios are dynamic classroom tools, used regularly to help students track their progress.
- Teachers and students mutually decide how and when to report data and growth to families, often during student-led conferences or passage presentations.

Advanced

- A comprehensive portfolio system enables students to house data about their progress and tell the story of their learning.
- Students are responsible for their own data analysis and share their findings with their teacher(s) and family.
- Student goals are specific and individual.
- Students are comfortable with and are expected to maintain their own work folders, portfolios, or digital data-collection systems.
- Data analysis is a daily or weekly routine.
- Student's goals and action plans are written independently and critiqued by teachers.
- Students prepare data analysis and visualizations for an audience beyond themselves and their teacher (e.g., at passage presentations).

COMMON CHALLENGES

Neglecting to Build a Safe, Skillful Environment for Data Analysis

Culture counts. Students and teachers may be afraid of data, feeling that data may bring bad news, highlight problems, and be hard to understand. It is key that the school as a whole and each classroom cultivates a positive, skilled data environment in which data inquiry is welcomed as a flashlight to uncover trends, not a club to punish people.

Not Enabling Teachers and Students to Discover Data Trends Themselves

Let them do the discovering. When school leaders tell teachers, "Here is where your students scored poorly," they often feel defensive. When they discover patterns in the raw data themselves, they are more motivated to address the issues. It's the same with students—discovering patterns themselves enables them to own the data and set goals for themselves.

Struggling to Manage Resources

Set up clear structures. It is critical to give students the time and the tools to become proficient in tracking and using data. Building routines and the time to do them well will enable students to be successful. The forms, tables, or digital tools used with students should be student friendly and developmentally appropriate. Whether using a work folder, portfolio, or database-driven data-collection system, be sure it is one that students can handle.

Collecting the Wrong Kinds of Data

Choose the right evidence. Be certain that the data being collected will help students move forward. Although a series of high-scoring math drill sheets might illuminate a student's strengths, it doesn't necessarily help her to extend herself. Help students identify the right pieces of evidence to use in their data analysis. Move beyond basic skills to include data on higher-order skills such as problem solving and critical thinking.

Generic or Vague Goals

Good goals are actionable. Many teachers starting to use data with students will create whole-class goals around a particular group need—but never move away from these. Likewise, goals created by teachers (or students) may be vague or too broad in terms of meeting the learning target. A goal of "I will get better at reading," says nothing of the child's particular needs. A better, more-specific goal would be, "I will increase my reading fluency to 160 words per minute by the next semester."

Data out of Synch with Learning Targets and Standards

Check the alignment. Collecting data not connected to a learning target or standard, or data extraneous to assessments, will make goal setting difficult. Be sure that there is a cohesive unity between the assessment methods and the learning target tracker students will be using to look for patterns. Learning target trackers should be built directly from standards and learning targets set at the beginning of a curriculum unit or learning expedition.

Missing an Audience

Data analysis should be public. Students should not be engaged in evidence collection and data analysis to please or do the work of a teacher. Students need to know that the data analysis and corresponding goals and action plans are to inform themselves as well as their teachers and families. In some schools, goals are posted publicly to reinforce a culture of critique and revision.

Not Enough Instruction in Seeing the Patterns

Students need explicit teaching. Although it comes almost as second nature for many teachers to pore over assignments and assessments to identify patterns that will help inform instruction, students will need time and specific lessons to learn to do this. Creating the right data trackers will enable students to see data visually (e.g., tables, graphs, charts) and see how their growth moves as they become more proficient in the goal.

Failure to Support Student Goals

Individualize and differentiate instructional support. As teachers confer with students about their goals, they will see patterns that should alert them to instructional needs for groups of students in certain skills and concepts. At times the support will need to be even more individual. For example, if a student recognizes that he lacks the academic vocabulary to support his comprehension and sets a goal to acquire three new academic terms per week, his teachers should acknowledge this goal and provide either lessons or supplemental work to help him meet the goal.

Time to Meet with Students to Set and Track Goals

Using data takes ongoing practice. Like any good coach, teachers need to make time available for students to practice the skills of data collection and analysis and get feedback on progress. It is not enough to have students "track data." Teachers must ensure that they are doing it right and doing it well. Examine student work and schedule data- and goal-setting conferences with them to help them stay on track.

Chapter 4

Models, Critique, and Descriptive Feedback

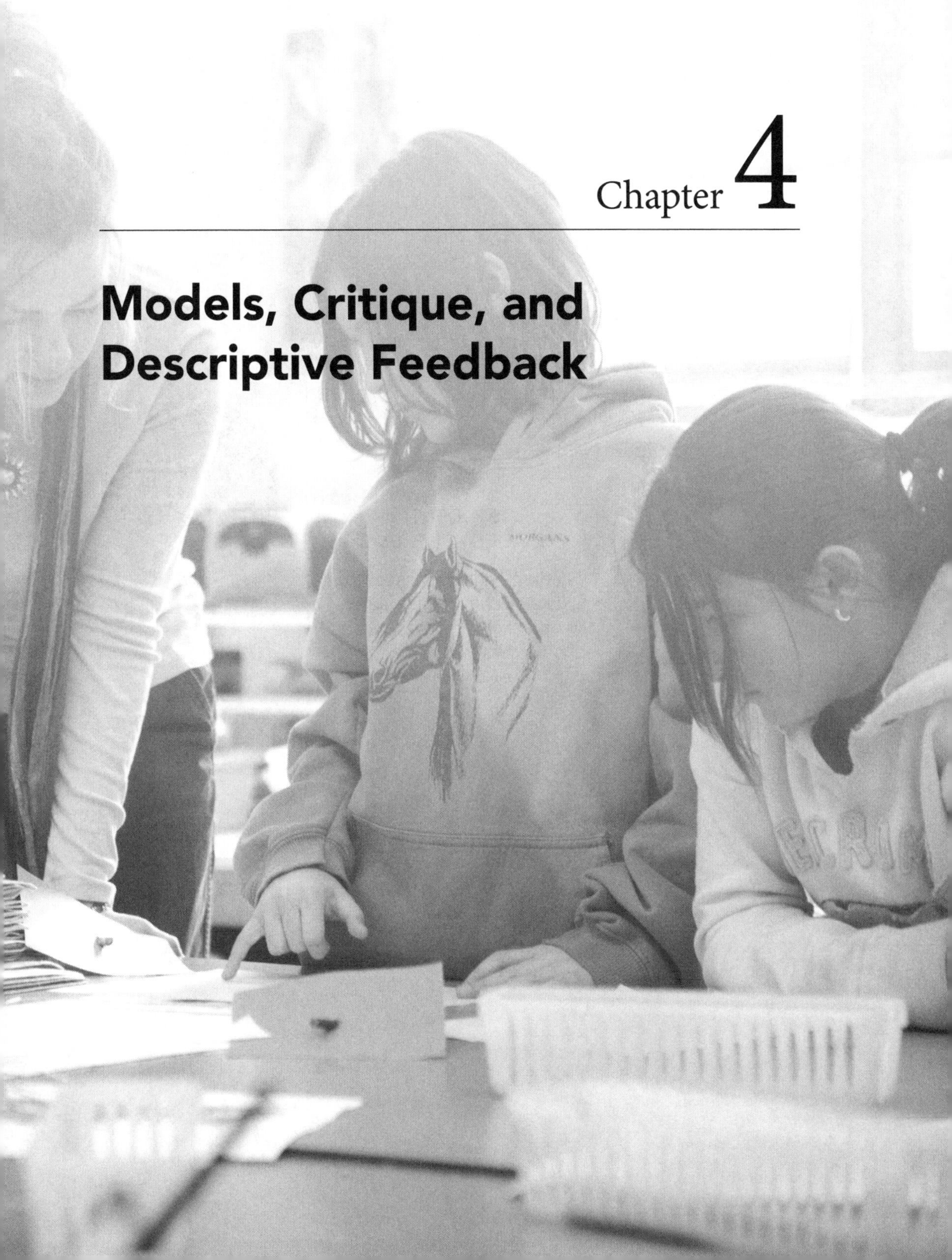

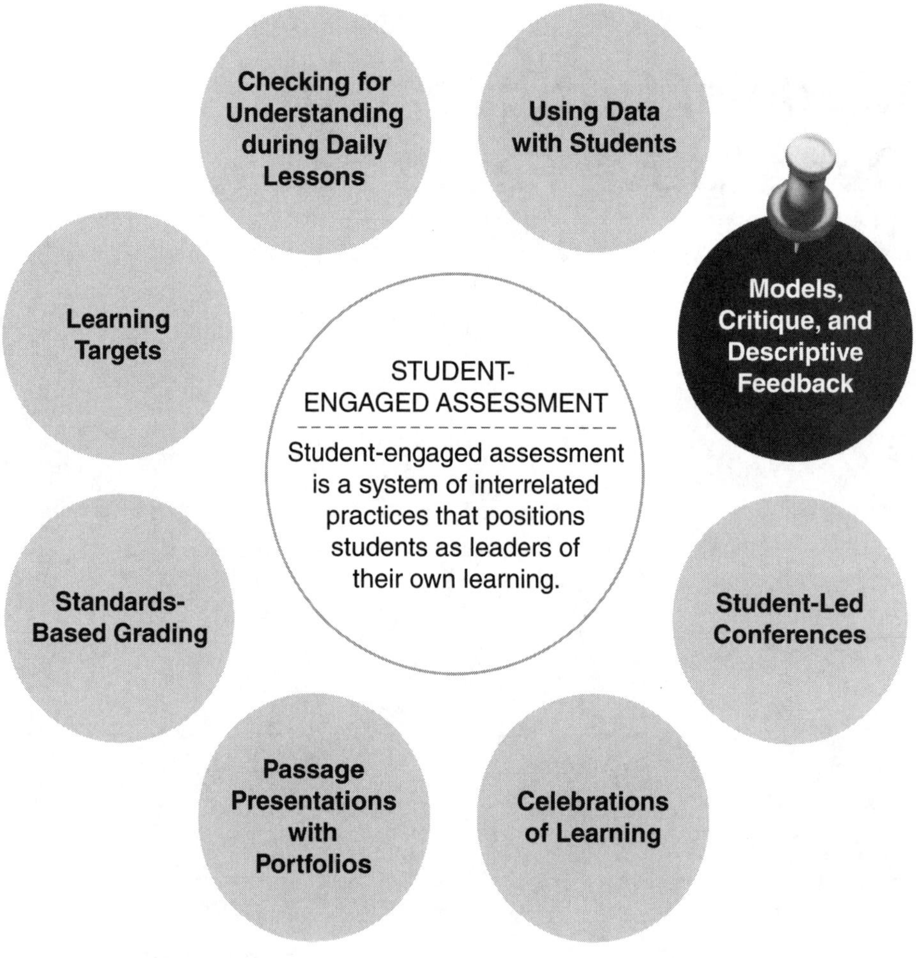

Checking for Understanding during Daily Lessons

Using Data with Students

Learning Targets

Models, Critique, and Descriptive Feedback

STUDENT-ENGAGED ASSESSMENT

Student-engaged assessment is a system of interrelated practices that positions students as leaders of their own learning.

Standards-Based Grading

Student-Led Conferences

Passage Presentations with Portfolios

Celebrations of Learning

Several years ago, I visited the classroom of a skilled and veteran high school physics teacher in Oregon who had sought my help as an instructional coach. Observing her classroom, I was hard-pressed to guess why she might be dissatisfied—the culture of the class and her lesson were excellent. Students were motivated and eager. After class she explained her need: "It's lab reports. Their lab reports are terrible! It's driving me crazy." I asked if this was a problem with just this section. "No, all my classes. I grade their papers and mark them up with comments and corrections and it's always the same. They don't know how to write in science."

I asked her if she had ever shown her students a model of a good lab report. She replied that she had not. We looked through student portfolios, and she found an example of a strong report from one of her students. We found that student and got her permission to use her work as a model—she was delighted. We removed her name, to avoid the distraction, and made photocopies for the next class.

We conducted the next class as a critique lesson on what makes a good lab report. Every student looked through the model report and text coded—marked it up with their thoughts about what was done well and what questions it raised. They conferred with each other, and then, as a whole group, we discussed the features of the lab report that they felt were strong.

Students were amazed at the depth and length of the report and the clarity of language. They admired the author's precision and vocabulary and quoted from the report when they spoke. It made their typical reports look, in their words, "pretty sorry." A number of them laughed about how low their standards had been for this work. One young man turned to the teacher and said, "Mrs. C., is this what you wanted to us to do? Why didn't you show us this in September?"

For all the correcting we do, directions we give, and rubrics we create about what good work looks like, students are often unclear about what they are aiming for until they actually see and analyze strong models.

—Ron Berger

Tools for Improvement

It is a challenge to think of a skilled profession that does not rely on models, critique, and descriptive feedback to improve performance. Imagine fields such as medicine, journalism, or software development without clear models, and without continual critique and revision. Professionals in these fields know what a high-quality product looks like—whether it's a Pulitzer Prize–winning article or a software application with record-breaking sales—and these models provide them with a reference point for productive critique and feedback that will enable them to improve their own work. Professional dancers have watched thousands of dance performances and have those etched in their minds. Professional basketball players have watched thousands of games. They have a clear picture of where they want to go, and they need continual critique from coaches and colleagues to get there.

Picture a ballet troupe without someone continually adjusting posture and position, or a basketball team never critiquing strategies during halftime or analyzing their play on video. These ongoing feedback practices, which help us improve, are essential in nearly every field. Despite its prevalence in the world, this kind of on-the-job, on-the-spot feedback, based on strong models, is still strangely absent from many schools and classrooms. To be sure, grades and test scores abound, and occasionally students get assignments returned with comments, but these "results" are often thin and too distant from the moment of learning or effort to be useful. Now more than ever, with the introduction of rigorous Common Core State Standards, students need models of work that meet standards, and they need structured opportunities for critique and descriptive feedback so that they too can produce work that meets the standards. Students and teachers alike will benefit from seeing—sometimes even holding in their hands—examples of what they are aiming for.

We distinguish between group critique lessons—sessions to build students' common understanding of skills and quality (think of a medical team observing and analyzing an expert surgeon performing an operation)—and descriptive feedback—to improve a particular piece of work by an individual student (think of an editor working with a technical writer to improve a draft of a manual). These practices are not discrete—many times they overlap. Both share the goal of helping students understand what they need to do to improve. It is useful, however, to distinguish between them, because there are purposes and strategies for group critique lessons that are distinct from individual descriptive feedback, and teachers need to be adept at both.

Both practices center on models of work that give students a clear vision of what they are aiming for and set standards for quality. It is difficult for students to understand what good work looks like in a genre unless they have seen and analyzed it. Scoring rubrics are helpful for detailing the qualities in the work for which students will be assessed, but they do not provide a picture of what those qualities look like. We can create a rubric for a good jump shot in basketball or for a vivid descriptive paragraph, but to understand them we need to see them. Models bring standards to life.

Models: Exemplars of work used to build a vision of quality within a genre. Models are generally strong in important dimensions, which are discussed in critique lessons. They can be drawn from current or prior student work or the professional world or can be teacher created.

Critique lessons: Through critique lessons, students and teachers work together to define the qualities of good work in a specific genre or to think about the ways all students can improve their work through revision. This form of critique is a lesson, with clear objectives, and is designed to support the learning of all students, not primarily to improve the work of one. Models, which serve as the reference point to generate criteria for quality work, are at the heart of critique lessons.

Descriptive feedback: Descriptive feedback may take place in the form of a teacher-student conference, written comments from the teacher, or during a peer-to-peer feedback session. The constructive, precise comments that make up descriptive feedback specifically address a particular piece of work by a single student and are articulated in a way to raise the quality of the work toward the gold standard of the model.

Why These Practices Matter

Models, critique, and descriptive feedback are critical components of student-engaged assessment. The practices help students meet standards by giving them the tools they need to answer the question that may paralyze them when they get their work back for revision: "now what?" Often, students simply copyedit for conventions based on teacher corrections—grammar, spelling, and punctuation—and don't actually revise the work.

Instead, picture a student participating in a group critique of a strong historical essay, chosen by his teacher as a model. The teacher has decided to focus only on the introductory paragraphs—each student reads and text codes the model for those paragraphs. The class then generates a list of the qualities that stand out as effective (e.g., thesis clearly stated). Those qualities are discussed and written on chart paper in the front of the room.

When his teacher returns the first draft of his essay the next day, the student also receives a copy of the list of qualities that make for a good introduction to an essay that he and his classmates generated. He must now revise the introduction to match those qualities. He looks over his own paper and the need for revision is clear, as is the substance of what he needs to add and change. Critique, descriptive feedback, and the use of models are all practices designed to give students a vision of quality so that they know what they are aiming for.

Making Standards Real and Tangible

Standards do not create a picture of what students are aiming for. They are typically dry technical descriptions. When a Common Core literacy standard requires that students "use organization that is appropriate to task and purpose" or "use a variety of transitional words and phrases to manage the sequence of events," what does that mean? What does that look like?

> "I like models because they give a visual representation for people who learn better visually than by reading or listening."
>
> —*Paige, seventh-grade student, Grass Valley Charter School, Grass Valley, California*

Within a student-engaged assessment system, we start with learning targets, which put the standards in concrete terms that students understand. Students should then be provided with models that make those targets come to life. Finally, they should analyze those models to build a shared understanding of what makes them effective.

Building a Mindset of Continuous Improvement

Critique and descriptive feedback help students understand that all work, learning, and performance can be improved. We can tell students that their potential to learn is great, but they won't believe it, especially in areas in which they don't feel confident, until they actually see themselves improve. There is nothing that does

Figure 4.1 Natalie's Grasshopper—Multiple Drafts

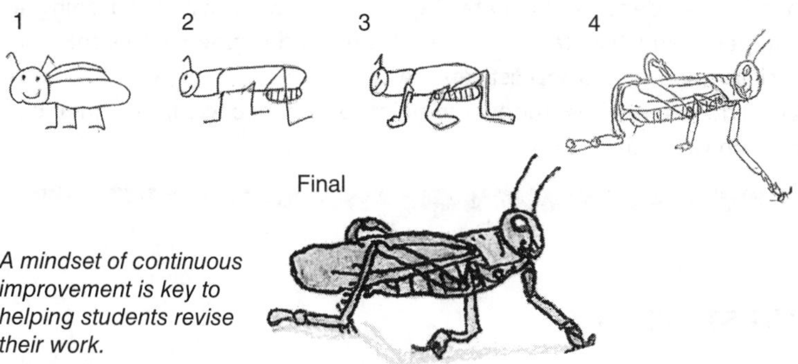

A mindset of continuous improvement is key to helping students revise their work.

this more effectively than when students work through multiple drafts, rehearsals, or practices and end up creating work or performing at a level that is beyond what they thought possible. Participating in critique and giving, receiving, and using feedback teaches students the value of effort and revision. Figure 4.1 is a great example of the power of a mindset of continuous improvement.

Instilling Responsibility and Ownership of Learning

Critique and descriptive feedback emphasize skills of critical analysis and self-assessment and ask students to make important decisions about their work and learning. Because the path to meeting learning targets is clearly defined by a shared vision of what quality looks like, students can work independently and build skills confidently.

Contributing to Collaboration and a Culture of Safety

To be effective, critique and descriptive feedback require a deliberate and sustained attention to emotional safety and depend on skills of collaboration. These practices help a classroom become a learning community dedicated to getting better together.

Common Core Connections

- Examining models and generating the criteria for success gives students a road map for meeting standards. They know what they are aiming for and how to get there.

(continued)

- Both the math and literacy standards explicitly demand that students become independent learners who can "critique the reasoning of others."
- The need for students to evaluate the validity and quality of reasoning and craftsmanship permeates the standards. The strategies described in this chapter build students' skills to do so in a sophisticated way.
- A quality critique requires students to point to evidence to support their claims, a key to Common Core success.

GETTING STARTED

Developing a Positive Culture for Critique and Descriptive Feedback

An essential starting point for critique and descriptive feedback in any classroom is ensuring that the guidelines *be kind, be specific,* and *be helpful* are the backbone of every class. Formal and informal feedback and critique flow from these. Safety and encouragement, as well as structure and clear learning targets, will set students up for success.

Just about everyone has a feedback nightmare, a time when they felt hurt or judged by someone's feedback or criticism. Some students are particularly vulnerable, especially if they have not experienced much school success and have received many messages of negative criticism (both implicit and explicit). School and classroom guidelines must be carefully built and reinforced, but individual feedback also must be tailored and shaped with the particular student in mind. There is not a template or cookie-cutter approach that will work for every student.

This kind of safety can be hard to monitor—teachers must be vigilant and firm, especially when building a classroom culture with a new group. Very young students often don't realize that their comments may be perceived as mean. They can be candid even when it's hurtful to others and need to learn how to word things carefully. Sometimes older students, particularly adolescents, may intentionally but subtly undermine a peer's work—such as complimenting work with a sarcastic tone or facial expression. It is imperative that the teacher stops the critique the moment problems happen, deals with unkind or untruthful comments or tone firmly, and reestablishes norms. Eventually, students will trust and reinforce the norms themselves.

Because group critique lessons often focus on exemplars from outside the classroom, they offer some distance from a student's personal feelings, and reinforce skills students will need in their future careers, a key Common Core connection. They also represent a rich opportunity for students to experience what constructive feedback looks and sounds like.

Snapshot: Building Culture with Fourth-Graders

"To build habits that establish a culture in which quality is the norm, I begin with a basic but demanding task that each student can accomplish, yet all can improve: the challenge of drawing freehand a straight line," says Steven Levy, EL Education school designer and former fourth-grade teacher at Bowman Elementary School in Lexington, Massachusetts. "I introduce standards of quality that guide our work throughout the year." Students develop the language, norms, and skills of describing quality through group critique as they analyze lines.

Levy assigns every student the task of drawing a straight line freehand and uses the work to demonstrate generating criteria, feedback and critique, revision, planning ahead, taking care of resources, and above all the norms of a safe, collaborative, constructive classroom. "Practicing these drawings is a particularly effective way to begin the year because everyone has equal access to the assignment. No one can do it perfectly, so everyone is challenged."

"When students have learned this process of producing quality work, they are ready to apply it to more complex tasks. We now go through the same process to develop standards for writing, for presentations, and for major projects. We do not follow the exact steps in the line exercises for everything we do. Sometimes I give more explicit instruction or direction at the beginning. At other times, depending on the effectiveness of the students' work, I recommend additional critique sessions or more practice of discrete skills between drafts. The steps are simply tools and processes designed to help students take more responsibility in producing quality work."

Choosing the Right Work Models

Because critique lessons are based on good models, the most important part of the lesson takes place before it even begins. Learning how to recognize and select powerful, generative models for critique lessons is essential and it takes practice. Models should show students where they are headed. The exemplars don't need to be perfect but must be good models of features that are connected to learning targets. The more compelling the models are, the more powerful the critique can be. Ideally, teachers will begin building an archive of good work models that are gathered and stored for specific purposes. When a teacher needs to teach the format or genre of a research paper, for example, she has a file of research papers by former or other students to draw from for critique lessons.

> "I think the difference in math is that our models aren't 'products,' but ways of thinking. We critique our class exit slips often as models of thinking with the intent of helping students identify common misconceptions. We look for 'brilliant mistakes' that students can learn from and that lead to deeper understanding of the learning target."
>
> *—Lin Tarr, math teacher, William Smith High School, Aurora, Colorado*

A teacher might choose to create exemplary models herself, or models with the types of problems she thinks her students will encounter. Models from the professional world can also be useful, and set a high and authentic bar, especially for older students. If models of current student work are used, it is important to choose samples that represent different approaches to the same assignment, or different strong features, so there is little duplication in what is viewed and discussed. There should be a specific reason for each piece chosen. If the class is going to spend valuable, whole-class time considering a piece, there should be a clear reason that relates to the goal of the critique.

Modeling with Weak Work

Although it is most important to have exemplary models, it can also be useful to have examples of pieces that are poorly done in different ways, particularly in those areas that the teacher feels her current students may find challenging. For example, to help students remember to be less repetitive with sentence structure in a composition, it can be very powerful to have them critique an anonymous student composition that is fraught with repetitive language. The image of this weak work will stay with them and can be discussed regularly to remind the group to be careful to avoid its pitfalls.

When using weak work, there are some cautions. First, the work must be anonymous. Students should never be able to recognize it as the work of a current or former student. Second, the work must be treated respectfully. Modeling mean-spirited critique will promote an unkind classroom climate. Last, not all weak work is a good choice. Ideally, the work is compelling in its flaws. For example, if it is very strong in some areas but confusing in others, it can invite wonder and analysis. The best weak work is not an example of a student who wasn't trying, but rather a student who was putting in effort and created something interesting to consider, but had confusions that resulted in problems that are likely to crop up for many students.

Turning Critique *Sessions* into Standards-Based Critique *Lessons*

A critique session becomes more than a simple exercise in closely examining student work when it leads students to new learning, application of knowledge and skills, and meeting standards. It then becomes a standards-driven critique lesson. As with all student-engaged assessment practices, standards-based learning targets are the foundation of every critique lesson. Critique lessons will not be effective without clear learning targets and models of what meeting the learning target looks like.

The following sample in-depth critique flows from a clear learning target, based on a fourth-grade Common Core math standard. It illustrates how effective critique can be as a lesson. Many concepts and areas of content that the teacher would be addressing in a more conventional lesson can be addressed more powerfully and concretely in a lesson connected to a critique of real work. Rather than a teacher telling students about the dimensions of good work in that genre, the students discover and name those features themselves. It is clearer, more engaging, and more memorable than a lecture-style lesson. Critique lessons like this actively involve students in analyzing work against learning targets and compel them to use academic vocabulary and cite evidence for their assertions. These are key skills for meeting Common Core standards.

Snapshot: In-Depth Critique in a Fourth-Grade Math Class

Common Core standard 4.MD.A.3: *Apply the area and perimeter formulas for rectangles in real world and mathematical problems.*

Long-term learning target: I can use formulas to find the area and perimeter of spaces in the real world and in math problems.

Supporting learning targets: (1) I can recognize when the formulas for rectangular areas and perimeters are used correctly in student work and can explain why, using evidence

(continued)

from the work. (2) I can describe what a good solution to a real-world area and perimeter problem looks like and explain why.

Step one: Choosing work samples for a clear purpose: The teacher has a collection of student work from prior years of students measuring rectangular spaces in the school, drawing labeled diagrams, and calculating area and perimeter. From this collection, she creates a packet with four work samples—two samples are fully accurate (though different in approach); one is partially accurate; one is fully inaccurate. All the work is anonymous and there are no labels as to which samples are accurate and which are not.

Step two: Individual challenge (five minutes): The teacher hands a packet of the four samples to each student. Students silently and individually analyze the samples and try to make sense of them, determining which they think are accurate and why.

Step three: Group analysis (ten minutes): The students are clustered into groups of four. Each group discusses which of the samples they feel is accurate and justifies their opinions with evidence from the work.

Step four: Whole-group critique (fifteen minutes): The teacher leads the class in an analysis of the samples. First, she introduces the long-term learning target and the supporting learning targets for the lesson. Next, she leads the class in analyzing each of the four student samples. She begins with what they noticed about the samples—without judgment—focusing on what strikes them about the work. She then focuses on accuracy, discussing which ones they feel are correct and why, citing evidence. After this, she leads the group in discussing which samples are good examples—those that are clear and correctly labeled and include well-explained reasoning.

Step five: Small group brainstorm (five minutes): Small groups brainstorm a list of the attributes of a good solution—accurate and well presented.

Step six: Synthesis: Building of collaborative criteria (fifteen minutes): The teacher runs a whole-class discussion, eliciting comments from each group. She charts their thinking about what a good solution to a real-world rectangular perimeter and area problem looks like.

Define the Purpose for Each Critique Lesson

Critique lessons can have a variety of specific purposes—setting standards of quality and developing criteria for work (as in the example), supporting focused revision, or fine-tuning final presentations, products, or performances. It is important to make the particular focus of the critique clear from the outset. The teacher frames the critique with learning targets so that she can keep track of guiding the inquiry to address them. Clarity about learning targets should not prevent the critique from producing unplanned discoveries, clarifications, and new ideas or directions, and it is important for the teacher to celebrate and identify these.

Teacher-facilitated critique lessons that include looking together at work models can be used to address learning in a variety of disciplines. The lesson could focus on the following:

- Content (e.g., simple machines, an historical timeline)
- Concepts (e.g., recurring themes in history, binary numbers)
- Skills (e.g., keyboarding, interpreting a bar chart, factoring equations)
- Product formats or genres (e.g., business letter, political map, watercolor portrait)
- Habits of scholarship (e.g., group collaboration during field work excursions, participation during literature circles, hallway behavior)

The following critique lesson snapshot is a good example of how clear focus and purpose can lead students to a productive understanding of expectations for quality. A similar lesson can also be viewed on the accompanying video of third-graders at Presumpscot Elementary School in Portland, Maine.

Watch video: "A Group Critique Lesson—Models, Critique, and Descriptive Feedback"

Snapshot: A Gallery Critique in a Third-Grade Classroom

Ron Berger visited Lori Andrusic's third-grade classroom at Capital City Charter School in Washington, DC, to conduct a guest critique. He led a whole-class gallery critique on story openings. The students were working to improve their skills in writing narratives, which corresponds to third-grade Common Core writing standards, W.3.3: *Write narratives to develop real or imagined experiences or events using effective techniques, descriptive details, and clear event sequences.* For this critique lesson, Berger narrowed the focus to one small but vital aspect of narratives—the opening lines. He asked Andrusic to cut and paste the first line (or lines, as warranted) of the first-draft story of each student into a single document. This document was in each student's hands at the beginning of the lesson.

With Andrusic prepared to list students' ideas on chart paper, the class read aloud all the opening lines of the stories. Berger then asked the students if there was one that really stood out and grabbed their interest.

A boy's hand shot up: "This one—written by Hector," he said. "I love this one: 'The haunted car. It all started when . . .'"

"What is it about that opening line you like so much?" Berger asked.

"I don't know. . . . I just do."

(continued)

"Is it a particular word? The flow of the language? An idea?"

He smiled. "It is a word—*haunted.* I love that word."

"Why do you think you love that word?"

"I don't know. It's powerful?"

Andrusic turned to her chart paper which she had titled, "Strategies for Good Story Openings," at the top and wrote the first of the class's discoveries: powerful words.

"Does anybody else see an opening with a powerful word?" Berger continued.

"I do," said a girl. "'Once there were some ninjas in China; they were magic ninjas.'"

"And what's the powerful word there?"

"*Magic.* If they were just plain ninjas . . . boring." (The class nodded their agreement.) "It's magic that makes you interested."

One boy raised his hand with concern: "I don't think I used any powerful words in my opening," he said. "I don't think my story has anything interesting until half-way down the first page. I'm going to do some rewriting."

Another girl raised her hand. "I think it's not just that *haunted* is a good word . . . it's also putting together haunted with car—that's unexpected. Haunted house, that's usual, but haunted car—that's weird, and interesting."

The class had additions for the list: combining words in unusual ways, using the unexpected.

The class was suddenly full of ideas, hands shooting up around the circle. The list grew longer. And then a quiet boy raised his hand tentatively. "Can we go back to Hector's—the haunted car?" he asked. "I think it's more than just the word *haunted.* I think that story opening has music."

"What do you mean, music?" Berger asked. "Can you describe it?"

He sang the opening theme to Beethoven's Fifth Symphony with dramatic flourish: "Da-da-da-DUM!" The class erupted in delight and repeated his notes.

"Tell us more. Where do you see that?"

"'It all started when . . . da-da-da-DUM!' I can tell it's a mystery! It has that mystery opening. Like a fairy tale opens with, 'Once upon a time,' but a mystery opens like this."

This really got the class thinking. Are there standard openings for genres of stories? Did they want to use them? The discussion took off and they were engaged in generating strategies for good story openings for half an hour. Eventually Berger had to say a regretful goodbye to lead critique lessons in other classes, but when he ran into these same students at lunch they gathered around quickly to resume the dialogue. "Hector isn't at lunch," they told Berger. "He's back in the room working on his story about the haunted car. He doesn't usually write so much, but now he just can't stop!'"

Determine the Right Timing in a Sequence of Curriculum for a Critique to Be Held

Depending on the goals and learning targets, critique can be useful at a variety of times in a curriculum or long-term study:

- Introductory teacher-facilitated lesson using previously collected models of work—to set a high standard for quality and to construct with students a framework of criteria for what constitutes good work in that domain or product format.
- In process, during the creation of work—to support focused revision, clarify and tune student efforts to apply criteria for quality, refocus student concentration and momentum, and introduce new concepts or next steps. The snapshot of good story openings on the previous pages is a good example of this.
- Just before final exhibition of work—to fine-tune the quality of the presentation, display, or performance for an audience. Often final details and touches make a major difference in quality.
- After completion of an assignment—to reflect on quality and learning and to set goals.

Depending also on the assignment or project being created, each of these points in the sequence of study suggests a different focus and style of critique lesson. Ideally a form of critique will be used at all points in the process.

Choose a Structured Format or Protocol to Match the Goals

A discussion protocol—a planned format or agenda—can help create a more productive conversation. Protocols help structure group discussions by accomplishing the following:

- Defining a sequence of discussion prompts
- Structuring time, allocating a set amount of minutes for each section of a discussion
- Defining roles, assigning particular perspectives or responsibilities to various group members
- Defining norms for the give-and-take of ideas and for listening habits

There are well-known protocols for critique, such as the collaborative assessment protocol[1] or the tuning protocol (McDonald, Mohr, Dichter, & McDonald, 2007). There is, however, no single protocol that works well in all

[1] Developed by Steve Seidel and Project Zero colleagues at the Harvard Graduate School of Education.

classroom settings. Critique protocols work best when they are designed or customized by classroom teachers to meet the particular needs of their lesson objectives and classroom settings. All protocols, whether established or invented, benefit from being tweaked and refashioned at times to suit particular situations.

Strategy Close Up: The Tuning Protocol

Purpose: To identify strengths and weaknesses of an anonymous work model

Time: Approximately thirty minutes

Grade level: Fifth and higher

Roles: Presenter or teacher, participants (ideally in small groups)

Steps

1. Presentation by presenter or teacher; participants are silent (four minutes)
   - Provide context for the work being discussed
   - Present a question to the group that will help them focus their feedback on one aspect
2. Reading and examination (three to eight minutes)
   Students examine the work, focusing on the question the presenter or teacher asked.
3. Clarifying questions (three minutes)
   Clarifying questions are matter of fact; save substantive issues for later. Clarifying questions are answerable with "yes," "no," or a single brief sentence. The teacher or presenter is responsible for making sure that clarifying questions are truly clarifying in nature.
4. Processing by participants (ten to fifteen minutes)
   Participants talk to each other about the teacher's or presenter's work, with particular attention to the focusing question, whereas the teacher or presenter remains quiet, taking notes as appropriate. The group begins dialogue by concentrating on the following:
   - Strengths
   - Disconnects and problems
   - Questions for probing or further reflection on the part of the presenter
5. Teacher's or presenter's response (five minutes)
   Presenter shares significant points, recognizes powerful feedback, and identifies next steps.

Two Types of Critique Lessons

Gallery Critique

In a gallery critique, all students post work for everyone to view closely. A gallery critique works best when the goal is to identify and capture only positive features in the selected work that can help everyone improve. Only a small set of the posted work may be cited. With work from the whole class, there is obviously going to be a lot of work with problems; this is not the time to try to point them all out. The point of a gallery critique is to find effective ideas and strategies in strong examples that students can borrow to improve their own work.

If the work is visual, it can be posted for viewing in a gallery style. If the work is written, it may be posted on a wall or copied and distributed. For written work, short pieces or a portion of a larger piece (e.g., a multistep word problem, the lead of a paper, a poem) work best. The critique of the first lines of stories featured previously is an example of this.

A silent gallery walk enables students to focus on how work does or does not meet learning targets and standards for quality.

Clearly there are advantages to sharing every student's work, such as building accountability, excitement, shared commitment, and a realistic sense of how one's work compares with others. However, it is important to create safety for students whose initial performance on the assignment was weak. A protocol for a gallery critique might look something like this:

Introduction: The teacher explains the steps of the protocol and the learning targets. He reminds students of the norms of giving feedback—*be kind, be specific,* and *be helpful.*

Step one: Posting the work (five minutes): Each student tapes his or her first draft to the wall.

Step two: Silent gallery walk (five minutes): Students view all the drafts in a silent walk, and take notes identifying strong examples of a predetermined focus (e.g., descriptive language, use of evidence, elegant problem solving, experiment design).

Step three: What did you notice? (five minutes): The teacher leads a discussion in which students are not allowed to make judgments or give opinions; they can comment only on things they noticed and identified.

Step four: What is working? (fifteen minutes): The teacher leads the class in a discussion of which aspects of the posted drafts grabbed their attention or impressed them. Each time students choose an example, they need to articulate exactly what they found compelling, citing evidence from the work itself. If they're not sure, the teacher draws them out until they can point to evidence in the work and name something specific. The teacher also points to examples he or she is impressed with, and explains why. The insights are charted by the teacher to codify specific strategies that students can use to improve their drafts.

In-Depth Critique

A single piece of work (or set of related pieces) is used to uncover strengths or to highlight common areas in need of revision or gaps in knowledge that need to be addressed (e.g., use of evidence, descriptive language, topic development). Unlike a gallery critique, wherein the focus is exclusively on positive aspects in the collection of work, an in-depth critique analyzes a particular piece to determine what aspects are working and which are not. The goal is to recognize and name particular features that are effective or ineffective so that the class can learn from them. The story that opened this chapter—high school physics students analyzing an exemplary lab report—is an example of in-depth critique.

Case Study

Critique and Descriptive Feedback at the Center of the Curriculum

Adapted from a piece written by Jane Dunbar, kindergarten teacher at ANSER Charter School in Boise, Idaho, during her class's learning expedition on birds, in this learning expedition, extensive fieldwork and research led students to their final product—beautiful, high-quality bird cards (see figure 4.2 for an example of one of the student's bird cards), which were sold throughout the state to raise money for bird habitats. The use of models and critique lessons were central to Dunbar's curriculum.

By February, we are ready to start the month-long project. Each child will research and draw a scientific representation of one bird. Although all kindergartners have the support of a fifth- or sixth-grade buddy for research, the drawings are all their own. Their exceptional drawings develop over time through carefully layered instructional practices, and a classroom climate that makes all things seem possible to these young, impassioned learners. By building a classroom community that supports strong character development (courage, compassion, respect, discipline, and integrity), children learn to challenge themselves, to give and receive constructive criticism, and to take risks as learners.

Steps to the Final Product

Best work: Kindergartners know that they must attend to lessons, practice, reflect on their work, and have the courage to take risks as learners and learn from their mistakes. I honor effort and intentions in this classroom each and every day. Kindergartners have been internalizing these behaviors since September.

A culture of quality: My role is to provide quality materials (paper, colored drawing pencils of every shade), exemplary photographs to work from, and modeling of how to visualize and then draw lines corresponding to the shape of a given bird.

Rubric: Students look at an exemplary bird drawing done by a former kindergartner. Next to this drawing is the photograph that was used as a model. "What do you notice?" I ask. Children look closely at similarities and differences. I help them tease generic comments into specific, explicit descriptions. After this close examination of work, I ask students what is important to notice when drawing a bird. The children develop criteria for the rubric. I use their words and add icons for each characteristic.

(continued)

Collaborative critique: Children continue to look closely at each other's work. This time, the rubric, the photo, and each draft of a peer's work is displayed. We focus our attention on the latest draft. I ask the children, "What do you notice?" I try to remind students that they only "notice" and that they do not make evaluative comments. I then ask the group, "What would you do on the next draft if this were yours?" And, "What would you change?" I challenge them for details. For example, "What about the eye?" and "What line, shape, color needs attention?" From this discussion the child whose work is displayed makes his or her own decision on what will be the focus of the next draft and writes an intention on a sticky note (see the following section). The child has been given many suggestions, but he or she has ownership of this next important decision of how to proceed. A collaborative critique of one child's work can take between ten and twenty minutes.

Compliment circle: A compliment circle follows the critique session. The student who has shown work calls on his or her peers for compliments. With both the critique and compliment circle, I have found it important to be sure each featured student gets the same number of constructive comments and compliments. Attention to balance saves any unintentional negative comparison between students and their work.

Sticky notes: Each child, using the rubric as a guide, sets an intention for the focus of his or her efforts on the next draft. Writing the word or drawing the icon given on the rubric, the kindergartner focuses now on his or her own work and sets an intention. I place the sticky note above a new white piece of drawing paper and alert teachers and other adults present as to what the child is attempting to accomplish with this next draft. Adults can then support the child's intentions.

Doing More Than They Thought Possible

Most children do four to five drafts before marking the rubric and formally assessing their own work. Each draft will take thirty to forty minutes. At this point in the process, children decide if they have accomplished "best work" or if they wish to try again. A surprising number will want to try again. They are hooked. This process has led them far beyond what they ever thought possible.

The Role of the Teacher in the Critique Lesson

The teacher must take an active role in facilitation throughout a critique lesson. This process works best when it looks organic (emerging entirely from student ideas) but is in fact skillfully shaped. The teacher chooses students strategically for comments, governs the flow of discussion and contributes enthusiasm, interjects compelling comments to build interest and makes key points, and reframes student observations when necessary to make them clear to the group and connected to the learning targets. The teacher needs to remember that the critique is

Figure 4.2 Sample Bird Card

Kindergartners in Boise, Idaho, created a beautiful boxed set of bird cards. This extraordinarily high-quality work by very young students was made possible by critique lessons at the heart of the curriculum.

a lesson, with clear learning targets, and should not hesitate to take charge of the flow to ensure the session is productive.

Be a Strong Guardian of Critique Norms

The most important teacher role is to foster and sustain a critique culture that is emotionally safe for students and productive for learning. The critique rules, or norms, must be explicit and tracked vigilantly during the lesson to ensure that all students feel protected from ridicule (even subtle sarcasm or facial expressions) and that comments are specific and instructive. The critique rules should require participants to *be kind, specific,* and *helpful* in their comments. In addition to guarding against any hurtful comments, this also means guarding against vague comments (e.g., "I like it," "It's good"). Participants must point to specific features (e.g., "I think the title is well chosen," "Including the graph makes it much clearer to me"). It means that repetitive comments or tangential comments that derail the momentum of learning should be avoided. The participants should be aware of the goals for the critique lesson, and their comments should relate to the group effort to build understanding.

To do this well, the teacher must convey that she is in absolute control of the rules and will tolerate nothing that is mean-spirited. At the same time, she must also encourage positive, helpful comments. It is also useful to "critique the critique," that is, for the teacher to continually note and compliment insightful or thoughtful comments and to lead the class in reflection about what constitutes good critique.

There are additional guideline suggestions that can help to build a positive climate. Examples of such guidelines include the following:

- It should always be clear that it is the work itself, not the author of the work, that is the subject of the critique.
- Use "I" statements (e.g., "I don't understand your first sentence" rather than "It doesn't make sense").

The teacher must ensure that students adhere to group norms.

- Begin comments, if possible, with a positive feature in the work before moving on to perceived weaknesses (e.g., "I think the eyes in your portrait are very powerful, but I think adding eyebrows would give it more feeling").
- Frame ideas, when possible, as questions rather than as statements (e.g., "Why did you choose to leave out the illustration on this draft?" rather than "It was better with an illustration").

These norms are especially important when students are sharing their own work with their classmates, but they apply even when the work is from outside of the class. Explicitly teaching and using critique rules will strengthen students' critique skills as well as their abilities to hear and use descriptive feedback.

Keep the Critique Moving at an Interesting, Energetic Pace

To keep the critique engaging, the teacher should be sure the work being analyzed is accessible and clear. Photocopies should be made for each student or posted and projected work should be close enough for students to easily see. This preparation will help the teacher keep the lesson lively, as will using the following strategies to compel student involvement: involving a range of voices in the discussion, reading work aloud with a strong voice or choosing selected students to read aloud, or calling students up to the board to point out exactly what they see in the posted work.

Distill, Shape, and Record the Insights from the Critique

Many of the insights that the teacher hopes students will come to may arise from student comments, but the teacher may need to jump on them, repeat them, reword, or reframe them. Later they may even be codified for the class in the form of criteria or next steps. It is helpful to return to these insights during the critique, explicitly attributing them to the original student ("Tamika's theory" or "Jonathan's observation"), even though the teacher has perhaps changed and deepened the original comment. If particular key insights don't arise, the teacher shouldn't hesitate to seed them as questions or discovery challenges in viewing the work ("Did anyone notice . . . ," "Can you see an example of . . .") or simply add them directly.

In a gallery critique, the teacher can't rely just on students picking the examples that are most useful and generative—she must direct attention to examples that are important bridges to the learning targets, and ones that will stimulate new insights. She can use gallery critiques for other purposes as well—to give public affirmation to students who have made particular progress, or conversely, to use the critique to push students who have exhibited less than best effort. If there is a guest critique expert from the professional community, the teacher can seed the critique by explaining to the expert the learning targets and goals for the session, and perhaps help to direct his or her attention beforehand to particular pieces of work. (For more on using guest critique experts, see "Strategy Close Up: Speed Feedback").

Focus on Naming the Specific Qualities and Strategies That Students Can Take Away with Them

It is not useful for students to leave the session with the idea that "Aliya is a good writer" or "The book review we read was great," but rather, "Aliya used eight strategies that made her piece good, and now I know them and can use them." Naming the effective qualities and strategies must be explicit, openly discussed and negotiated, and must result in terms that students understand—in their language. Sometimes it is not even clear to the teacher at first what feature in the work is being cited as strong—this is a perfect opportunity to engage the class in a spirited discussion to define and name the feature. The more concrete the naming of features, the better. Charting the names of features and hanging them on the wall for reference helps. Vague insights put on a chart, such as "Use 'voice'" are less helpful, particularly to weaker writers, than specific suggestions such as "Include dialogue," "Use verbs other than *said,*" "Use punctuation marks other than periods." Again, the teacher should not hesitate to reshape student ideas into words that she feels will be clear and helpful, and to add to the list if students have omitted important qualities or strategies.

> "Since the 1990s all California students in fourth and seventh grades take a state writing assessment. As part of the preparation for this summative exam, students examine available sample writing against the four-point rubric. Both the samples and the rubric are available from the California Department of education website. As a result of this consistent instructional practice, students' writing skills have improved. More important though, students are better prepared to look critically for evidence of excellence in their own writing compared to a rubric. They can name their own strengths and hone in on specific needs in their own writing."
>
> —*Brian Martinez, principal, Grass Valley Charter School, Grass Valley, California*

The process of naming qualities and strategies can also be a step in creating a rubric of what constitutes quality for this genre or skill, or can refer to an existing rubric that the class uses, supporting that rubric with specific strategies. The critique lesson is most effective in creating specific, rather than general, criteria lists or rubrics—instead of "what makes good writing," the list would address "features of a good research paper." Table 4.1 shows an excerpt from a sample rubric for a letter-writing assignment with specific, detailed criteria for proficiency on one learning target. Additional learning targets for this assignment (not shown) focus on domain-specific vocabulary, organization, and writing conventions.

Table 4.1 Sample Rubric

Writing invitation:
You are an individual who wants to affect what kids eat in school. Write a letter to the superintendent to persuade her to change the school food policy.
Long-term learning target:
I can write an analysis of substantive topics or texts using valid reasoning and sufficient evidence.

Learning Target	Beginning	Developing	Proficient	Advanced
I can develop a clear position or claim about food policy and support it with valid reasoning and sufficient evidence (derived from Common Core writing standard, W.9–10.1.	• Topic is only loosely about school food policy or is muddled. • No counter-claims are presented. • Evidence only loosely supports the position or claim or counterclaim and there is minimal evidence or no evidence cited.	• Topic addresses school food policy but lacks a clear position statement. • Claims and counterclaims are present but lack coherence and do not build on the position or claim. • Evidence only loosely supports the position or claim or counterclaim or there is minimal evidence present.	• Author develops a clear position on school food policy. • Author demonstrates an ability to anticipate audience's knowledge and concerns through the development of the claims and counterclaims. • Author includes well-chosen, relevant, and sufficient evidence from text to support the position or claim and counterclaim.	• Position is clear and provides a unique perspective. • Multiple related claims and counterclaims flow seamlessly together. • Extensive and varied evidence (e.g., quotes, data) from a variety of sources back the position for each claim or counterclaim.

Teach the Vocabulary

The Common Core State Standards require students to "acquire new vocabulary, particularly general academic and domain-specific words and phrases." In line with the Common Core, this kind of vocabulary acquisition is the foundation of effective critique. Imagine a fifth-grade writing lesson with the following learning target: "I can use teacher feedback to make decisions about how to revise my script," derived from Common Core writing standard, W.5.5: *With guidance and support from peers and adults, develop and strengthen writing as needed by planning, revising, editing, rewriting, or trying a new approach.* In order to meet this learning target, students must understand the academic vocabulary words *feedback* and *revise.* The teacher may support students in deconstructing a word like *revise*—identifying the prefix *re-* and explaining its meaning as *again* and the root *vise* as derived from the word *vision,* which means to *see.* Additionally, students must use domain-specific vocabulary such as *script, narrator, character, lines, conflict,* and *theme* to give effective feedback.

> "Rubrics help you understand what quality work is. They tell you the truth. You may have thought you did very good, but then you get your score and you see what you need to work on."
>
> *—Alex, third-grade student, Grass Valley Charter School, Grass Valley, California*

To use a metaphor, if critique is like surgery, carefully cutting into a piece of work to determine what is working well and what is not, then the surgical tools are the words we use to dissect the piece. If a student can only use simple terms to describe a piece (e.g., "It's good. I like it"), it's like attempting surgery with a butter knife. Students need sharp precision in their language to be effective surgeons (e.g., "I think the narrator's voice sounds too much like a kid our age and not like someone his character's age," "There is a confusion here between correlation and causation"). The need for precision gives students an authentic reason and immediate application for learning new vocabulary and putting it to use.

Providing Descriptive Feedback to Individual Students

There is a great deal of overlap between whole-class critique lessons and individual descriptive feedback in the mindset, skills, and practices that teachers must bring to this work. As the story from the physics classroom illustrates, showing

Feedback is typically a private exchange between teacher and student.

students an excellent model can in fact be a powerful form of feedback (e.g., "Why didn't you show us this in September?"). Teachers give students feedback all the time. In this section, we propose that teachers think more analytically and strategically about the nature of the feedback they provide.

Descriptive feedback is distinguished by these features:

- The focus is on supporting the growth of an individual student or small group, improving a particular piece of work, performance, skill, or disposition.
- It is typically an exchange between teacher and student, or student and student, not a public learning experience for the class.
- It is nested in a long-term relationship (e.g., teacher-student, coach-player, supervisor-worker). Maintaining a constructive relationship must be an implicit focus in all feedback conversations, whether spoken or written.
- Individuals are sensitive when receiving personal feedback. It is much more likely that strategic, positive comments will result in improvements than will criticism.
- Feedback ideally flows from strong knowledge of the student—knowing the student's strengths and weaknesses, knowing where she is in her growth and what she needs to spark the next step of growth.

In some cases, feedback will come from a guest expert or someone a student doesn't know well. For example, a martial arts class might be visited by a highly honored sensei. This teacher knows nothing about the students but can watch a class and offer highly specific feedback to each student. Because of his expertise and fresh eyes, this expert is able to offer advice that may be new and constructive. It builds excitement when students know they will receive feedback from an authentic expert, impels them to work harder, and models for them the concepts and vocabulary of the field. It is important to structure these sessions carefully and prepare the guest experts and students for a successful experience.

Strategy Close Up: Speed Feedback

In our schools, students frequently produce work modeled after a real-world format. For example, rather than a typical book report, students might instead write book reviews and maintain a blog for other students their age. In such cases, bringing a professional into the classroom to offer feedback can add huge value for the students who are motivated to make their work mirror that of professionals in the field.

In Ron Berger's former sixth-grade classroom, where students were working on architectural blueprints of residential homes for fictional clients, a different local architect visited the classroom for ninety minutes on three consecutive Fridays. Each architect began with a fifteen-minute presentation to the class, followed by a work period during which he or she circulated the room offering feedback to students.

To ensure that all twenty-four students had the chance to meet with the architect, the class used a "speed feedback" protocol, based on speed chess. The architect met with each student for three minutes, looking over the plans and pointing out positive or problematic features. To monitor time, a student ambassador stood behind the architect with a stopwatch and gave a signal when time was up. Using this protocol, every student received feedback from three different architects, which enabled them to produce high-quality work that mirrored the work of real architects as closely as possible.

Planning for Effective Feedback

Analyze and Adapt Your Current Means of Giving Feedback

Every teacher spends much of the day giving students feedback—collectively and individually. The question is, how much of this feedback is actually used by students to improve their learning? Figure 4.3 is a continuum of how a student might hear and use feedback.

Figure 4.3 Continuum of How Students Hear Feedback

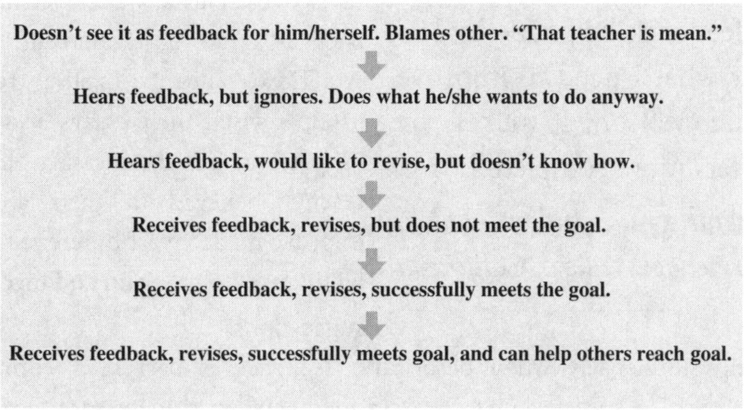

Doesn't see it as feedback for him/herself. Blames other. "That teacher is mean."

↓

Hears feedback, but ignores. Does what he/she wants to do anyway.

↓

Hears feedback, would like to revise, but doesn't know how.

↓

Receives feedback, revises, but does not meet the goal.

↓

Receives feedback, revises, successfully meets the goal.

↓

Receives feedback, revises, successfully meets goal, and can help others reach goal.

Often the students most readily able to meet the final two points on the continuum are already the most capable, skilled, and successful. "Students can't hear something that's beyond their comprehension; nor can they hear something if they are not listening or are feeling like it would be useless to listen. Because students' feelings of control and self-efficacy are involved, even well-intentioned feedback can be very destructive ('See? I knew I was stupid!'). The research on feedback shows its Jekyll-and-Hyde character. Not all studies about feedback show positive effects. The nature of the feedback and the context in which it is given matter a great deal" (Brookhart, 2008, p. 2).

Recent research related to student mindsets highlights that without the right mindset, students are often incapable or unwilling to act on feedback, however accurate and useful it may seem to be. For example, teachers regularly read student essays and provide feedback for revisions, then are surprised that the students either don't choose to revise or incorporate only surface copyedits instead of real revisions. Researchers David Yeager and colleagues (2013) created a randomized experiment in which middle school student essays that had been marked by teachers with suggested revisions had a sticky note added to the paper. Half the students received a control message: "I'm giving you these comments so that you'll have feedback on your paper." The other random half was given the treatment message: "I'm giving you these comments because I have very high expectations and I know that you can reach them."

The difference in the sticky note messages is subtle. It would hardly seem possible that it would have an effect. However, the effect was dramatic. African American students in the control group revised their essays after getting them back at a rate of 17 percent. African American students in the treatment group revised their essays at a rate of 71 percent. Just the message that their teacher believed in their ability to improve made a vast difference in their willingness to try again and incorporate suggestions.

"Descriptive feedback helps me by letting me know what I need to improve and what I did well on. It makes my final product feel more complete."

—Rachael, seventh-grade student, Vallejo Charter School, Vallejo, California

It helps immensely when descriptive feedback is part of a comprehensive approach to student-engaged assessment—when students are clear about the learning targets and are asked to set goals for their learning, and when they are taught the language and norms of critique and shown positive models of giving and receiving feedback. In essence, when students are treated as partners in assessment from the outset, they will be in a much stronger position to make use of a teacher's feedback.

The good news is that like every other important instructional practice, feedback can be fine-tuned and improved through careful attention to its content and delivery. As students become more proficient using feedback, they become more independent learners.

Consider the "How"[2]

Timing: How Often and When Should Feedback Be Given?

- Always be sure that there will be time and opportunity for the student to use the feedback.
- Immediate feedback is best for factual knowledge (yes-no, right-wrong), but delaying a bit will make sense for more complex assessments of comprehension and thinking processes.
- Provide feedback as often as you can for major assignments. The best feedback is ongoing.

Quantity: How Much Feedback Should Be Given?

- Choose priority points that relate to learning targets.
- Consider the individual student's developmental needs and how much he or she can take in at once.

Written versus Oral: What's the Right Balance between These Modes?

- Oral feedback, provided as students are working, is often the most effective and efficient.
- If giving oral feedback, it is often useful to ask the student to repeat back what he or she heard to guard against misinterpretations.

---

[2] This section is based on the work of Susan Brookhart and Connie Moss (Brookhart, 2008; Moss & Brookhart, 2009).

- Use individual conferences for more substantive feedback.
- Provide targeted written feedback on the work itself or on an assignment sheet, rubric, or criteria sheet.

Audience: What Is the Right Balance between Group and Individual Feedback?

- Individual feedback conveys the message that the teacher cares about the individual's learning. It is also most tailored and responsive to an individual's needs.
- Group or whole-class feedback works if everyone has missed the same thing or a clear pattern of weakness has emerged.

Tone: How Words Are Used Matters a Great Deal in Giving Effective Feedback.

- Effective tone:
  - Be positive
  - Be constructive when critical
  - Make suggestions not prescriptions or mandates
- Ineffective tone:
  - Finding fault
  - Describing what is wrong but offering no suggestions
  - Punishing or denigrating students for poor work

  Clarity: Feedback should be understandable and user-friendly. Similar to learning targets, feedback should be framed in language students can readily understand. Assessment expert and author Grant Wiggins tells a useful story: "A student came up to [a teacher] at year's end and said, 'Miss Jones, you kept writing this same word on my English papers all year, and I still don't know what it means.' 'What's the word?' she asked. 'Vag-oo', he said. (The word was *vague!*)" (Wiggins, 2012, p. 11).

Consider the What—the Content of Feedback

Focus: Feedback can be focused on the work or task, on the process of learning, or on the way a student self-regulates and uses his or her thought processes to accomplish a task. It should not be focused on the student personally and personal comments should be avoided. Feedback should always be connected to the goals for learning and be actionable, offering specific ideas for what to do next and how to improve.

Comparison: Effective feedback compares student work or performance with criteria and with past performance, benchmarks, and personal goals. Norm-referenced feedback, which compares a student's performance with that of other students, is generally not useful. It doesn't help a student improve and often damages the motivation of unsuccessful students.

Function: The function or purpose of feedback is to describe how the student has done in order to identify ways and provide information about how to improve. Evaluating or judging performance does not help students improve. (For example, grading work in a draft stage tends to shut down motivation to revise as does stating that the work is simply "good" or "bad.")

"If only using 'descriptive' vs. 'evaluative' feedback were simply a matter of wordsmithing! We could all learn how to write descriptive feedback just as we learned to write descriptive paragraphs in elementary school. Unfortunately, part of the issue is how the student understands the comment. Students filter what they hear through their own past experiences, good and bad" (Brookhart, 2008, p. 24). This brings us back to the importance of fostering strong collaborative cultures, building relationships with students, and setting the work in the context of student-engaged assessment more broadly. There are many strategies and techniques but unfortunately no shortcuts.

IN PRACTICE

Developing Structures to Make Feedback and Critique a Part of Daily Lessons

At the classroom level, respectful and helpful critique and descriptive feedback can be incorporated every day into all aspects of schooling, improving the quality of student understanding, work, effort, and character. Students learn to self-critique and critique others, respectfully and helpfully, as part of a productive learning environment. As the practices are implemented more consistently across classrooms in a school and understood and used more effectively by teachers, they are tightly aligned to standards and more closely integrated as part of a student-engaged assessment system.

Identify Teacher-to-Student Feedback Strategies for Daily Lessons and Long-Term Assignments

- Structure individual conference times (can be as brief as several minutes) during work time. Focus on brief, clear, specific comments and on interactions with students as they work.
- Use small-group mini-lessons to address common areas of weakness.
- Target one skill at a time. Focus comments on one or two important areas (don't copyedit!). Connect feedback to learning targets, using rubrics to highlight areas for improvement.
- Assess effectiveness of feedback—examine student work and performance to see if feedback was used. Are students moving toward meeting learning targets and standards?

Identify Peer and Self-Assessment Strategies

- Teach students the purpose and language of feedback.
- Return frequently to learning targets and ensure that students understand them.
- Model giving effective feedback for students. Ask students to self-assess using similar language.
- Emphasize self-assessment over peer assessment—research has demonstrated it is more effective in improving learning (Brookhart, 2008).

As the following case study of Susan McCray's eleventh-grade English class illustrates, the use of learning targets, goal setting, descriptive feedback, group critique, and mini-lessons on needs highlighted in the feedback fit together to support all students in meeting the standards. This lesson can be viewed in the accompanying video.

Watch video: "Descriptive Feedback Helps All Students Meet Proficiency—Standards-Based Grading"

Case Study

Descriptive Feedback in a High School English Class at Casco Bay High School in Portland, Maine

As students enter Susan McCray's eleventh-grade English classroom, they are handed back the first drafts of their oral histories. They quietly digest the descriptive feedback from McCray while they wait for class to begin. McCray starts them off by reminding them of the long-term learning target for the assignment, "I can write a quality oral history," and the supporting learning target for the day, "I can use my feedback effectively to identify changes to make in revising my oral history."

McCray uses a rubric to provide highly focused and descriptive feedback to each student. Along with their drafts, she has given them a copy of the rubric, on which she has highlighted particular areas that each student needs to address, filled in with concise written comments. One student explained, "We were handed back our first drafts with feedback. Right now we're looking at what changes we need to make it the best possible piece."

Students then write entrance tickets to review the learning targets and to set specific work goals for the class period. Next, McCray asks two students to read their drafts and has students listen for evidence of quality oral histories. One student observes her classmate and notes, "She really went after description of every move they made." This condensed version of a group critique lesson primed the pump for students to make use of their own individual feedback.

Her reading of the first drafts enabled McCray to identify three common needs among the students—descriptive detail, ideas, and organization. She forms small mini-lesson groups on those topics. The mini-lessons run consecutively so that students can choose to attend more than one if they wish. Though students choose whether or not to attend the mini-lessons, McCray's feedback points them in the right direction.

Following the mini-lessons, McCray circulates and offers students individual feedback. "Because they've had the mini-lessons, those are much shorter conversations," explains McCray. "I've been working to come up with structures that allow me to get to more kids and help everyone to meet the standards."

Preparing Students to Be Effective at Giving Peer-to-Peer Feedback

One of the most common structures for feedback and critique in classrooms is the use of student-to-student peer feedback conversations. Many teachers will ask their students to "find your writing critique partners and give them advice on their first draft" or something similar. In most cases, this practice is largely unproductive. Strategic, effective, specific feedback is a difficult enough practice for adults. For most students, it is impossible without guidance. If we listen in to those peer-to-peer conversations in many classrooms, we will find the following:

- Students who can only give vague comments
- A confusing mix of copyediting (suggestions for spelling, grammar, and punctuation) with content or language suggestions (*Note:* Helping students distinguish between these two types of feedback supports them in better understanding Common Core language standards—about conventions and grammar—and Common Core writing standards—about student thinking.)
- Students who finish their comments quickly and then engage in off-task discussions

Peer-to-peer feedback can be effective when the conditions are right, when students are practiced in giving targeted feedback, and they have clarity on the specific dimension of the work they are analyzing. For example, in a science class where students have been collecting data and creating spreadsheets to categorize those data, the teacher discovers problems with how students have constructed their spreadsheets. Using models, she runs a class critique lesson in which the students analyze models of strong and weak work, and identify in the weaker work the problems she has noticed. Students then work with a partner to analyze each other's current spreadsheets to see if any of those problems are present. In this case, the class is likely to be very effective in giving helpful feedback to each other. The snapshot of Austin's butterfly is a good example of students having the skills focus, as well as the appropriate vocabulary, to provide their classmate with feedback that supported him to do exemplary work.

> "One of the greatest challenges is to get students to want feedback. I'll ask students, 'How did your peer help you?' And if a student's reply is, 'They said it was good enough,' I say, 'Then go get them to help you! You don't want to be 'good enough.' You want to be great! Go to them and say you really want their help and their ideas. Don't let your peer 'critiquer' get away with not helping you.' "
>
> —*Tracy Horner, teacher, Vallejo Charter School, Vallejo, California*

Snapshot: Peer Feedback in Small Groups

At ANSER Charter School in Boise, Idaho, first-grade student Austin was preparing a scientific illustration of a Western Tiger Swallowtail, a local butterfly (see figure 4.4). The class had looked together at models of butterfly illustrations and had created criteria and a rubric for a strong illustration. In fact, they created two rubrics: one for the shape of the wings and one for the pattern inside the wings. Students were charged with using the eyes of scientists to examine a photograph and make sure its features and details were accurately presented in their illustration.

The problem was that Austin was just a first-grader, and when he began, he didn't look that carefully at the photograph; he defaulted to the icon of a butterfly shape that was in his head, and his first draft was a generic first-grade butterfly outline that looked nothing like a Tiger Swallowtail. Austin met with a small group on the carpet in front of the whiteboard, and, using the criteria for wing shape, his peers gave him *kind, specific, helpful* suggestions of what he could change to make his drawing look more like the photograph. (For example, they suggested that the wing shape in the photo was triangular, whereas his drawing had rounded wings).

Austin was happy to take their advice and quickly created a second draft that had more angular wings, and included the "swallowtails" at the base of the wings, as his peers suggested. The growth in his second draft was appreciated by his peers, and they suggested he include both an upper and lower wing on each side, which he then did in his third draft. His peers again appreciated his growth but pointed out that he had "gotten round again" on the upper wings, and so on his fourth draft he made the upper wings more angular. His peers were delighted that the shape looked right now and suggested that he add the pattern, which he did for draft five. His sixth and final draft was a beautiful and accurate colored illustration and showed remarkable growth from his first draft, thanks to the help of excellent peer feedback.

Figure 4.4 Austin's Butterfly

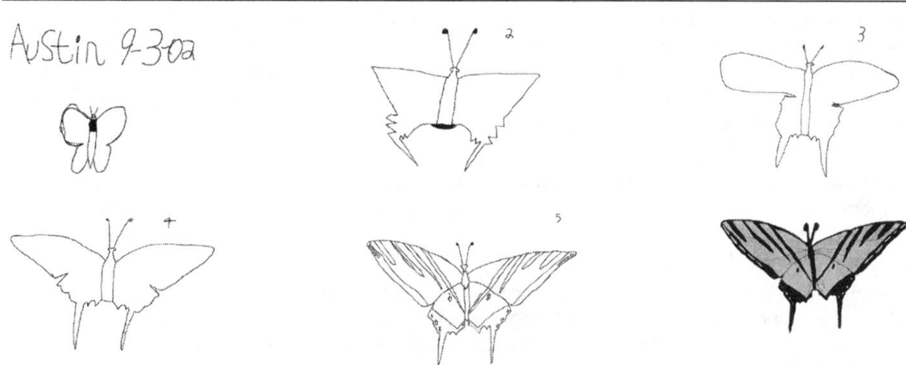

Once students have learned the process of giving specific feedback effectively in these formal protocols, there is a positive phenomenon that can develop in which students begin giving each other informal critique, appropriately and respectfully throughout the day.

Critical Moves for Deepening Student Engagement

Critique and descriptive feedback cannot be effective practices unless students fully own them. In fact, both practices involve a dynamic partnership between teachers and students as they critically analyze work, give, receive, and use feedback. It takes strong models, time, and practice before critique and descriptive feedback truly take root in a classroom. Table 4.2 illustrates the who, what, and

Table 4.2 The Who, What, and Why of Models, Critique, and Descriptive Feedback

What Do Teachers Do?	What Do Students Do?	What's the Result?
Create quality learning targets and assessments—based on state and Common Core standards—and use models of what work that meets the standards looks like.	Understand what it looks like to meet standards.	Students have greater engagement and ownership of learning because they know what they are working toward.
Establish strong norms for giving and receiving feedback and critique: *be kind, be helpful,* and *be specific.* Follow up and be vigilant about using the norms.	Practice the norms when participating in critique or giving feedback to peers.	Students experience a safe culture that deepens each time they repeat the feedback and critique process.
Conduct group critique lessons to identify the qualities of work models that meet learning targets. At first, explicitly teach and model critique, and critique the critique until students are adept.	Analyze models and identify characteristics of quality work that meets learning targets. Identify how they can apply this learning to their own work.	Student work improves as they learn to identify what quality means in any given genre.
Build a collection of exemplary student work that is reflective of common assignment formats. Analyze that work with students in order to create criteria lists and rubrics for quality work in each format, based on student- and teacher-designated strengths.	Look closely at work models and identify the qualities that make it strong.	Students learn disciplinary and academic vocabulary and critique skills. They build a common vision of quality work and learn to use criteria lists and rubrics to improve drafts of their work.
Build lessons that include frequent opportunities for descriptive feedback. Strategize how to give feedback and what feedback to give.	Listen to feedback and apply it to their work.	Because feedback is targeted toward specific needs, students can use it productively to improve their work.
Over time, build a repertoire of structures and protocols for feedback and critique. Engage students in self-assessment and peer-to-peer feedback.	Become more proficient at giving, receiving, and using feedback. Take ownership of the process.	An effective culture of descriptive feedback and critique is established in the classroom. This leads to higher levels of achievement and student ownership of learning.

why of how models, critique, and descriptive feedback can increase engagement and achievement.

SCHOOLWIDE IMPLEMENTATION

A strong and consistent schoolwide practice of critique and descriptive feedback is an essential component of a student-engaged assessment system. School leaders establish the vision and rationale for the practice through modeling and focused professional development. The culture of positive, constructive critique must permeate the building, modeled by adults and students.

All of the norms, purposes, and processes of good critique and descriptive feedback can be practiced by the adults in the community—in team meetings, faculty sessions, and one-on-one interactions—which builds the dispositions and skills of a schoolwide culture of critique. A principal who allows faculty members to revise her plans or decisions during faculty meetings, for example, can model a culture of critique. This sends a powerful message about the school's ethic of continuous improvement.

School leaders also play an important role in supporting teachers to collect and archive models of strong student work. This starts by ensuring that teachers have deep knowledge of state and Common Core standards and strong accompanying learning targets. It is important that models are aligned to these learning targets and supported by criteria lists and rubrics. The collection of models should grow and change over time. When it is an expectation in a building that the geometry teachers will have a file drawer of high-quality, student-written proofs, and a history teacher will have a similar file of strong student-written essays, then both students and teachers in the school will come to expect to see and discuss models of quality to improve their understanding and work. We have highlighted some of the key leadership actions that will support school leaders to build a culture of critique and descriptive feedback throughout the school.

Lay the Groundwork

- Provide time for staff to know their standards deeply, including the instructional shifts required by the Common Core. Support them in developing strong accompanying learning targets.

- Conduct professional development and establish norms and strategies of critique and descriptive feedback that the staff agrees to practice.
- Embed critique and descriptive feedback into a coherent plan for student-engaged assessment.
- Model self-critique and descriptive feedback in faculty meetings and professional learning settings. It is powerful for faculty members to see leaders who publicly appreciate and use critique of their decisions to improve.

Build Teacher Capacity

- Establish a regular and consistent practice of collaboratively looking at student work against learning targets to ensure that critique and descriptive feedback are effectively improving student performance.
- Support the creation of grade-level libraries of student work as well as benchmarked exemplars to be used as models for teachers and students.
- Provide professional development to help teachers develop standards-based critique lessons that build skill and content knowledge through the critique process.

Support Teachers to Deepen Their Practice

- Establish structures that promote feedback, critique, revision, and sharing of work (e.g., galleries of student work, portfolios that show the evolution of a project over time in response to feedback).
- Provide time and space for teachers to engage in protocols for presenting their work (e.g., a proposed unit study, project, or lesson) to peers on the faculty, receiving feedback and perhaps suggested resources. This might even be followed by a protocol for peer observation or lesson study, with teachers observing each other's instruction.
- Document critique lessons through video and other means to help foster the ongoing use and refinement of practice.

WHAT TO EXPECT

When teachers use work models to show students what's possible, it can be magical. In the accompanying video, Ron Berger shows young students several drafts of "Austin's butterfly." When he reveals Austin's accurate and beautiful final draft, the children gasp. They lean in, look closer, and make comments like, "Oh, my gosh!" Their subsequent discussion, in which they develop the criteria for a quality final draft, is testament to the power of the practices described in this chapter to help students be leaders of their own learning.

Watch video: "Austin's Butterfly: Building Excellence in Student Work—Models, Critique, and Descriptive Feedback"

Despite the transformational power of these practices, teachers and school leaders must take care (and time) to develop the habits and skills students need to make the most of them. As with all student-engagement practices, nurturing a growth mindset is an essential foundation. Students must believe in their own power to improve their work—with this belief in place, the use of models, critique, and descriptive feedback will give them the skills they need to do so. Teachers must also start from a place of deep understanding of state and Common Core standards so that they can choose models, build critique lessons, and provide feedback that will enable students to meet the standards.

With time and practice, teachers will experience the power of these practices to guide their curriculum. Critique lessons won't be special events; they will be a key part of teaching students content and skills and engaging them in thinking critically about their progress toward quality work. Over time, teachers will gather and use a collection of student work models to use again and again, and the practice will take hold throughout the school, in classrooms, and in professional development.

We have identified some of the benchmarks that teachers and school leaders can expect at the beginning, intermediate, and advanced phases of implementing a robust practice of using models, critique, and descriptive feedback.

Beginning

- Students learn the basic guidelines of critique and descriptive feedback: *be kind, be specific,* and *be helpful.* Teachers and school leaders begin to internalize these norms in professional settings as well.
- Through the use of models, students expand their preconceived notions of what quality work can look like at their grade level.

- Students learn to identify the key steps involved in producing high-quality work. This gives them greater ownership of the path to producing their own high-quality work.
- Teachers develop a repertoire of protocols to structure critique lessons.
- Teachers use learning targets to guide their critique lessons and descriptive feedback.
- As students see how the practices help them meet their learning goals, they begin to exhibit confidence in participating in critique and using feedback.

Intermediate

- Teachers see the opportunities critique *lessons* (as opposed to critique *sessions*) hold for teaching content and skills and helping students meet state and Common Core standards.
- The interrelationship of models, critique, and descriptive feedback supports students to do their best work. Models give them a vision of what quality looks like. Critique lessons involve them in identifying the criteria for success. Descriptive feedback supports them to revise and improve their work.
- Teachers are strong guardians of critique norms, ensuring that the lessons are productive.
- Lessons based on models, critique, and descriptive feedback are routine.
- Faculty members are more comfortable and proficient in using critique and descriptive feedback in their professional interactions.
- Teachers build and use a collection of student work models.

Advanced

- Student work models and exemplars are documented and shared extensively throughout the school.
- With scaffolding, norm setting, and skill building, students can engage in effective peer feedback.

- Students exhibit pride and ownership of their work and learning. Quality student work is visible throughout the school and important student and teacher discussions about quality are commonplace.
- School leaders model critique and descriptive feedback practices in faculty meetings and other professional settings.
- There is a strong culture of continuous improvement with every member of the community asking, "How are we doing?" "What's the evidence?" and "How can we improve?"
- Teachers, students, and families can clearly see the ways in which quality student work demonstrates evidence of students meeting state and Common Core standards.

COMMON CHALLENGES

Not Spending Enough Time on Culture Building and Norms Setting to Create Safety

Time is a critical investment. The pressure to get to the heart of content and skills standards in critique and descriptive feedback can lead teachers to shortchange valuable culture-building and norms-setting activities. This is a serious mistake because the time spent on creating a culture of safety and skills of critique will make the sessions much more effective and will also serve students well as lifelong strategies for success in the workplace.

Lack of Clarity about Goals, Learning Targets, and What Work That Meets Standards Looks Like

Know where you are headed. The learning targets and models that bring standards to life give critique and descriptive feedback power and focus. Once students understand and can reflect on where they are headed, they are prepared to receive and use feedback. Being clear about what success looks like, and the steps necessary to get there, will help more students meet standards.

Choosing the Wrong Work to Critique

Good critique depends on compelling work models. If work is chosen haphazardly or for the wrong reasons, the critique lesson will flounder. At the most basic level, interesting and engaging critique lessons require interesting work. Even if it is flawed or full of mistakes, it should be flawed in an interesting way—a way that can lead to learning for all students.

Neglecting the Teacher Role (Thinking That Critiques Will Run Themselves)

The teacher remains a teacher. It is not enough to choose a good protocol and a compelling piece of work for the critique. The teacher must constantly pay attention to the pace and flow of discussion and the range of participation and focus on capturing and shaping the insights from the discussion. Pushing for clarity and substance, being vigilant about the norms, adding insights, and naming and charting takeaways are all vital roles for the teacher.

Neglecting the Student Role

Student ownership is key. If the process drags or is too focused on a small number of needs, or if the teacher dominates the discussion, student engagement in the critique won't be sustained. Teachers need to ensure that the critique lesson has an energetic pace, that every student understands his or her role and participates, and that the learning targets are clear.

Underestimating Student Mindsets and Sensitivities to Hearing Feedback

Feelings and mindsets matter. Students bring a wide range of experiences—both positive and negative—and different personalities and mindsets to the classroom. Some are more confident and receptive to feedback and others may be anxious or sensitive. It is vital to nurture a growth mindset in all students so that they believe in their capacity to improve. Teachers must get to know individual students and the range of emotions they bring to the learning process. The selection of approaches to feedback and critique should be shaped by individual needs. Specific, strategic, positive feedback is almost always more effective than criticism.

Underestimating the Power of Language and Timing

Strive for balance in feedback. There are many potential pitfalls in teacher-to-student feedback. It can be too much, too little, too late, too judgmental, or too hard to understand. Take time in solo planning and team discussions to consider what feedback is effective, what is not, and how you can tell the difference.

Asking Students to Engage in Peer Feedback When They Are Unprepared to Succeed

Students need tools. Giving strategic, effective feedback is difficult for adults. For unprepared students, it is almost impossible. Peer feedback is often vague and unproductive for both students. Useful peer feedback occurs when students are clear on specific skills and can apply that clarity to a specific focus for the feedback.

Chapter 5

Student-Led Conferences

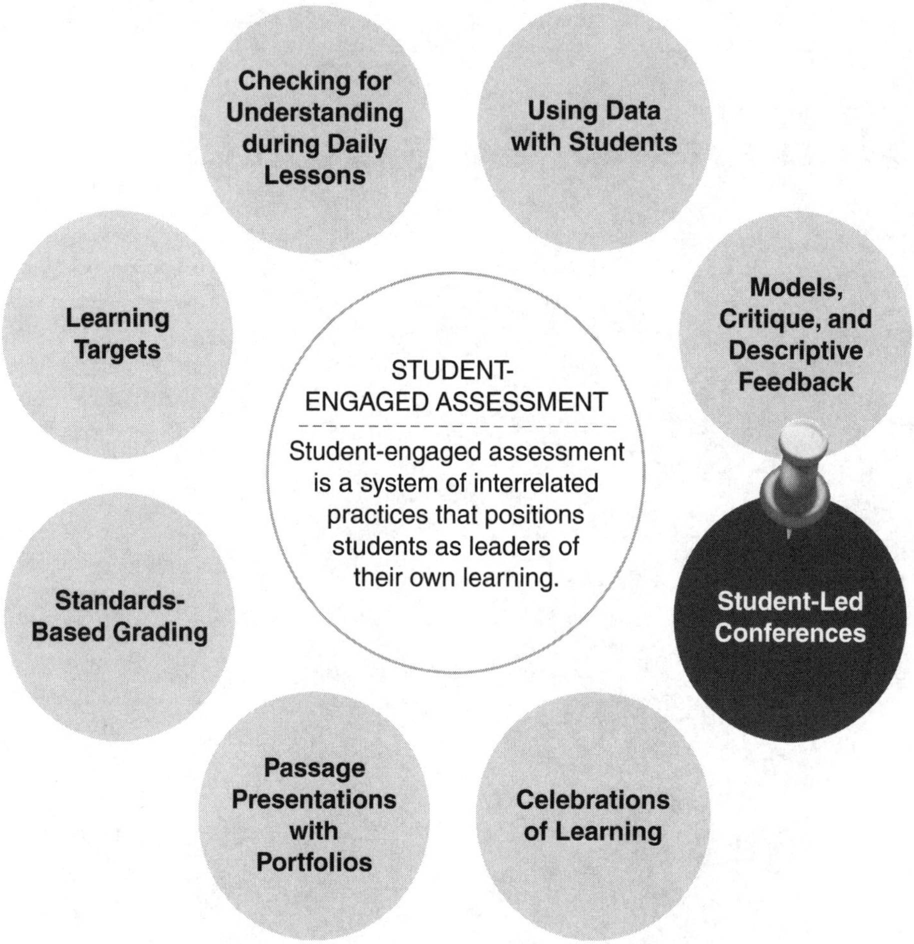

Checking for Understanding during Daily Lessons

Using Data with Students

Learning Targets

STUDENT-ENGAGED ASSESSMENT

Student-engaged assessment is a system of interrelated practices that positions students as leaders of their own learning.

Models, Critique, and Descriptive Feedback

Student-Led Conferences

Standards-Based Grading

Passage Presentations with Portfolios

Celebrations of Learning

I walked into the first-grade room at Delaware Ridge Elementary School in Kansas City, Kansas, a little unsure. I had been told that it was all right to observe student-led conferences in this room, but it seemed a bit intrusive in what seemed such a personal family event. The conference had not yet begun. A tiny girl was seated in a miniature blue plastic chair, and her mother and teacher were awkwardly lowering themselves into similar chairs. Before I could ask for permission, the young student, Elandria, rose from her seat, her fat portfolio binder clutched to her chest, and extended her small hand to me.

"Welcome to my student-led conference. My name is Elandria. Thank you for coming." I shook her hand, thanked her, her mother, and her teacher, and pulled a small chair to the edge of the short trapezoid table. Elandria turned to her mother, "Mama, this is Mr. Berger. He will be observing conferences in our school today." I was a bit shocked. I had not introduced myself yet. Had she noticed my name tag? Then I noticed my name on the whiteboard and realized that her teacher must have explained my visit. Still, her composure in introducing me was startling. She turned to me. "Mr. Berger, I will be sharing my learning targets with my mother and you today and I will show you which ones I have reached. I hope you will see evidence in my work that I have succeeded."

Elandria led us through her portfolio of work for twenty minutes. She explained each learning target, read aloud her writing, analyzed her projects in multiple drafts, and showed us a set of assessments in math, vocabulary, and reading proficiency. She explained her progress, her challenges, and her goals. Her mother asked few questions but was obviously very proud. I asked many questions, even difficult ones, and Elandria was never rattled. Twice she paused after I asked something and replied, "I don't understand that question." I wondered if I had ever responded so sensibly to a confusing question.

When the conference ended and Elandria rose again to shake my hand and thank me for coming, she looked up and asked, "Do you have any advice for me?" All I could offer for advice was to encourage her to keep up the great work. But I did have one request for her—would she be willing to share some of her beautiful work with me and could I make copies of it? For the first time she turned off her serious presentation face and smiled as she said, "Of course, I would. That's a silly question."

> It's hard to imagine a more high-leverage practice for improving learning than this. It brings the family in as a partner in the child's growth—instead of being intimidated by facing news from a teacher, the family members are proud to listen to their child present herself with candor and clarity, even when there are challenges. It makes the teacher accountable for getting every child ready to be an articulate, informed presenter who knows her own learning. And most of all, it puts students at the helm of their growth as learners.
>
> —Ron Berger

A Key to Building Student Ownership of Learning

For Gabriella, a seventh-grade student at Washington Heights Expeditionary Learning School (WHEELS) in New York City, student-led conferences have helped her develop confidence in her academics and communication skills. After sharing her progress with her dad, noting her strengths in math and habits of scholarship, she commented that the conferences have shown her and her classmates that "kids can actually talk to their parents about their work." Her dad, Miguel, marveled at "how much confidence she has built" since she started leading her own conferences when she entered sixth grade at WHEELS. See Gabriella and her dad in the accompanying video.

Watch video: "Middle School Student-Led Conference"

A **student-led conference** is a meeting with a student and his or her family and teachers during which the student shares his or her portfolio of work and discusses progress with family members. The student facilitates the meeting from start to finish. Student-led conferences can be implemented at all grade levels, K–12.

Student-led conferences put students in charge of sharing information about their progress with their families. The earlier student-led conferences begin in a child's learning career, the more the benefits they can accrue over time. As Cindy Kapeller, principal of Delaware Ridge Elementary School in Kansas City, Kansas, puts it, "Setting that standard in kindergarten is the best time. They learn to advocate for themselves. When they are responsible for their learning, they are not going to sit quietly and not ask a question." Preparation for a conference creates an authentic purpose for good organizational and communication skills. The structure builds students' sense of responsibility and accountability for their own learning, and it helps to hone their understanding of what it means to meet learning targets.

> "Student-led conferences have tentacles into so many different things that you get tremendous bang for your buck. The student-led conference is a game changer when influencing a kid's trajectory toward college."
>
> *—Brett Kimmel, principal, Washington Heights Expeditionary Learning School, New York City*

Student-led conferences also greatly enhance family engagement. Schools report that parents are more likely to participate in conferences when students are the leaders. The conference structure builds family members' interest and understanding in what has been happening in the classroom. Relationships among students, family members, and teachers are strengthened. Ryan Maxwell, the instructional guide at EPIC Academy in Chicago, says, "The most important thing is that the student-led conference really puts the kid[s] at the center of their own learning, and they become the bridge between the school and parents."

Why This Practice Matters

Student-led conferences require and empower students to take the lead role in communicating their learning. The practice helps to build dispositions and skills—such as adapting speech to the appropriate context and organizing and presenting information—that will be vital for students in college and careers and is at the center of the Common Core speaking and listening standards. Sharing work and reflecting on learning with one's family helps to bridge the divide that often exists between school and home and enables parents to understand their children's progress more deeply.

Building Student Engagement

When students are asked to play a leadership role in selecting and presenting work to share with their families, they begin to take greater pride in the quality of what they do. A "progress report" becomes not just something given to them, but is actually something students have a hand in creating.

Building Responsibility, Organization, and Decision Making

Students have ownership of much of the process and are required to make key decisions of what work to include in their portfolios and what to say about it at the conference. They are compelled and supported to understand themselves as learners and advocate for themselves. This helps to build personal agency in students that can be a foundation of college and career success. It also teaches higher-order skills of metacognition and analysis, because students reflect on their work and learning and assess their own strengths, challenges, and next steps.

Creating a Culture of Evidence

As students guide their families through their portfolios, they provide evidence of their learning and their progress toward state and Common Core standards and habits of scholarship, such as revision and collaboration. This affirms and teaches

Most EL Education schools report 100 percent parent attendance at student-led conferences.

the evidence-based academic mindset that is at the center of the Common Core. Passing classes is not about pleasing a teacher; it is about providing evidence of understanding and skill.

Building Strong Home-School Partnerships

Student-led conferences connect families and the school around the real work of students. They put family members in an authentic, helpful role and can build an important level of understanding and connection to the school. Rather than being simple observers of their children's school experience, student-led conferences enable family members to participate actively and even contribute to the academic growth of their children.

Common Core Connections

- Student-led conferences are an ideal way for students to show evidence of meeting standards—they deeply know and engage with the standards as they prepare for and conduct the conferences.
- The conferences are a meaningful and practical way to teach students to justify their conclusions with evidence, a key to Common Core success.
- Parents have a heightened awareness of the standards their students are working toward, increasing their ability to provide support for meeting them. Many parents are unsure of the relevancy of standards until they take part in a student-led conference.
- Student-led conferences provide an authentic and direct opportunity to address the Common Core's speaking and listening standards at all grade levels.

GETTING STARTED

Developing the Structures to Get Started with Student-Led Conferences

Depending on the grade level and school context, student-led conferences can have slightly different structures. For example, some schools include report cards as part of the conference. At other schools, conferences are held midway through a grading period to provide feedback that can be used to improve grades before report cards are issued. Before getting started with student-led conferences, there are many choices for teachers and school leaders to make so that this new structure can be seamlessly integrated into the culture of the school.

Key Decisions

- How many times per year will student-led conferences occur?
- Will the conferences take place at the end of a grading period or in the middle?
- How long should each conference last? Conferences for elementary age students are generally shorter than for secondary students. The typical range is twenty minutes for younger students to forty-five minutes for older students.
- What will be shared at the conference? How will students be supported to create a strong portfolio?
  - Will all subjects be discussed?
  - What will be the balance between students providing a general overview of their performance in all subjects versus discussing specific examples of their work in depth?
  - What kinds of evidence will students present?
  - How will character growth and habits of scholarship be addressed?
  - To what degree will extracurricular activities be shared and discussed? Which staff members should attend? At the elementary level the classroom teacher is a given, but it also may be appropriate for art and music teachers, counselors, or special education teachers to attend. At the secondary level, an advisory teacher is usually the lead staff person.
- How will the conferences be scheduled to enable 100 percent of families to attend? Offering some evening time slots may be important. What is the school's plan B if families don't show up for conferences?
- How can parents be encouraged to actively participate?
- How will teachers handle discussing issues that can't be discussed in front of students? (e.g., some schools have the option of a five-minute period during the conference when the student leaves the room).

Communicating with Families about Student-Led Conferences

For many students and families, student-led conferences are a very different structure than they are used to. Not only are students in charge of facilitating the conferences, schools expect 100 percent of families to attend and they make this

Portfolios of student work are the centerpiece of the student-led conference.

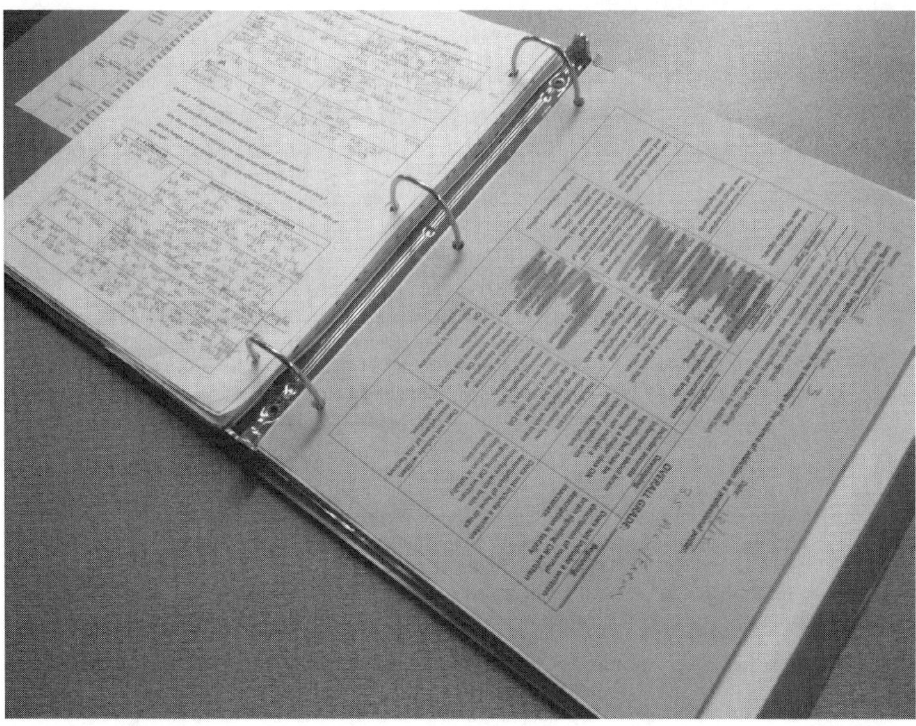

expectation known from the start. Unlike elementary schools, many secondary schools don't usually schedule parent conferences, so the idea of requiring secondary students and parents to join this process may be surprising. It is important that the school inform families about student-led conferences so that they know why they are important and what to expect. Figure 5.1 is a sample letter to families informing them of what to expect.

It is also important to set up structures that enable the greatest turnout at student-led conferences. Schools must make every effort to make appointments available that accommodate parents' schedules, to have translators available if necessary, and to plan ahead for how to handle situations when parents are unable to attend. There are many ways to go about scheduling conferences—from sending letters home with sign-up options, to direct phone calls, to online programs such as SignUpGenius (www.signupgenius.com/index.cfm). Schools should set up a system that will best meet the needs of their families. Approaching this process

Figure 5.1 Sample Letter Introducing Student-Led Conferences to Families

Dear Families,

Welcome back to school! As you help your child get adjusted to a new school year, I want to introduce an exciting and important new practice we have decided to launch this year—student-led conferences. In place of the traditional parent–teacher conferences, your child will lead two conferences this year to reflect on his or her progress, show you his or her work, and receive feedback. You, your child, your child's teacher, and any other adult your student or the teacher would like to invite, will participate in the conference.

Members of the faculty visited several schools where these conferences are in place and felt convinced by the results they observed. We feel that student-led conferences are a very important way to engage children in understanding and taking ownership of their learning. We also believe this conference structure will help us to build better communication and stronger relationships with all families. Of course, anyone who feels they need a private meeting with a teacher will still be able to schedule one.

As parents and family members, you are critical partners in helping support your child's learning and growth. Our new conference structure will be a very important way to show this support. In the coming weeks your child's teacher will send home more detailed information describing the conferences. Please respond to the request for information about scheduling. We are counting on 100% participation as we launch student-led conferences.

Sincerely,
Principal Kerry

with clear guidelines but a flexible approach will ensure high attendance and that parents will get the most from the experience.

Determining the Agenda for Student-Led Conferences

As previously mentioned, student-led conferences can take anywhere from twenty to forty-five minutes, depending on the age of the students and the constraints of the schedule. Creating and sticking to an agenda is essential to keep things running smoothly. What follows are two sample agendas—one at the elementary level and one at the middle school level.

Elementary School Conference Agenda from Delaware Ridge Elementary School in Kansas City, Kansas

1. Teacher will welcome the families at the classroom door and ask them to sign in.
2. Students will lead their families through a guided tour of the student work on display for the grade-level learning expedition. (five minutes)
   a. The tour will have specific stops to emphasize the learning targets and evidence of learning in the student work on display, including draft work and reflections. At each stop, parents will have the opportunity to ask questions.
3. Student-led conference with portfolio (ten minutes)
   a. Students will share progress made toward their goals and highlight artifacts in their portfolios that demonstrate their learning (e.g., assessment data, daily work, project work, a series of drafts leading to a final product).
   b. Students share work, do demonstrations, and provide evidence of learning in all of their "specials" classes (e.g., art, PE).
   c. The teacher will actively listen, support the student if necessary, and provide feedback to the student at a later time.
   d. If parents struggle to think of questions to ask their child, the teacher will make suggestions (e.g., "What piece are you most proud of? What challenges did you face?").
   e. At the conclusion of the conference, students ask their parents if they have any questions.
   f. Parents are asked to give their child feedback on the student-led conference either verbally or in writing.
4. If parents wish to conference directly with the teacher, a meeting is scheduled at a later date.

Total time: approximately twenty minutes

Middle School Conference Agenda from WHEELS in New York City

1. Arrive on time.
2. Sit outside the classroom with family members until invited in by teacher.
3. Re-introduce teacher and family members.
4. Thank family for coming.

(continued)

5. Briefly explain the format and objectives of the student-led conference, reminding family to save questions for the end. (steps 1–5, five minutes)
6. Show family progress report and point out academic grades and habits of scholarship grades, as well as teacher comments and attendance and tardiness.
7. Discuss which subject seems to be the strongest and which is the greatest struggle. (steps 6–7, five minutes)
8. Present portfolio of work from each subject, showing work samples, explaining learning target mastery, and sharing goals and action plan for improvement. (fifteen minutes)
9. Share with family how they can help at home.
10. Ask parents if they have any questions.
11. Give time for paperwork.
12. Thank family and teacher.
13. Help family to refreshments. (steps 9–13, five minutes)
14. Make sure family fills out the conference survey.
15. Make changes if needed to goals and action plan.
16. Put the survey and action plan in the return box.

Total time: approximately thirty minutes

Covering the Basics

It is essential that teachers schedule all conferences well in advance and that everything is ready for the students and families. The following crew advisor checklist reprinted from the WHEELS student-led conference handbook provides a sense of the scope of preparation. (In EL Education schools, advisories are called *crew.* For a further explanation of crew and the advisory structure, see the "Defining the Roles of Student-Led Conference Participants" section of this chapter.)

Crew Advisor Preparation Checklist Adapted from WHEELS in New York City

Preconference and Scheduling Logistics

- ❑ I have scheduled a conference for each student in my crew, paying specific attention to families with multiple children in attendance at WHEELS.
- ❑ Each family knows when to arrive and where the conference will be held.
- ❑ I know the first and last names of [all] adults [who] will be attending the conference.
- ❑ I have created other arrangements for parents who cannot attend the regular conference times.
- ❑ If I don't speak Spanish I know there will be a translator available for me.

Preconference and Student Logistics

- ❑ I have helped students organize assignments and prepare for conferences by reviewing student self-evaluation forms, helping students set new goals, and guiding students in the creation of action plans to meet those goals.
- ❑ I have helped students develop agendas for the conference time and have helped them learn to manage time wisely when speaking.
- ❑ I have helped students learn appropriate speaking skills.
- ❑ I have set aside crew time for students to practice student-led conferences with peers.
- ❑ I have reviewed the student-led conference assessment rubric with students. They know what they need to do!
- ❑ I know my crew! I know what classes they are excelling in and those in which they struggle. I know if they are having trouble with behavior in a specific class. I know if the child's family is going through a difficult time. I know with whom each student lives and if there has been a change in the home environment. Nothing is a surprise to me.

Materials for Conferences

- ❑ I have a copy of the conference schedule posted outside my classroom.
- ❑ I have set up chairs in the hallway for families that arrive early.
- ❑ I have a container next to me filled with portfolio materials arranged in the order of the conference schedule. I do not waste time by looking for work.
- ❑ The students' report cards, evaluations, and other important documents are in the folders.
- ❑ I have a group of desks arranged to promote small-group discussion. Multiple chairs are available. There is a place for smaller children to sit and play quietly. My crew may have provided refreshments.
- ❑ I have a copy of the conference schedule in front of me.

Case Study

Building Responsibility for Student-Led Conferences in Preschool Students at Delaware Ridge Elementary School in Kansas City, Kansas

When Cindy Kapeller, principal of Delaware Ridge Elementary, reflects on the school's decision to implement student-led conferences, she sees it as one of their most important decisions. "It set an early foundation that this is how our school would operate, and that the most important thing is the ownership and accountability students develop for their own learning. Too often as educators we decide what students are capable of doing and set a low bar. Student-led conferences open that up."

(continued)

At Delaware Ridge Elementary, conferences take place twice a year, in October and February, during release days allocated by the district for that purpose. Most conferences are twenty to thirty minutes long. They vary somewhat in structure and focus depending on the grade level, but all teachers are guided by common expectations in five areas: presentation, preparation, evidence of learning based on learning targets, goal setting, and reflection.

For Kapeller and her faculty, reflection is the linchpin of student-led conferences and it links to everything they do in the classroom. "The process builds self-esteem. I have watched students who were very timid and shy, but as they've grown, they have developed much stronger voices. They set goals and learn to monitor their own progress, and they have developed critical thinking and problem-solving skills as they figure out their own learning styles and what they need to improve."

In Molly Dykman's kindergarten classroom, reflection is embedded in the curriculum all year to make preparation for conferences less stressful. "From the beginning, we focus on what the evidence of learning is and keep those in portfolios. Every artifact we share with parents has a reflection on it."

Dykman sees the benefit for her students in how they learn to be responsible for their learning. "They are not afraid to talk about what they know and what they don't know. They learn to take control of their learning, and that's one of the greatest gifts we can give them."

Defining the Roles of Student-Led Conference Participants

For conferences to be successful, everyone needs to understand and commit to his or her role.

Role of the student: Whether in third grade or tenth grade, the role of the student is to lead the conference, presenting his or her learning in sufficient detail and depth. Preparation for the conference is key, as is the completion of solid work that is evidence of meeting learning targets. Throughout the year, students keep their work and organize it in portfolios. They continually self-assess their progress based on learning targets. Before the conference, students follow classroom guidelines to prepare and practice. Selections of work are made and mock conferences held. Students give and receive feedback on speaking and presentation skills.

Role of the teacher: The teacher is responsible for using student-engaged assessment practices, such as learning targets, portfolios, and using data with students, that set students up for success during the student-led conference. Learning targets, which are derived from state and Common Core standards, enable students to talk about their progress and help families understand the standards being addressed in school.

Teachers are also responsible for creating clear expectations and guidelines for student-led conferences, helping students understand and practice their role. The teacher makes time and provides structure for students to make selections of their work, prepare reflections, and practice presentation skills. She or he ensures clear and timely communication with families, and creates the opportunity for family members to schedule follow-up conferences with them if desired.

Strategy Close Up: Using an Advisory Structure for Student-Led Conferences in Secondary Schools

Arranging and preparing for student-led conferences in an elementary classroom of twenty-five students is one thing; it's another thing entirely for a secondary teacher who may teach more than one hundred students every day. How can that teacher possibly manage the student-led conferences of so many students? The most efficient way to solve this dilemma is through an advisory structure (called *crew* in the EL Education schools highlighted throughout this book).

An advisor, or crew leader, meets daily with a small group of ten to fifteen students. The advisor monitors and supports student progress, serves as student advocate in difficult academic and social situations, and acts as the primary contact between families and the school. An advisory ensures that each student has a consistent relationship with an adult in the school as well as a consistent and ongoing small-scale peer community. The group usually stays together over multiple years. The advisor is responsible for the student-led conferences for his or her advisees only; not for every student he or she teaches. The advisor's role is to arrange the logistics of the conferences and collaborate with classroom teachers to prepare students. Information about advisees' progress in classes, including behavioral or social issues, is usually shared during team meetings, on progress tracker forms, or through an online intranet so that advisors are well informed about each of their advisees.

A structure like this not only solves the problem of conducting student-led conferences with a large number of students but it also strengthens advisors' abilities to support the progress of their advisees. Too often secondary school advisors have only cursory knowledge about their advisees' progress in their classes. Being a part of the student-led conferences enhances advisors' abilities to be supportive of their advisees' strengths and challenges and to be an effective bridge between families and the school. This same structure is key to the success of passage presentations in secondary schools (see chapter 7).

Role of family members: The role of family members is to attend the conference and pay close attention to the student's presentation, offering reflections and questions at the appropriate time. Family member involvement can be enhanced through guidelines for participation provided in advance. Family members support the conference by arriving on time, listening closely, and following the guidelines. Family members may decide they need to arrange a follow-up meeting with the teacher to share any concerns that have not been addressed during the conference. Of course, the most important role of family members is to support the student's learning goals and academic progress at home.

It is sometimes challenging for students to speak about their work and for family members to know what to ask. At Fitchburg Arts Academy in Fitchburg, Massachusetts, teachers provide family members with possible questions in case they struggle to find ways to participate:

- Can you tell me why this piece is important to you? What does it say about you?
- What were you thinking about when you chose this piece of work for your conference portfolio?
- What did you learn from that assignment? Is there anything you might have changed?

Role of school leadership: The school's leaders and office staff support student-led conferences through clear communication and logistical assistance. They make sure that families understand the format for the conferences and they provide translators when needed. They provide scheduling support and ensure that families receive timely notification. They ensure that the importance of student-led conferences is communicated clearly and linked to student-engaged assessment more broadly.

Preparing Students for Student-Led Conferences

One of the benefits of the student-led conference is that it creates an authentic opportunity for students to meet presentation, speaking, and communication standards. Common Core speaking and listening anchor standards, SL.4 and SL.6 are particularly germane to the conference:

- SL.4: *Present information, findings, and supporting evidence such that listeners can follow the line of reasoning and the organization, development, and style are appropriate to task, purpose, and audience.*
- SL.6: *Adapt speech to a variety of contexts and communicative tasks, demonstrating command of formal English when indicated or appropriate.*

Students need ample time to practice before the conference in order to hone their skills. Teachers can use a variety of techniques, such as fishbowls and critique sessions, to help students learn the skills needed to look closely at their work and cite evidence of meeting standards. Tawanna Billingsley-Patton, a tenth-grade teacher at EPIC Academy, offers this advice: "Preparation on the front end really helps with the final presentation. Give the students the time to practice, using sentence starts. Give them the opportunity to see [a conference] and critique it."

Particularly at the early stages of implementing student-led conferences, a conference script can be a very helpful support for students. Scripts are great scaffolds to help students develop public speaking skills. Figure 5.2 is an excerpt

Figure 5.2 Sample Ninth-Grade Conference Script

1. My name is ________________ . I would like to welcome and thank you, ________ and ________ for taking the time to come to my trimester ________ student-led conference. The classes included in my portfolio are ________ ________________________.	2. I would like to start by telling you about __________ class. The expedition for this class was about __________________. One learning target I met for this class is ________________________ ________________________ ________________________.
3. This assignment/project shows my level of understanding of the learning target. This assignment is a good example of the learning target because I had to ________________________ ________________________.	4. This is what I will do academically next trimester, I will ________________________ ________________________ ________________________ ________________________.
5. Do you have any questions about my work on this learning target? My academic grade for this class is ________________________.	6. In order to improve my Habits of Mind for this class, I will ________________________ ________________________ ________________________.

of a script used by EPIC ninth-graders to keep them on track during the conference.

Setting well-defined, high expectations is also important. At WHEELS, a student-led conference is evaluated on par with a major assignment and comes with its own set of learning targets. Table 5.1 shows WHEELS's student-led conference learning targets for both habits of scholarship and content and skills. The Common Core standards describe a "portrait of students who meets the standards" in literacy. This portrait, along with the math practice standards, describes habits of scholarship like those listed in table 5.1 that set students up for college and career success. The student-led conference is an opportunity for students to reflect on habits of scholarship such as problem solving, communication skills, and responsibility. Although it wouldn't necessarily be appropriate for a student to work on all of these learning targets during one conference, teachers can help students identify two or three character learning targets and two or three content and skills learning targets to work toward during the conference.

Table 5.1 Learning Targets for the Student-Led Conference

Habits of Scholarship	Content and Skills
• I can make consistent eye contact when speaking. • I can speak clearly, audibly, and at an appropriate pace. • I can use an appropriate and respectful tone. • I can answer questions directly and honestly. • I can communicate ideas in an organized and coherent manner with appropriate and precise vocabulary. • I can take responsibility for progress, explaining how and why I have improved. • I can take ownership of my failures and mistakes. • I can reflect on my work habits. • I can create and share a plan for improvement or continued success.	• I can explain the learning targets I met in each of my academic subjects. • I can share examples and evidence from specific assignments in each of my academic subjects. • I can use notes and outlines to help me present. • I can include details and examples relative to the audience. • I can conclude my presentation by reviewing the main points. • I can synthesize and paraphrase information. • I can make connections between sources of information. • I can persuade my audience by substantiating claims with evidence. • I can use language and grammar appropriate for my purpose and audience. • I can use grammatically correct sentences when speaking. • I can use facial expressions and gestures that help in communicating my point.

IN PRACTICE

Deepening Student Reflection and Learning

There are many schoolwide decisions involved in getting started with student-led conferences. The logistics deserve significant time and attention to ensure that the experience is smooth for students, families, and teachers. One of the most important decisions for a school to make, however, is one that has ripple effects on classroom instruction and curriculum—determining what students will share during the conference and how to prepare them to reflect deeply on their learning. There are many different structures that can help students reflect on their progress. No matter the structure, if students are going to learn to reflect thoughtfully and well, it will need to be an ongoing and thorough part of instructional practice.

Portfolios

A strong portfolio structure will support strong student-led conferences. Portfolios should be updated on a regular basis and include work that shows evidence

Portfolios are a powerful way for students to share their work with their families.

of meeting standards, self-reflections, feedback, and rubrics. They should tell the story of student growth toward academic learning targets, which are based on state and Common Core standards, as well as character learning targets. An established portfolio system is helpful when it is time for student-led conferences because it serves as a historical record of student work, self-reflections, and teacher feedback.

Absent a portfolio structure, students may need to write reflections on work that they haven't looked at in a long while. If they wait until days before their conference, it will be difficult for them to remember and reflect back on work from multiple subject areas. Students will do more thoughtful reflecting if it is an ongoing process. Reflection must be taught as a distinct form of writing, thinking, and speaking. Providing models, criteria, feedback, and critique will help students develop increasingly thoughtful and probing reflections.

Some schools set up their portfolios by subject area with students pulling their best work from each subject area to represent their progress in that area. Other schools set them up by learning targets. In this case, students pull work that demonstrates their mastery of each learning target (either academic or character learning targets), regardless of what subject area it is from. In the accompanying video, we see Trinity, a kindergartner from Delaware Ridge Elementary School, leading her parents through her portfolio during the student-led conference. She explains each learning target and points to evidence in her work that she met the target.

Watch video: "Kindergarten Student-Led Conference"

There are myriad ways to set up portfolios (for a more detailed discussion of portfolios, see chapter 7). Regardless of format, students should be prepared to reflect on their work and performance. What follows is an excerpt from a student-preparation checklist at WHEELS.

Student Preparation Checklist—Excerpted from WHEELS in New York City

- ❑ I have work from each of my academic classes in my crew folder.
- ❑ I have completed evaluations for each academic class.
- ❑ I understand how my work and mastery of learning targets have resulted in my final grade in each academic subject.

- ❑ I know my strengths and weaknesses as a student.
- ❑ I know how I can improve for next quarter: I have set goals and created an action plan for each class.
- ❑ I know how my behavior, attendance, and tardiness are affecting my academic progress.
- ❑ I have practiced speaking about my work in my home language.
- ❑ I feel comfortable talking about my progress.
- ❑ I understand how my performance during student-led conferences will be assessed.
- ❑ I am familiar with the conference agenda.

Goal Setting

An important component of any student-led conference is student goal setting. Based on academic or character learning targets, the opportunity to set goals in the presence of teachers and family members is a powerful way for students to engage their community in helping them make progress. As with reflection, students must be taught how to set effective goals for their learning. Goal setting should be a regular, if not daily, part of teaching and learning. The process of formulating a goal helps students translate learning targets into personal terms. To be effective, goals should be specific and doable (challenging enough to advance learning but not so challenging as to overwhelm or frustrate). If setting goals is a regular part of the learning process, the longer-term goals students create for student-led conferences will be grounded and powerful. In the accompanying video we see a tenth-grade student Rafael coming to terms with an area of weakness and setting goals with the support and participation of his mother.

Watch video: "High School Student-Led Conference"

Case Study

Two Stories of Student Success with Student-Led Conferences at EPIC Academy in Chicago

Student-led conferences gain power over time as students grow in their capacity to reflect on their learning. According to Ryan Maxwell, instructional guide and crew leader

(continued)

at EPIC, the investment of time and preparation is well worth it. He described the experiences of two very different students who each grew a great deal through the practice.

Carmella, a capable and motivated learner, emigrated from Mexico at around age eleven. "When she started in ninth grade, she was really shy, and when it came to reflection she didn't speak," Maxwell reflects. "She was very good at following directions. She would do what was expected and then wait for the next instructions. What she didn't do in her conferences was discuss what the work meant, or what she had learned. She would say, 'I don't know. I did good. I got a good grade.'" "But what did you learn?" Maxwell would counter. Maxwell was persistent and over time it got better, little by little. "Carmella really took learning targets to heart, and when she presented her reflection for her passage portfolio it was forty-five minutes long (and most kids took fifteen or twenty [minutes]). With no prompting or questions, she talked about what worked for her as a learner and what she needed. Her reflections were in-depth and really got to successes and challenges." Carmella's two years at EPIC represented a real transformation.

Another EPIC student, Efrain, comes to school but has a difficult time getting work done. He has an IEP and needs additional time and support to process information and directions. "He needs all the structures and supports to reflect," says Maxwell. For example, Maxwell would provide many prompts such as, "Here is a way to start the first sentence." Efrain's progress over the two years was also very good. "At first, his reflections were very minimal. He would do the minimum requirement." It was also difficult to engage his family. Several times Maxwell went to his house to facilitate the conference. The persistence paid off. For Efrain's passage presentation, his mom came to the school. Efrain wore a linen suit. "He had excellent reflections both about skills and subjects in general and work habits." The conferences had become his way of really seeing what he needed to work on and what support would help him continue to grow.

Critical Moves for Deepening Student Engagement

The student-led conference integrates many dimensions of student-engaged assessment. It is an opportunity for students to reflect on their progress toward learning targets and standards, to ask for help, and to set goals for improvement. Students are in the driver's seat, making connections between effort and performance, between standards and achievement, between engagement with school and enjoyment of it, and between life in school and life at home. Table 5.2 describes the who, what, and why of student-led conferences as a tool for increasing student engagement.

Table 5.2 The Who, What, and Why of Student-Led Conferences

What Do Teachers Do?	What Do Students Do?	What's the Result?
Create quality learning targets and assessments based on state and Common Core standards. Plan curriculum and instruction around meeting the targets.	Understand that each lesson and learning activity is connected to learning targets.	Students have greater engagement and ownership of learning. They understand the purpose of their work.
Prepare students to be reflective about their work and progress toward learning targets. Make reflection an ongoing classroom practice. Model and teach reflections using written or video exemplars.	Engage in reflection and commit to making a strong effort to improve.	Over time student reflections grow deeper and more self-aware.
Establish student portfolios as a way to organize student work and reflections.	Keep track of and regularly update portfolios with new work and reflections.	Students use portfolios to tell the story of their learning journey. Students, teachers, and families have a visual reference point for discussion.
Establish a culture and practice of ongoing communication with families about the goals and work of the class and each student's individual progress.	Understand their progress and communicate with families about goals, learning, and progress.	Teachers, families, and students are stronger allies and partners in improving learning.
Plan a schedule for student-led conferences well in advance that includes preparation time for students, communication home, and conferences with debriefs.	Understand how structure and preparation will help make the student-led conference successful.	Student-led conferences are focused and productive and lead to greater student engagement and achievement.
Allow ample time to reach out to families and schedule conferences. Advance timing and flexibility of hours will permit maximum participation. Use multiple communication formats (e.g., e-mail, website, online programs, phone, mailings).	Assist teachers in understanding family needs and communicating about scheduling conferences.	Family participation and investment in student-led conferences is high.

(continued)

Table 5.2 Continued

What Do Teachers Do?	What Do Students Do?	What's the Result?
In preparation for student-led conferences, develop learning targets tied directly to Common Core speaking and listening standards (SL.4, SL.6) and provide students with time to practice these skills.	Understand what good speaking skills look like and sound like. Practice with and support other students to hone these skills.	Students meet Common Core speaking and listening standards and run a student-led conference that demonstrates their ability to organize and present information effectively.
Plan at least one class devoted to modeling and practicing a conference. Review roles, identify criteria for success, and give students an opportunity to practice in small groups and give each other feedback using the criteria.	Engage in preparation for the conference and understand what it takes to make it a successful experience for everyone.	Students have a clear understanding of their role in the conference and are confident and well prepared.
On the day of the conferences, make sure families are welcomed by name and the format and goals of the conference are reviewed by the student.	Help to welcome families and guide them in understanding the conference structure. Model graciousness, respect, and leadership.	Families feel welcomed and prepared to contribute to their child's learning.
Follow a structured agenda or protocol for the conference, and ensure the student has the lead role.	Stick to the agenda and use it to reflect on learning and goals. Strive to articulate honestly and deeply their strengths and challenges.	Students are able to share their work and reflect on their learning through preparation and a structured process.
In addition to a verbal reflection on the conference, give family members the opportunity to provide written feedback (e.g., through a simple questionnaire) and reflect on goals for their children. Give families the opportunity to sign up for a follow-up meeting with the teacher if they wish.	Assist in collecting feedback from families.	Family members feel encouraged to contribute and participate in their child's learning. The relationships among families, teachers, and students are strengthened.
Debrief the conference experience with the students through group discussion or individual writing.	Participate in the conference debrief and share ideas for improvement.	Students and teachers share ownership for effective student-led conferences.

SCHOOLWIDE IMPLEMENTATION

School leaders play a critical role in the successful launch of student-led conferences. From the logistics of scheduling the conference within the yearly calendar, to communicating with families, to providing professional development for teachers, school leaders must set the tone for student-led conferences as a key component of a student-engaged assessment system. As students gain confidence and skill collecting evidence of and speaking about their progress, they not only become more engaged learners but their reflections also become an important source of data about the progress of the whole school. Leaders will need to understand and frame the practice as part of the larger effort to communicate more effectively about progress toward standards.

One of the leader's most essential jobs related to student-led conferences is communicating the importance of the conferences to families, students, and teachers. Leaders can ensure that the conferences are viewed as powerful levers for engaging students in understanding their progress toward standards and that families buy into their critical role in the process. Leaders must also help teachers see the potential of student-led conferences to help students meet Common Core speaking and listening standards. Supporting students to be better communicators—able to ask and answer questions, make appropriate eye contact, and present information in an organized manner—is an important outcome of student-led conferences. We have highlighted some of the key leadership actions that will support smooth implementation of student-led conferences throughout a school.

Lay the Groundwork

- Set the vision and create the sense of purpose for student-engaged assessment and a data-driven culture. Embed student-led conferences in a broader plan for student-engaged assessment and ensure that they are linked to state and Common Core standards.

- Collect data on current assessment and communication practices and analyze data with faculty members. For example, track how many families currently come to traditional conferences and what they say about the usefulness of home-school communication. Use this data to create a plan.

- Create a master schedule that allocates time for planning, preparation, and implementation of student-led conferences. Ensure that there is adequate administrative support for all necessary logistics.

Build Teacher Capacity

- Set up a structure to enable new teachers to observe student-led conferences in person or on video. Debrief the observations with them and make a plan that supports them to implement the practice fully.
- Create professional development time and support for teachers to learn to facilitate and prepare for student-led conferences.
- Identify the Common Core speaking and listening standards that students can work toward in their student-led conference. Develop schoolwide learning targets for the conferences aligned with these standards.

Communicate with Stakeholders

- Communicate the purpose and vision of student-led conferences and the expectation of 100 percent participation with families.
    - Share the student-led conference format with the parents and be clear about the objectives of the conferences.
    - Encourage parent questions about the conference format.
    - Send multiple reminders home to families in both English and other appropriate languages.
    - Provide translators when necessary.
- Inform district or charter leaders about the student-led conference structure and expectations for family participation.

Support Teachers to Deepen Their Practice

- Facilitate faculty conversations about lessons learned from student-led conferences—identify strengths and challenges of the process and the work that students share and make any necessary changes.
- Celebrate success. Track data about conferences and document successes as well as challenges. Share student and family stories and insights.

"Number one is letting people see a student-led conference (video or observation). It is such a different process from what many people have experienced, and it can be hard for teachers to give up a role where they are in control."

—*Ryan Maxwell, instructional guide, EPIC Academy, Chicago*

Case Study

Establishing a Vision for Student-Led Conferences at WHEELS in New York City

When Brett Kimmel, principal of WHEELS, talks about student-led conferences, his voice is full of conviction about their efficacy. "Student-led conferences have tentacles into so many different things that you get tremendous bang for your buck. The student-led conference is a game changer when influencing a kid's trajectory towards college." It powerfully connects student reflection on learning targets, accountability and responsibility for learning, and family communication.

According to Kimmel, there are three critical pieces to schoolwide implementation: setting high expectations and communicating them clearly, providing the structure and time to make it work, and providing professional development for faculty.

High Expectations and Communication

"When WHEELS first began implementing student-led conferences, they were not sure what they would ultimately look like," said Joe Catalanotti, instructional guide, "so we mucked around for a while. Even if you don't have everything perfect from the beginning, you get positive feedback right away." Setting clear and high expectations for students, families, and teachers is key.

Expectations for students came first. "We give students learning targets for the student-led conference," says Kimmel (see table 5.1). "There is preparation and practice, and our expectation is that they treat the student-led conference the same way they would a final project or test. It's how they start taking responsibility for their own work. We tell them 'you are part of it.'" He acknowledges that at first, establishing expectations for families is a heavy lift. "You have to be very clear and communicative through PTA meetings, phone, e-mail. We make them think that student-led conferences are the most important thing to hit this earth."

Structure and Schedule

For secondary schools, having an established crew (advisory) structure and the time to schedule the conferences is a critical piece. At WHEELS, conferences take place three times a year, from noon to eight. Crew leaders are responsible for setting up and attending the conferences for each member of their crew (approximately fifteen students). According to Kimmel, instituting an advisory structure like crew and giving crew leaders the time and support to prepare student-led conferences is the key structure to making the practice work. The time for conferences is consistent and predictable. They always occur on Thursdays. Teachers are responsible for scheduling conferences during the noon-to-eight time frame for their crew students. Then there is a week and a day to schedule any make-up conferences.

(continued)

Professional Development

Kimmel says, "The most effective thing is for teachers to see it." Ideally teachers new to the practice can observe it live. They invite faculty members who are joining the school in the fall to observe the May conferences. But they have also developed a video "How to Do a Student-Led Conference." "In the beginning we focused all of our energy on faculty professional development, but now that we have a critical mass of teachers and students who have participated in student-led conferences, we rely more heavily on our grade teams to guide the work," says Catalanotti.

Continuous Improvement

Though WHEELS now has a highly functioning student-led conference process in place, they are continually refining the structure. Recently they decided to shift the timing of the conferences. Instead of coming at the end of the trimester and including a report card review, now the conference comes in the middle and serves as a review of progress. Catalanotti explains, "We hold student-led conferences in the middle of each trimester. This way, the conferences serve as a progress report through which students actually have time to reflect on their performance, identify successes, and remedy what might not be going well before they earn their final grades." Action plans created at the conference can affect achievement. See an interview with Principal Kimmel in the accompanying video.

Watch video: "Schoolwide Structures for Student-Led Conferences"

WHAT TO EXPECT

As any teacher or school leader can tell you, setting up conferences, whether they are student-led or more traditional parent-teacher conferences, is a lot of work. There are many logistics to consider. Communicating early and often with families is key to the success of student-led conferences, especially in the early phase of implementation. The school must emphasize the importance of their attendance and participation.

A key marker for when a school has moved out of the beginning phases of this work and into the more advanced phase is when structures for student reflection are a part of the classroom routine on a daily or weekly basis. Preparation for a student-led conference shouldn't be a last-minute scramble, full of hurried reflections. At its best, preparation should involve synthesizing learning and culling representative pieces from an existing portfolio of work, rather than pulling work from binders and trying to reflect on it after the fact. Ongoing reflection and connection to other components of a student-engaged assessment system will enrich the practice for everyone involved.

We have identified some of the benchmarks that teachers and school leaders can expect at the beginning, intermediate, and advanced phases of implementing student-led conferences.

> "In year one we established expectations as a group. We didn't have much literature on it but felt our way through trial and error. Our goal was that we wanted students to be able to communicate with parents about work and progress."
>
> —*Cindy Kapeller, principal, Delaware Ridge Elementary School, Kansas City, Kansas*

Beginning

- The school makes the key decisions necessary to set up student-led conferences (e.g., what time of year and how many times per year they will occur).
- Students gather and reflect on work that they will share at the conference.
- Agendas are built for the conferences that give students ownership of the entire process.
- School leadership communicates with families about the new structure.
- Teachers provide students with time to practice leading a conference.
- Family participation rates are good (90 percent).

Intermediate

- Students are well prepared for conferences and family participation is high (95 to 100 percent).
- Student reflection and goal setting are classroom routines that are in place all year round, not just in preparation for conferences.
- Students prepare portfolios of their work to share at the conference.
- Students and teachers are well prepared for all logistical considerations.

- New teachers are introduced to student-led conferences early on in the orientation process and are supported in implementing them.
- Teachers, students, and families begin to see the natural connections between student-led conferences and other student-engaged assessment practices, such as learning targets, portfolios, celebrations of learning, and standards-based grading.
- All teachers help students understand and work toward mastery of Common Core speaking and listening standards. Students are able to modulate their speech for the audience and organize and present evidence of their learning.

Advanced

- Students engage in deep reflection on their progress toward meeting standards. Reflection is evidenced throughout all classrooms and stages of curriculum.
- Students' reflection on their work demonstrates deep conceptual understandings.
- Teachers, families, and students see conferences as an opportunity to support students in their growth as learners.
- A dynamic portfolio system supports students' reflection on their work and learning all year round and serves as an anchor of the student-led conference.
- Family participation in conferences is consistently high (98 to 100 percent) and family members, and students can articulate the purpose and value of the conferences. Family members actively participate in the conference, asking probing questions and sharing in the reflection process.

COMMON CHALLENGES

Student-Led Conferences Not Tied to Standards and Learning Targets

Alignment is critical. If the learning targets or standards in a class are not clearly articulated, the conference will not be as reflective and rigorous as it should be. Likewise, students who are not taught to use and reflect on learning targets will not be able to reflect productively on their learning during conferences.

Student-Led Conferences That Lack Meaningful Work

Work must be worth sharing. A large part of what will make a conference successful is that the student shares work he or she is rightly proud of. The work should be reflective of quality learning targets—intellectually rich, challenging, and engaging. If a student has not met expectations in a class, the conference can still be a positive experience, but the lack of progress should never be a surprise to family members or the student.

Student-Led Conferences with a Poor Balance of Overview and In-Depth Evidence

Balance is key. If the entire conference consists of looking at a few pieces of student work in depth, the family will not get a good overview of how the student is doing. Conversely, if students present overview materials such as report cards, test scores, or learning target grades without looking closely at work examples, families will lose the opportunity to see and understand how student work reflects learning.

Students Describe the Work Rather Than How the Work Reflects Learning

Describe the learning, not the doing. Without preparation, discussion, and coaching, students tend to show work and describe assignments, rather than explain what they learned. Simply describing work does not convey the level of quality the student achieved, what skills and content they acquired, and what their next steps for learning are.

Not Enough Time Is Allocated to Prepare for Student-Led Conferences

Preparation is essential. Successful conferences cannot be thrown together at the last minute. They require forethought and planning for all aspects—student preparation, communication with families, and scheduling. Rehearsing is essential. Observing video of model conferences or conducting mock conferences will help students know what to expect. Students will also benefit from clear criteria for success related to the Common Core speaking and listening standards.

Adults (Teachers or Family Members) Take Over Student-Led Conferences

Adults must take a back seat. Student-led conferences are about student leadership. With the right support and in the context of ongoing student-engaged assessment, students can develop invaluable skills of reflection, goal setting, and presentation. Student-led conferences run into trouble when adults take over or dominate during the conference.

Student-Led Conferences That Lack Logistical Coordination

It's all about the details. Because student-led conferences often involve coordination among teacher team members and school staff, and always involve reaching out to families, the details are critical. School teams should decide early how they will keep track of who does what, manage multiple forms of communication, and follow up on tasks. Creating a common handbook for a school's approach to conferences is a good idea.

A Key Family Member Doesn't Come to the Student-Led Conference

Flexibility is key. Sometimes, despite all efforts, a parent or family member may be unable to attend a student's conference. Schools have handled this in different ways. One possibility is that a well-prepared student could conduct a conference at home and ask a family member to record comments and reflections. Another possibility is that a supportive adult from the school community (e.g., counselor, physical education or music teacher, administrator) can fill in for a family member. The most important thing is that every student has a chance to reflect on his or her learning and present to a caring adult who is not one of his or her teachers.

Chapter 6

Celebrations of Learning

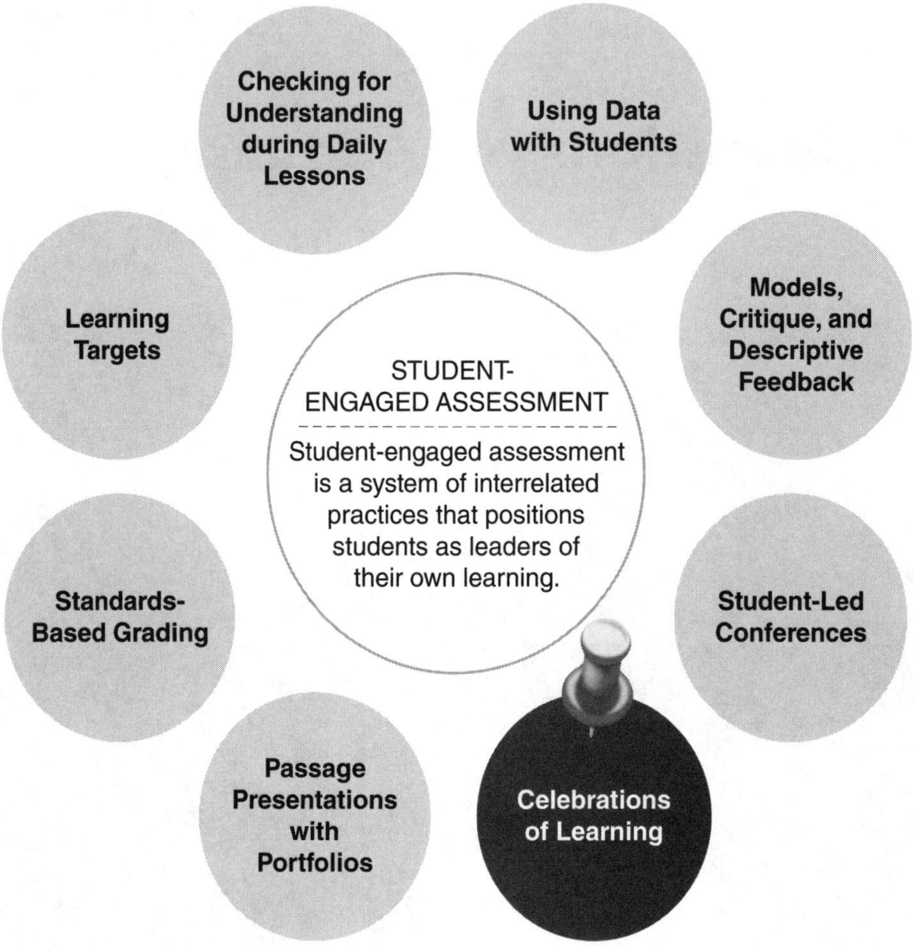

Checking for Understanding during Daily Lessons

Using Data with Students

Learning Targets

Models, Critique, and Descriptive Feedback

STUDENT-ENGAGED ASSESSMENT

Student-engaged assessment is a system of interrelated practices that positions students as leaders of their own learning.

Standards-Based Grading

Student-Led Conferences

Passage Presentations with Portfolios

Celebrations of Learning

Fifth-graders at the Alice B. Beal Elementary School in Springfield, Massachusetts, were studying bones and skeletons, a requirement of the district curriculum. They were very excited about an idea they had to deepen and share their learning—they wanted to open a museum of bones and skeletons. "Not a dorky school museum," they said, "where you go into a classroom and there are posters on desks, and it's just a boring classroom. A real, cool museum." They even had a name—*The Skeleseum.*

I was fortunate to work with them and their talented teacher, Pat Pio, supporting their museum idea. They studied in the classroom and also engaged in fieldwork with researchers and medical professionals who studied and worked with human and animal bones. They visited a science museum in their city and analyzed the features that made it compelling. With Pat's and my help, they assembled a wealth of hands-on resources to go along with their informational writing and posters, including actual human and animal bones and skeletons, models of human and animal bones and skeletons, and x-rays.

We found a seldom-used room in the school that was filled with storage items and, with the permission of the custodian, students cleaned out the entire room to set up the museum. It was a windowless room. The students wanted spooky lighting, so we set it up as mostly dark, with spotlights covered with x-rays, table lamps, and black fabric dividers. The students set up interactive exhibits where younger students could handle bones, build joints, explore animal skeletons, fill out cards, and attend lectures. There was a gift shop, the Skelestore, where visitors could buy miniature skeleton kits and Skelecookies created by fifth-graders.

On the opening day, every student in the school was excited. They paid their museum admission (one penny), got their hand stamped, and entered a spooky, dark world with exciting activities everywhere. Young students were shrieking with discoveries—holding bones, drawing bones, filling out bone cards. They sat motionless as fifth-graders gave lessons and demonstrations of skeletons and joints, and explained how they learned about bones. The fifth-graders, dressed impeccably in black pants or skirts and white shirts, were like professional museum staff.

I saw one of those students this year. Shanice is now a senior in high school. She asked if I remembered the Skeleseum. "How could I forget?" I asked. She nodded excitedly and said, "I still remember everything about bones and skeletons. That was the coolest thing ever!"

—Ron Berger

Making Learning Public

It is not uncommon for students to be in the spotlight in front of their communities from time to time. Almost always this happens in one of two formats: a performance, such as a school play or concert, or a sporting event. The pressure of preparing for a big concert, play, or game compels students to practice and to strive to improve. Some students literally push themselves to total exhaustion in football or soccer practice every afternoon to be ready for a big game. For some reason, however, schools have not typically harnessed this incredible motivating structure and connected it to academic learning.

With a focus on showcasing academics, celebrations of learning capture that power—not just for some students—but for all students, and these experiences fuel their learning all year long. When they know that the work they are doing will culminate in high-quality final products for display in front of their community, students approach their learning with the same commitment and focus as they would in preparation for a performance or big game. They are more willing to revise, meet deadlines, and take responsibility for their learning. Whether the event is at the school, town library, or museum, students beam with pride when their families, community members, and professional experts look closely at their work, and students can articulate what they have learned and how they have grown.

Celebrations of learning showcase and honor the work of all students, empowering them to take the lead role in communicating about their learning. At a celebration of learning, students make the connections among their work, habits of scholarship—such as perseverance and responsibility—and state and Common Core standards. It is an opportunity for students to reflect and assess themselves. The events give them a unique opportunity to say, "These are the standards we met, here's the work I did that proves I met them, and here's how I did it." This is powerful self-knowledge.

A **celebration of learning** is a culminating grade-level or schoolwide event in which students present high-quality work to the school community, families, and members of the greater community. Although we use the term *celebration,* and there is always joy in the event, it is not like the cast party after a play—it is the play itself. It is a public exhibition of student learning in academics and the arts that features student work and student reflection on learning. *Expedition nights, culminating events, authors' nights,* and many other names all fall under the umbrella term *celebrations of learning.* Celebrations of learning can include presentations, original performances, and demonstrations. The events enable students to articulate their learning and achievement and demonstrate college- and career-ready skills to an authentic audience.

> "It felt really great sharing my work and I feel like I know enough about this that I can present it to people, and I think people in the community want to see what kids are learning."
>
> *—Sophie, sixth-grade student, King Middle School, Portland, Maine*

Celebrations of learning are also an essential component in building bridges among the school, community members, families, and school partners. Inviting the community into the academic culture of the school and enabling them to see the quality of work being done by students builds interest and helps schools sustain important relationships with families and the community. Celebrations of learning are infused with joy when students take pride in their work and that of their peers as they share their achievements with the community.

Celebrations of learning may occur at the end of the year, the end of a unit or long-term project, or at designated times throughout the year (e.g., prior to winter break, at the end of each semester). Schools have many choices to make for how they want to customize the events. A celebration may be a formal presentation or performance, a more free-flowing gallery opening, an interactive museum, or even a simulation experience that puts guests into active roles. In every case, the focus is different from an exhibit opening or concert in the adult world—the focus is not only on the work displayed but also on what students learned in the process. Although the celebrations of learning we discuss in this chapter are typically special events, beyond a single classroom, the principles behind the practice can transform small-scale events, such as classroom open houses, into celebrations of learning as well. Making learning public is the key.

Why This Practice Matters

Celebrations of learning are more than a display of student work and more than a party at the end of the year. The events compel students to reflect on and articulate what they have learned, how they learned, questions they answered, research they conducted, and areas of strength and struggles. They are powerful opportunities to make learning public.

High-Quality Work

At the center of celebrations of learning are high-quality products and performances that reflect the content and skills that students have learned. Typically, products are modeled after real-world formats, guided by professional models, and created for an audience beyond the classroom. For example, during a study of the Civil War, a traditional school assignment might be a report on an aspect of the war—not a bad assignment, but not necessarily motivating for high-quality research or compelling to students and the community. In this case, the audience for the work is really the teacher. By contrast, if students followed their study of the war by researching local sites that were a part of the war and prepared professional brochures or interpretive signs that could teach the community about it, there would be a genuine audience and a reason for the community to take interest in the work.

Students are supported in producing high-quality work in preparation for celebrations of learning and take their work through multiple drafts. With feedback from teachers, professionals, and peers, students are motivated to meet rigorous standards and engage in revision. It is clear to students why the product matters, and they are held to high expectations (see figure 6.1).

Authentic Audience

Celebrations of learning are created for an audience beyond the classroom. Preparing work to be shared with the public—the authentic audience—motivates students and creates a purpose for them to care about the quality of their work. Presenting work to an authentic audience also raises the stakes and sets the expectation that all students, not just a select group, will share their high-quality products. It motivates students to push themselves as learners. Caitlin LeClair, seventh-grade social studies teacher at King Middle School in Portland, Maine, reflects on her students' experience interviewing local

Figure 6.1 Field Guide Page Created by a Seventh-Grader in Portland, Maine

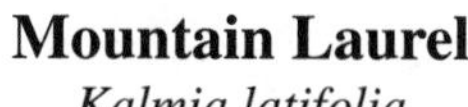

citizens and writing their stories during a study of the Civil Rights Movement: "The experience students had with their interviewees created an emotional connection to the content that they cannot get in the classroom or from books and research. It motivates them to work hard to write their stories and present their work to their interviewees." An authentic audience demonstrates for students that their work is real and important and increases their motivation and engagement (see figure 6.2).

> "Any time you make the work public, set the bar high, and are transparent about the steps to make a high-quality product, kids will deliver."
>
> —*Mike McCarthy, principal, King Middle School, Portland, Maine*

Figure 6.2 Hierarchy of Audience

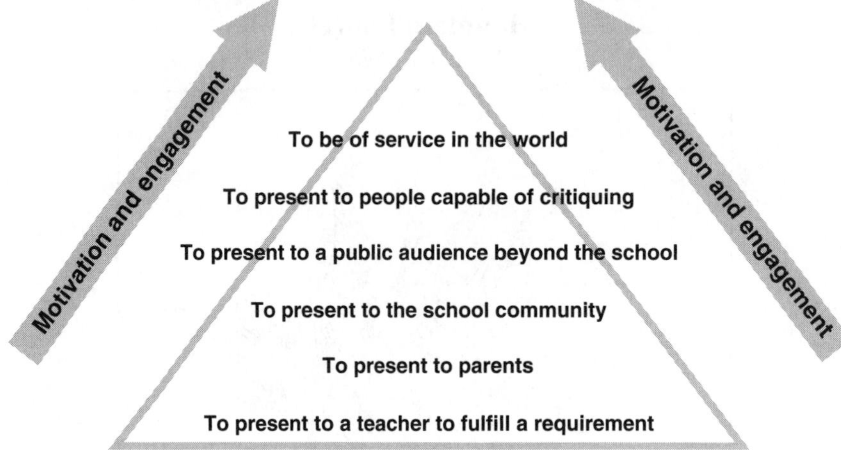

Communicating Learning

Celebrations of learning feature students as the communicators. They are front and center, articulating their learning, the process of learning, and their strengths and struggles. These skills are strongly emphasized in the speaking and listening strand of the Common Core State Standards, and celebrations of learning are a powerful way for students of all ages to master these standards. Being effective communicators is essential to Common Core success and will support college and career readiness for all students.

Reflection

In order for students to effectively communicate their achievement and learning, they must have regular opportunities to assess and articulate their progress toward learning targets. Regular reflection on progress creates opportunities for students to set goals and become partners with their teachers in meeting the standards. To help prepare students for a celebration of learning it is essential for them to reflect on key learning experiences. Journals are a great tool to house reflections and can accompany student work at a celebration of learning to help illustrate parts of the learning journey.

Common Core Connections

- Celebrations of learning are an ideal way to meet the Common Core speaking and listening standards at all grade levels. The introduction to the literacy standards states, "The Common Core Speaking and Listening Standards require students to develop a range of broadly useful oral communication and interpersonal skills. Students must learn to work together, express and listen carefully to ideas, integrate information from oral, visual, quantitative, and media sources, evaluate what they hear, use media and visual displays strategically to help achieve communicative purposes, and adapt speech to context and task" (National Governors Association Center for Best Practices and Council of Chief State School Officers, 2010, p. 8).
- Preparing for a celebration of learning requires that students know their standards-based content, independently use higher-order thinking skills such as synthesis or transfer to interact with audience members about that content, and cite evidence that demonstrates their learning.
- The standards require students throughout the grades to engage in research projects—very often the central focus of a celebration of learning. Students present their research and give evidence-based descriptions of their results.
- Celebrations of learning open the door for meaningful conversations among families, students, and teachers about standards and achievement.

GETTING STARTED

Developing the Structures to Get Started with Celebrations of Learning

Celebrations of learning can be structured in a variety of ways and can look very different depending on grade level, content area, school context, and school traditions. Before getting started with celebrations of learning, school leaders and teachers will need to decide how they will customize the events and support students in creating a culture of excellence in the school.

In some schools, celebrations of learning are schoolwide, showcasing work at all grade levels, and occur at key moments throughout the year (e.g., the end of each trimester). Other kinds of celebrations may occur at the end of a unit, learning expedition, or long-term project. Celebrations of learning can be schoolwide, grade level, or thematic. Regardless of the time, name, or type of celebration, the event needs to be thoughtfully planned and structured so that all students are supported to communicate their learning and present high-quality work to an authentic audience.

Key Decisions

- When will celebrations of learning occur throughout the year?
- What spaces will be used to showcase student learning?
- What can be done to ensure high levels of attendance from families and community members?
- In what ways will families and community members be encouraged to become active participants in the celebration of learning?
- How will teachers ensure that students demonstrate mastery of state and Common Core standards at the celebration of learning?
- What will be shared at the celebration of learning?
  - How will evidence of drafts, revisions, and craftsmanship be included?
  - How will documentation panels tell the story of student learning?
  - How will accompanying learning targets and standards be represented so that families and visitors see their connections to student work?
  - How will rubrics and reflections be shared?
- What steps need to be taken to prepare students for celebrations of learning?
- How will students discuss habits of scholarship?
  - How will students demonstrate the ways in which character growth and habits of scholarship are linked to aspects of their work?
  - How will students show evidence of progress toward character and academic learning targets during the celebration of learning?
- How will teachers be supported in creating powerful celebrations of learning?

Determining the Focus of the Celebration of Learning

When planning a celebration of learning, it is first necessary to determine the purpose of the event and then decide which format will best fit that purpose. For example, if the purpose of the celebration is to share high-quality, museum-style displays of scientists in the community who tenth-grade chemistry students researched, a grade-level celebration of learning hosted at a local science

Considerations for the size and scope of student displays will affect decisions about the space used for the event.

museum might be appropriate. However, if the purpose is to celebrate arts across the curriculum, at all grade levels, a year-end event involving the entire school population and the entire physical space of the school building is perhaps a better choice. What follows are snapshots of two of the most common structures for celebrations of learning.

Classroom- or Grade-Level-Based Celebrations of Learning at the Conclusion of a Unit, Learning Expedition, or Long-Term Project

This type of celebration of learning might feature the final product or performance created by students and would be presented to an audience that is connected to the work. For example, if students were engaged in an in-depth study of WWII for which they interviewed local WWII veterans and wrote an oral history capturing the stories, the celebration of learning could take place at the local veterans' home with students presenting their work to the interviewees.

At Vergennes Union Middle School, in Vergennes, Vermont, seventh-grade students participated in a learning expedition called "Reducing the Carbon Footprint of Vergennes Union Middle and High School." Their goal was to determine the amount of energy used on a yearly basis by students and staff at the school. Students conducted an energy audit and calculated the carbon footprint of the building. Students also traveled to different sites in Vermont to study systems being used to reduce the use of fossil fuels. They met with building managers and principals to interview them about the process of implementing an alternative energy source and the impact it had on their school or business. Students compiled their findings into an alternative energy report and presented it along with a recommendation to the school board. The presentation was open to the public—with special invitations sent to experts and professionals directly involved in student learning—and included student presentations on various alternative energy sources.

The celebration of learning at Vergennes had a dual purpose of showcasing student learning and serving as a pitch to local officials to make energy-saving changes in the school. Choosing a final product like this is an opportunity for schools to help students see the connection between schoolwork and meaningful service. The celebration of learning is an opportunity to highlight the real contributions that students can make to their communities.

Schoolwide Celebrations of Learning

Celebrations of learning can occur at designated times in the year and showcase work across multiple grade levels and disciplines. Often a common thread ties together the work of students at all grade levels. For example, at the Raphael Hernandez School in Boston, students at all grade levels wrote books, but the content and genre of each book was different depending on grade level, which skills they were working on, and what content they were studying. All students learned about the authoring process in writing a book and worked toward established schoolwide criteria. The celebration of learning was an authors' night held at the school. Students shared their books with families and community members who then had the opportunity to interview the authors. Although the content of each book was different, there was a common purpose and a common format. All students

Schoolwide celebrations of learning often bring the audience together for a performance or a welcome from students.

shared a similar learning experience, and the work was celebrated as a whole community in which students could appreciate each other's work.

At Genesee Community Charter School in Rochester, New York, where the curriculum is organized around six different time periods in history, the celebrations of learning have a similar flavor. All grade levels focus on the same historical time period each trimester, and all learning expeditions focus on that time period. Celebrations of learning feature student products and performances that demonstrate student learning about that time in history, but the content and complexity of the student work differs depending on grade-level standards. For example, one year when the school was studying prehistory, the K–1 classroom studied fossils and the 4–5 classroom studied volcanoes and land formations. At the celebration of learning K–1 students displayed and discussed the final product of their learning expedition, a book titled *Get a Clue: The Story of What Lived Here Long Ago and How We Know,* whereas 4–5 students displayed and discussed their field guide to local geological destinations called *Rock-On 'Rock'chester.* See figure 6.3 for samples of this work.

Figure 6.3 Student Work from a Celebration of Learning with a Common Academic Thread

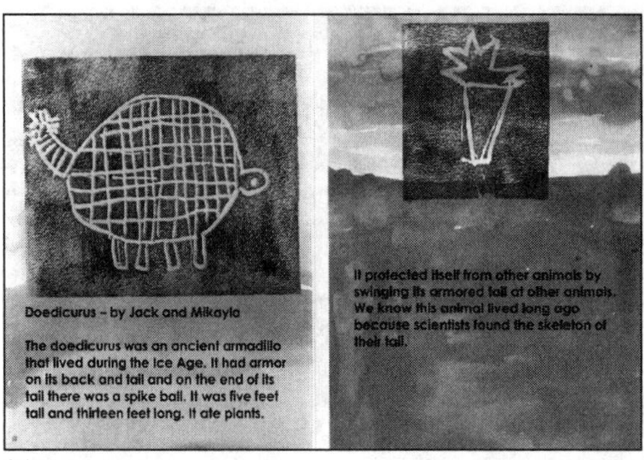

(a)

Although all students in the school studied prehistory, the content focus of each class was different based on grade-level standards. At the celebration of learning, K–1 students displayed work based on their study of fossils (a), whereas 4–5 students displayed work based on their study of land formations (b).

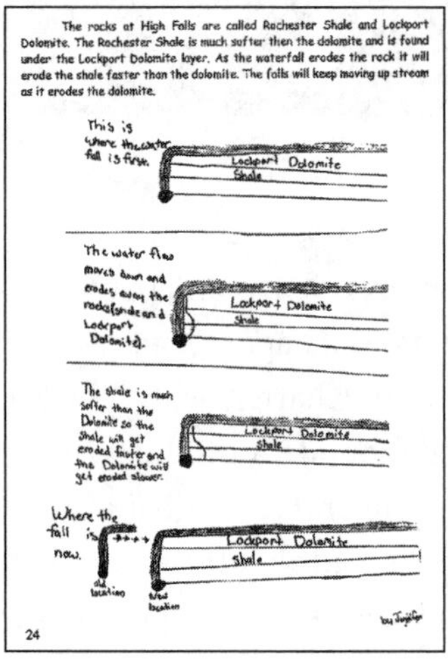

(b)

It is also possible to host a celebration of learning that is not tied with a common academic thread but that still has a common focus—such as art—that knits the content areas together. Figure 6.4 is an example of a program for visitors at a celebration of learning in which the content areas on display at each grade level are very different, but all student work is united by a focus on arts across the curriculum. When the purpose of the event is clear, the right structure will emerge.

Figure 6.4 Sample Exhibition Night Program

Mary O. Pottenger School
Presents:

Arts Across the Curriculum
Exhibition Night

Wednesday, June 3, 2009
6-7 p.m.

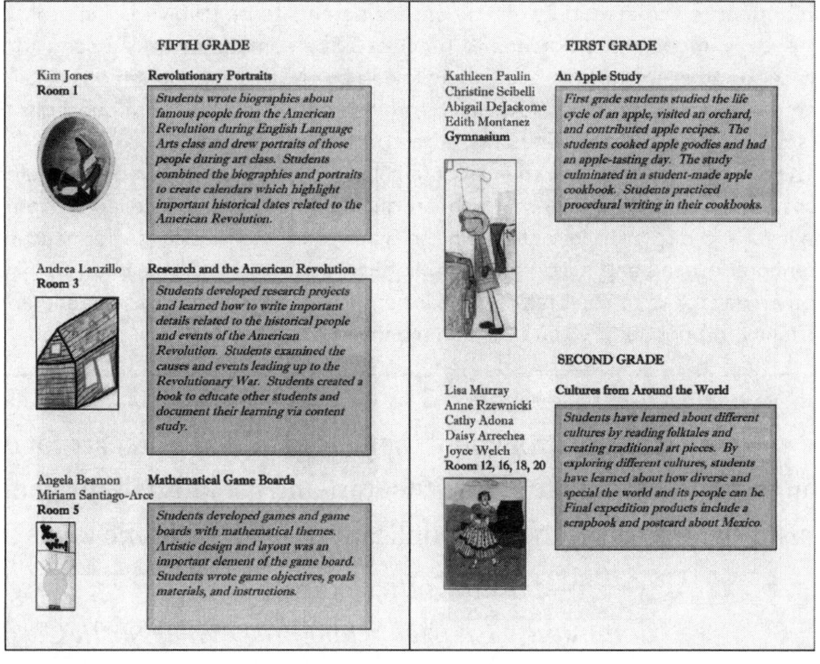

FIFTH GRADE

Kim Jones
Room 1

Revolutionary Portraits

Students wrote biographies about famous people from the American Revolution during English Language Arts class and drew portraits of those people during art class. Students combined the biographies and portraits to create calendars which highlight important historical dates related to the American Revolution.

Andrea Lanzillo
Room 3

Research and the American Revolution

Students developed research projects and learned how to write important details related to the historical people and events of the American Revolution. Students examined the causes and events leading up to the Revolutionary War. Students created a book to educate other students and document their learning via content study.

Angela Beamon
Miriam Santiago-Arce
Room 5

Mathematical Game Boards

Students developed games and game boards with mathematical themes. Artistic design and layout was an important element of the game board. Students wrote game objectives, goals materials, and instructions.

FIRST GRADE

Kathleen Paulin
Christine Scibelli
Abigail DeJackome
Edith Montanez
Gymnasium

An Apple Study

First grade students studied the life cycle of an apple, visited an orchard, and contributed apple recipes. The students cooked apple goodies and had an apple-tasting day. The study culminated in a student-made apple cookbook. Students practiced procedural writing in their cookbooks.

SECOND GRADE

Lisa Murray
Anne Rzewnicki
Cathy Adona
Daisy Arrechea
Joyce Welch
Room 12, 16, 18, 20

Cultures from Around the World

Students have learned about different cultures by reading folktales and creating traditional art pieces. By exploring different cultures, students have learned about how diverse and special the world and its people can be. Final expedition products include a scrapbook and postcard about Mexico.

Case Study

Using a Variety of Formats to Celebrate Learning at Evergreen Community Charter School in Asheville, North Carolina

At Evergreen, a K–8 school, students engage in celebrations of learning three times throughout the year. Each celebration of learning has a different focus, but each shares the common purpose of celebrating student work with parents and the community. At fall family night parents and other family members are invited to view student work in progress. They visit classrooms and see demonstrations of what students are learning. Susan Gottfried, executive director, says, "The purpose is to share with parents and give them an inside view of what has been happening during the first few months of school. It allows them to see that kids are continuously revising work until they reach high quality. It is also very helpful for new families to see what EL Education looks like; it engages them and helps them see the bigger picture."

At the spring exhibition night, each classroom showcases final products, learning targets, guiding questions, and interactive demonstrations. Students in Ona Armstrong's kindergarten class, for example, displayed work from their "Helping Hands, Helping Hearts" learning expedition, in which they studied professionals in the community. Visitors were given questions to prompt students such as, "What tools are used in your profession?" or "What does your job do to help the community?" Armstrong feels that it is important to "create high expectations for parents to be involved. Their role in the experience is important and needs to be clear." She sometimes uses a song to bring everyone together to start the evening, followed by visits to various stations to talk with students. Armstrong also finds it helpful to provide parents with a list of questions to ask each student and a place for feedback at the bottom of the page.

The spring arts festival is a chance for families and community members to celebrate student work in enrichment classes. Final products from art class are collected from each grade level and displayed in a gallery in the gym. There are musical performances from different grade levels and a slide show highlighting what students have been learning. "It is another way for us to celebrate what happens in our enrichment classes, and another opportunity to bring families and the community into the school," says Gottfried.

"The energy builds up throughout the year as students prepare for exhibition night. We build it up from the start and get kids talking about it. We also advertise it in a weekly publication that goes home to parents."

—Susan Gottfried, executive director, Evergreen Community Charter School, Asheville, North Carolina

Communicating with Families and Community Members

At the core of a powerful celebration of learning is the audience. It is the audience that motivates students, inspiring them to do their best work and to care about quality. Traditionally, families come to school for sporting events, music concerts, or performances. Inviting families and community members into the academic culture of the school is a powerful shift and needs to be planned so that it is meaningful for students and audience members (see figure 6.5).

Figure 6.5 A Beautiful Invitation Generates Enthusiasm for the Event

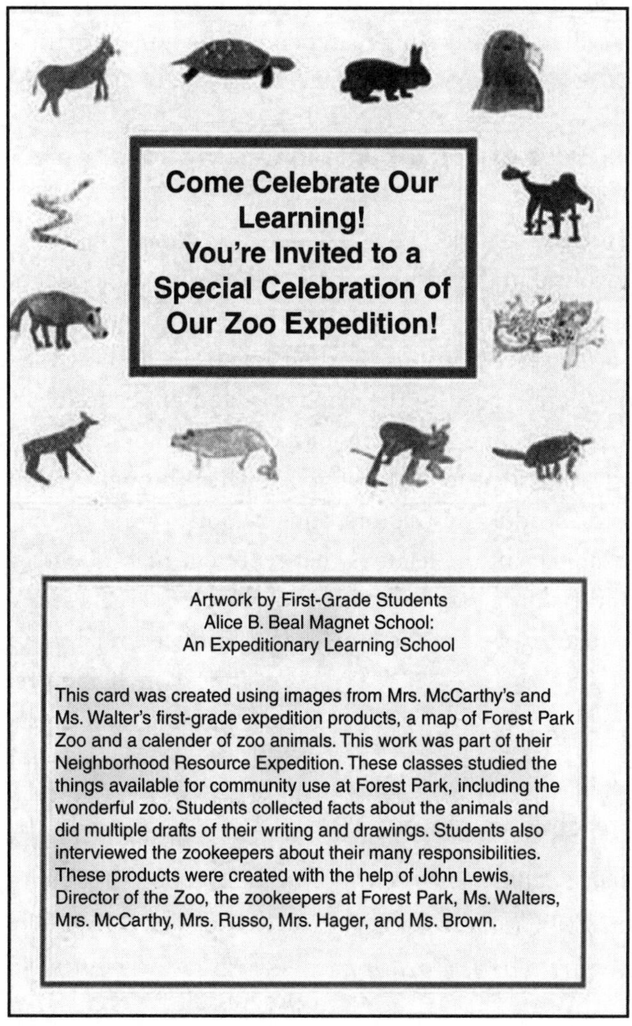

It is essential to communicate the logistics of the celebration with the intended audience well in advance of the celebration to ensure a good turnout. Also, deciding whether to schedule the event during the day or at night needs to be taken into consideration, especially if the celebration will be held off-site. Special efforts at communication with professionals, experts, and community members who have worked with students can go a long way toward a successful event. Presenting their work to experts and professionals elevates students' sense of pride and accomplishment. Schools also need structures to guarantee that parents are informed in a timely manner and supported in being able to attend, including the use of translators if needed and transportation to and from the venue. Attention to details will help ensure high attendance and a meaningful celebration of learning.

Defining the Roles of Participants in Celebrations of Learning

Role of the Student

Students are involved in the entire process of preparing for a celebration of learning. From the beginning they understand the structure and purpose of the celebration of learning, expectations for their involvement, how the learning process and product are related to the standards, and opportunities for leadership and involvement. During preparation for a celebration of learning, students take the work that is intended for the public audience through multiple drafts and revision. Rubrics, product descriptors, and exemplars are used to guide students and provide examples of the features that represent high quality. Students continually assess their progress and mastery of learning targets and standards that are connected to all aspects of the project and product. Preparation and practice are critical in helping students hone their speaking and presentation skills. Students play the lead role in communicating their learning and guide the audience through the process that led to the creation of a high-quality product. They are responsible for presenting their work and reflecting on their progress.

> "Celebrations of learning give kids the opportunity to talk about what they've learned. If you can teach it, you know it."
>
> —*Susan Gottfried, executive director, Evergreen Community Charter School, Asheville, North Carolina*

The celebration of learning is not "teacher work." Students partner with teachers in all aspects of preparing for the celebration of learning. Choosing work that will be highlighted and preparing visual displays is an important role for students. They also understand the logistics of the event and take on different roles, including greeting and guiding adults; helping with the design and creation of programs, flyers, posters, and signs; helping with food, music, and displays; and setting up and cleaning up. A checklist or agenda can help students remember their various roles during the celebration of learning. Students may be required to discuss the work of their peers in addition to their own, which demands an added layer of preparation. The snapshot that follows reveals the important role that students can play in discussing their own work and learning, as well as that of other students.

Snapshot: Connecting Learning across the School

The celebration of learning at Mary O. Pottenger Elementary School in Springfield, Massachusetts, was a schoolwide event, showcasing the best work and learning of every student, K–5. Visual and performing arts deepened student learning in core academic subjects throughout the spring, and this was the focus of the celebration. Principal Valerie Williams personally welcomed more than five hundred visitors as they entered, handing out programs (see figure 6.4) that described what was going on in every classroom and when performances were taking place.

The genius in the evening was that families did not simply visit the classroom of their child—they were given a learning tour. Fifth-grade students led their families into the kindergarten classrooms, where giant banners related to the students' study of color hung from the windows. First-grade students led their families into third-grade classrooms, where projects and work related to Native American Indians filled the rooms. During the day, students had visited every classroom and learned from every grade level so that they could show the learning throughout the school to their families. During the evening event, students toured the building in shifts so that some students were always in the classroom to explain the work and so that every student had a chance to share his or her learning with guests.

The structure enabled powerful conversations among students, teachers, and families about learning and high-quality work across grades and content areas.

Role of the Teacher

The teacher has myriad roles in a celebration of learning. Careful planning will ensure that all students experience success. The teacher does the following:

- Holds the vision for the celebration of learning, understands the logistics, and delegates responsibilities to students and other staff

- Helps students understand and practice their roles
- Creates opportunities for students to be involved in decision making about the celebration of learning as well as directing aspects of the project and product
- Guides students in creating high-quality work for a public audience and differentiates support for students as they work toward a common product
- Provides students with models of quality work, rubrics, product descriptors, and descriptive feedback to help them improve their work
- Plans backward from the celebration of learning and identifies the knowledge and skills students will need
- Creates appropriate learning targets and assesses student progress during all phases of learning, leading to the final product and celebration of learning
- Teaches presentation skills and provides opportunities for students to practice before sharing their work with the public
- Makes reflection a part of the classroom culture and supports students in identifying strengths and struggles and setting goals
- Familiarizes students with the format of the celebration of learning and provides them with multiple opportunities to go through the process of what will happen at the event
- Communicates with the intended audience to ensure they understand the purpose of the celebration and are prepared to interact with students
- Creates structures to support the audience in interacting with students

What follows is a sample checklist to help teachers keep organized.

Teacher Checklist—From the "Small Acts of Courage" Celebration at King Middle School in Portland, Maine

- ❑ Reserve cafeteria for three dress rehearsals and the culminating event
- ❑ Check with custodial staff about set up and break down—give them an estimate for number of chairs
- ❑ Reserve chairs for interviewees in the front two rows
- ❑ Invitations—pick a crew time to give to students to take home
- ❑ Other invitations—administration, superintendent, interviewees (sent at time of interview)

- ❑ Send an e-mail to remind interviewees about the date and time
- ❑ E-mail staff about the change in our schedule
- ❑ Materials—two microphones, soundboard, projector, speakers, screen
- ❑ For the reception—reserve the library, buy food
- ❑ Plan for someone to photograph and videotape the presentation
- ❑ Choose five students to be greeters before the presentation
- ❑ Choose two students to set up technology
- ❑ Make a reflection for students to complete after the presentation

Role of the Audience

It is important to first consider who will comprise the audience. The less close and familiar the audience is—particularly with older students—the more important the event will feel. For example, if the audience includes professionals, civic leaders, educators, or dignitaries from other places, then there is real reason to take the celebration preparation seriously. There is a similar phenomenon with the setting—although holding an event in the classroom is easiest, it may feel less important to students than presenting in a university, museum, city hall, public library, or the lobby of a business institution. As the story that opens this chapter illustrates, a class museum is one thing if it is set up in the classroom; it can be quite a different thing if it is held in a space that is set up to feel like a real museum, with different lighting, display formats, and sections.

If the audience is to include a variety of types of guests, it is important to consider different roles for different audience members. For example, parents may observe and interview students about their work (see figure 6.6); guest professionals may assess and give feedback on the work; guest dignitaries (e.g., the superintendent, mayor, school board) may get guided tours of the event. At Springville K–8 School in Portland, Oregon, teachers provide the audience members with possible talking points, questions, and a checklist to guide them through the celebration of learning and help them engage with students. At the conclusion of the event, they give parents a rating card (table 6.1) and have them turn it in before they leave. Teachers, students, and school leaders use this information when debriefing the event. In the accompanying video, we see family members and other guests at a celebration of learning at Anser Charter School in Boise, Idaho, fully engaged in learning about birds because of the students' interactive display boards.

Watch video: "Kindergartners as Experts—Celebrations of Learning"

Figure 6.6 Teacher-Prepared Questions Help to Engage Families and Guests with Student Learning.

Families and Friends,

Here are some questions to ask students about their learning:

1. Name the Colorado fish you have learned about?
2. What is special about your Colorado fish?
3. Why does a fish need its ___________ to help it survive?
   a. Fins
   b. Gills
   c. Tail
   d. Scales
4. Where did you get your information as a scientist?
5. What was your favorite part about our field work to the Denver Aquarium?

Table 6.1 Rating Card for Parents

	1 Not at all	2 Somewhat	3 Fairly well	4 Completely
I can identify the learning targets involved in the expedition in my child's classroom.				
I can identify experiences or teaching tools in the classroom that have helped my child with the content and craftsmanship of the product (charts, books, experts, field studies).				
I can see evidence of how my child perseveres in developing high-quality work.				
I can describe how my child used literacy skills (reading, writing) during the expedition.				
I can identify the purpose of my child's product (how it can be used in our school or real-world situation).				

Role of School Leadership

The school leadership supports celebrations of learning by aiding teachers with logistics and planning, including communication with custodians and food services personnel if appropriate. They provide support with scheduling and create ongoing structures such as newsletters, websites, or blogs to inform families and the community about celebrations of learning. More information about the role school leaders play in using celebrations of learning as an opportunity to deepen and improve teacher practice can be found in the "Schoolwide Implementation" section of this chapter.

IN PRACTICE

Deepening Student Learning

There are multiple logistical details and schoolwide decisions that need to be made when getting started with celebrations of learning. Building the traditions and customizing the manner in which student work will be celebrated needs attention to ensure success. As teachers gain experience with celebrations of learning, they grow more experienced in preparing their students to present work to a public audience and reflect on progress toward learning targets, state and Common Core standards, and habits of scholarship. Students see how their work meets standards and take ownership of their learning journey.

Connect Student Work and Celebrations of Learning to Standards

An essential component of preparing students to articulate their learning is to clearly define the skills and content they will be held accountable for throughout the learning process. The work needs to be rigorous and tied to the standards. Although the completion of the final product and the celebration of learning are in the future, the connection to the standards, skills, and content needs to be clear and consistently reinforced from the beginning. Planning backward from the completion of the final product and the celebration of learning strengthens the link between student work and state and Common Core standards.

It is important to create a road map for students to see where they start, what they will learn along the way, and how the standards and targets are linked to the project, final product, and presentation of learning. Sixth-grade Common Core English language arts standard, SL.6.4 asks students to *present claims and findings, sequencing ideas logically and using pertinent descriptions, facts, and details to accentuate main ideas or themes; use appropriate eye contact, adequate volume, and clear pronunciation.* An accompanying learning target for this standard is, "I can present a summary of my research using effective speaking techniques." It is powerful when students understand that this learning target is linked directly to the expectation that they will use speaking techniques to present their work at the celebration of learning. It makes the target come alive and have meaning. This process shifts the student focus from "I met the target" to "This is how I met the target and why it is important." It is critical that students understand that their practice and work matters.

In addition to supporting students to meet Common Core standards, celebrations of learning provide an opportunity for students to demonstrate their progress toward content area standards as well. A seventh-grade standard from the National Council of Social Studies Standards requires students to *understand the contribution of key persons and events and the influences of social, geographic, economic, and cultural factors on history.* A long-term learning target to support this standard is, "I can synthesize information from primary and secondary sources

Understanding the standards will help students think on their feet and respond to questions.

about an important person and event connected to the Civil Rights Movement." A celebration of learning that features student writing and presentations about an influential person and his or her contribution to the Civil Rights Movement demonstrates for teachers, parents, and community members how students have met this and the Common Core standard. Figure 6.7 demonstrates this process.

Figure 6.7 Planning the Focus of the Celebration of Learning Based on Content and Literacy Standards

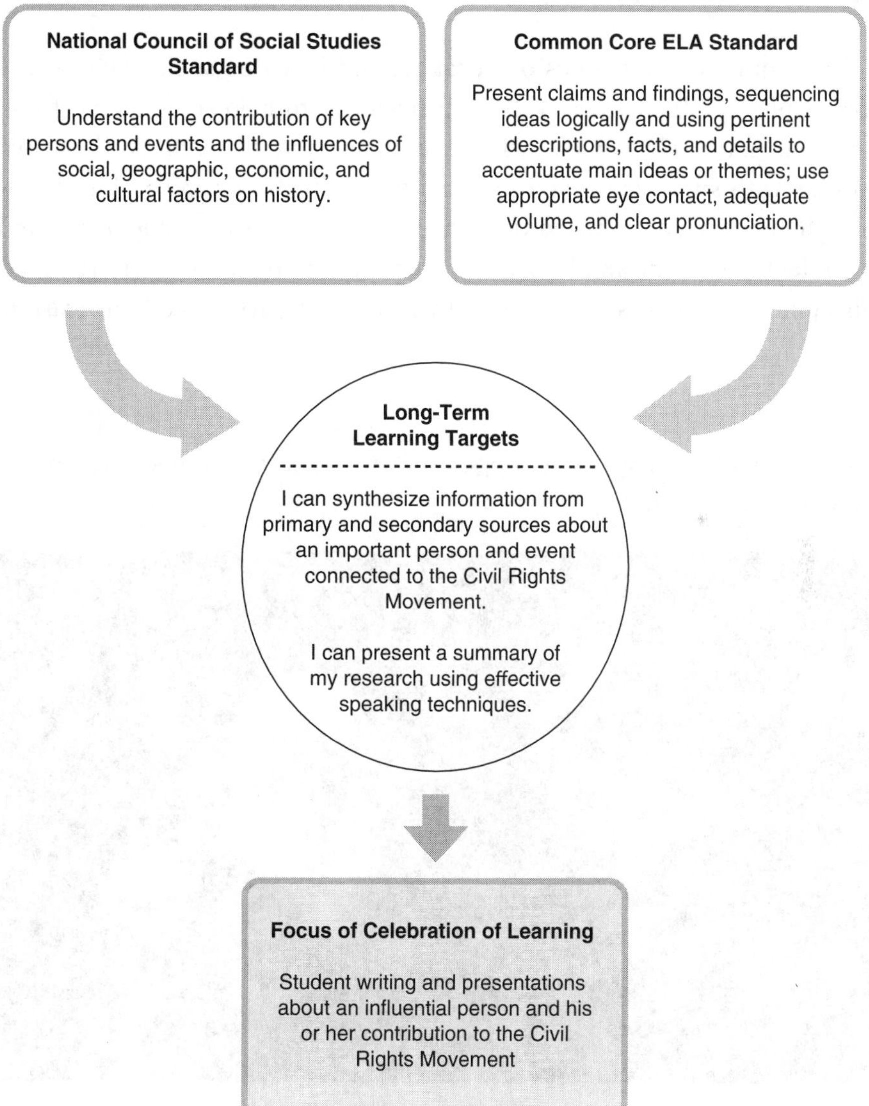

Teaching Students Oral Presentation and Communication Skills

It is crucial that students are prepared to present their work orally. Whether they are presenting their documentation panel to visitors as they browse or standing at the microphone before a large audience, public speaking is challenging for most students. They need to learn oral presentation skills that will enable them to effectively present to a public audience. As representatives of their learning—and the school—they need ample time and preparation for this aspect of the celebration of learning.

The Common Core's focus on speaking and listening skills makes it even more imperative that teachers develop strategies to help students meet these important standards, which will serve them well throughout their lives. Working with students on oral presentation skills can be woven into lessons throughout a project or expedition. Preparation creates a unique opportunity for students to review and hear the content of the project or learning expedition numerous times, strengthening their ability to articulate their learning.

Celebrations of learning are an opportunity for students to meet presentation and speaking and listening standards.

What follows are examples of structures to help prepare students for an oral presentation:

- Use rubrics to define expectations for students and to paint a picture of what a quality presentation looks like. Create opportunities for students to work in pairs and small groups to practice and critique based on the criteria in the rubric.
- Create a "fishbowl" experience and model characteristics of a quality presentation and a weak presentation. Focus on the content of what is being presented as well as how it is being presented. Model positive body language, tone, and volume of voice, posture, eye contact, and appropriate ways to greet guests.
- Allow students to critique an oral presentation done by someone else (e.g., the teacher, video from previous years), using the rubric with which they will be assessed.
- Provide multiple opportunities for students to practice. The more confident students feel in their roles, the more successful the celebration of learning will be. Invite support staff, colleagues, and administration to practice with students one-on-one. Give students positive feedback with one or two areas to work on and improve.
- Make sure that all students understand the sequence of events at a celebration of learning. If possible take students through the process of what will happen and provide an agenda for students to follow. It can also be helpful to provide students with a script to support them during the celebration of learning.

> "We took students through the process of what would happen at the culminating event and it all felt very familiar to them. They understood what it would take to make that experience successful."
>
> —*Karen MacDonald, seventh-grade language arts teacher, King Middle School, Portland, Maine*

The accompanying video and the next case study portray similar strategies teachers used to prepare their students for a celebration of learning.

Watch video: "Students Share Work That Matters with an Authentic Audience—Celebrations of Learning"

Case Study

Preparing Students for Celebrations of Learning at King Middle School in Portland, Maine

Celebrations of learning strengthen over time as teachers gain experience in preparing students to be successful. A seventh-grade learning expedition, "Small Acts of Courage," illustrates how preparation and support are key to setting students up for success. The expedition was an inquiry into important events and people involved in the Civil Rights Movement. Students interviewed local citizens who were connected to the movement in some way and wrote the story of their interviewees, taking their work through multiple drafts and revisions. The stories were compiled into a four-volume oral history that was presented to the interviewees and donated to the African American Special Collection for the state of Maine.

The culminating event featured ninety students on stage, sharing excerpts from their biographical narratives, accompanied by images and period music. It was not by chance that all students were able to successfully present their work with confidence at the celebration of learning. Preparation for the culminating event began in the early stages of the learning expedition when teachers identified the content and skills that needed to be taught and made the targets clear for all students. As figure 6.7 demonstrates, a celebration of learning should be a forum for students to show evidence of meeting standards. The standards for the "Small Acts of Courage" learning expedition flowed into student-friendly, long-term learning targets, and the celebration of learning was designed to showcase students' mastery of standards. Students knew from the very start what the purpose of the event was and what it would take to be ready for it.

Preparation for the event itself began several weeks in advance. In language arts class, students viewed video of a similar presentation by a class two years previous. Using a rubric, they critiqued the former students against speaking and oral presentation criteria (e.g., eye contact, voice projection, posture). Students then moved to selecting and practicing their lines with their teachers and peers in language arts and social studies classes. As the event got closer, the seventh-grade teaching team arranged their class schedules so that all ninety students could come together for four full rehearsals. Students rehearsed each part of the presentation, including the introduction, all individual student speaking parts, the conclusion, and the protocols for entering and exiting the stage. All media—pictures and music—were also incorporated into the rehearsals. As students recited their lines on stage, language arts and social studies teachers Karen MacDonald and Caitlin LeClair took notes and gave each student a sticky note with feedback. Students who were not on stage also provided feedback to their classmates.

The expectation that all students will participate in a celebration of learning raises the bar for teachers and students and creates a need for teachers to build a culture in which students feel safe, supported in taking risks, and will persevere to do their best work. Social studies teacher Caitlin LeClair stresses the importance of supporting all students to be successful: "Teachers need to know their students and differentiate so that students feel like the goal is attainable. It is important for students to understand the expectation that everyone will participate in the culminating event and that they will get the support they need to be successful. It sends the message that we are in this together and we will work together to reach our goal." The culture of the school supports students to take risks and persevere when they meet challenges. Preparation for celebrations of learning is an opportunity for students to meet challenges, learn from mistakes, and move forward. "Students persevere because they know the expectations and feel supported in being successful. Celebrations of learning are a time when we want all kids to succeed and we do everything we can to make that happen."

The "Small Acts of Courage" culminating event was a success for the students. It was also an emotional experience for many of the interviewees who were in the audience. Ida Gammon Wilson, an interviewee, reflected on the experience at a reception following the formal presentation: "Textbooks are often behind the times. They do not reflect who we are, where we have come from, and where we have come to. This kind of presentation by these young people would be an absolutely wonderful experience for everyone to have."

Prepare Students to Engage in a Professional Role at the Celebration of Learning

If students are mirroring or assuming a professional role at the celebration of learning, they need to be explicitly taught the skills required for that role. In addition to feeling pride in their work, students take pride in their ability to take on a professional role successfully. Picture a celebration of learning in which sixth-grade students create a museum in the school library to display their original artwork and writing. At the celebration of learning students assume the role of docents guiding guests through the displays and discussing their work and that of their peers. These kinds of authentic opportunities to practice communication skills in stride help students seamlessly master their Common Core speaking and listening skills. To support students

Teaching students to be professional hosts will enhance the experience for them and their guests.

in being successful, teachers might include some of the following learning experiences:

- Visits from the curator of a local museum to inform students about the choices made in setting up a display
- Trips to a local museum to work with docents and learn the necessary skills to be successful
- Opportunities for students to evaluate and learn about the work of their peers so that they can effectively speak about multiple displays in the museum
- Time to practice the role of a docent with an audience before the celebration—maybe another classroom or grade level

Snapshot: Gallery Opening at Casco Bay High School in Portland, Maine

Tenth-grade students at Casco Bay High School participated in an expedition called "The Human Face of Human Rights." Students conducted in-depth investigations into a human rights crisis that affected people in Portland. They completed research projects and worked in small groups to interview a subject and captured the subject's story in writing and photographs. Each student wrote an oral history of his or her subject. The class created displays of images and text that were featured at a local gallery where students teamed with gallery staff and hosted an evening gallery opening. Students were divided into committees to organize the opening—including a panel—and create professional invitations for the show. Community members, families, and interview subjects gathered at the gallery to view the displays and hear a selection of student readings.

Reflecting on Learning and Achievement

Reflection is a key component of a student's ability to articulate achievement. Students need to engage in regular reflection practices, explaining what they have learned and who they are as learners, and how they are progressing toward meeting learning targets and standards.

Documentation panels are visual representations of students' learning journey.

Figure 6.8 Documentation Panel Template

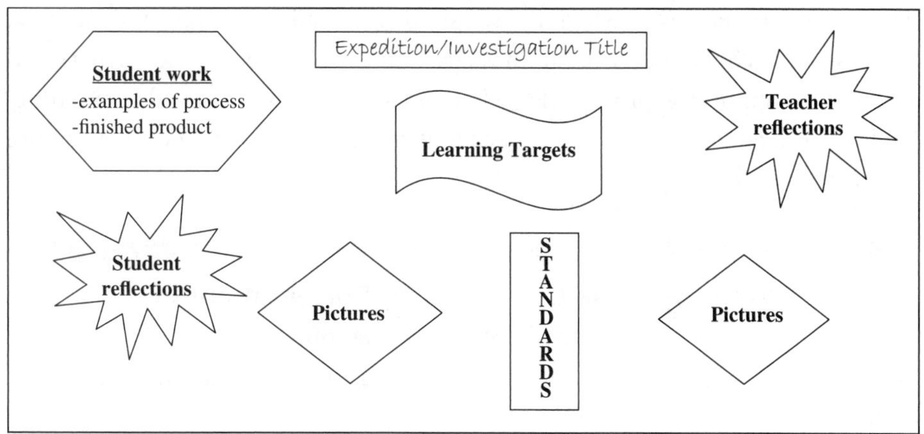

Documentation Panels

Documentation panels—visual representations of the learning journey—are a great way to help students tell the story of their learning. When students are thoughtful about reviewing the learning of the expedition or project and the artifacts they choose to portray it, they further reinforce the content and skills.

In addition to supporting students, documentation panels help enhance audience engagement and provide guests with an overview of the learning they are about to experience with students. They also include parts of the learning process that students may not touch on in their presentations, therefore enriching the experience for the audience. Figure 6.8 shows a documentation panel template from EPIC Academy in Chicago. In this template, teacher and student reflections, photographs, learning targets, and standards surround student work. Schools should consider whether or not to save strong documentation panels from celebrations of learning to mount or frame for long-term display on classroom or hallway walls. Panels from previous classes can be used as models for students when they create their own.

Reflecting on the Celebration of Learning Itself

Debriefing the celebration of learning is an important part of the process. It helps students connect the purpose of the event to the standards one more time and to self-assess against learning targets. Celebrations of learning are also opportunities to have families and community members engage in reflection around what the standards are, what students are learning, and how student work reflects the standards. It is another way in which the standards come alive through student work. Some schools choose to have families share their reflections with teachers and students to support the process of teacher and student reflection and goal setting. Table 6.1 is a good example of feedback that can be useful as schools plan future celebrations of learning.

Strategy Close Up: Assessing Presentations of Student Work and Learning

The following framework may be a useful guide for teachers in assessing students' presentations of their work and learning.

Representing the Learning Journey

- The story being told through student work
- The way in which students share their learning with others, including the public speaking skills they have mastered
- Rubrics or product descriptors that explain the expectations for the project or assignment
- Photos, videos, and documentation of the work in progress
- Documentation panels or handouts

Evidence of Skill Building and Content Knowledge

- The research or in-depth study leading up to the final product
- Applications of content and skills
- Meaningful connections to standards and curriculum
- Embedded literacy skills
- Work that demonstrates every student's learning (i.e., assessing individuals even if students worked in groups)

Quality and Craftsmanship

- Evidence of revision and quality work
- Reflection on progress and growth

Critical Moves for Deepening Student Engagement

A celebration of learning is not just an event; it is a process. The journey begins with quality learning targets based on state and Common Core standards and ends with high-quality work and students who are well prepared to articulate their learning journey. Student learning is the star of the show. Table 6.2 illustrates the who, what, and why of celebrations of learning as a tool for increasing student engagement and achievement.

Table 6.2 The Who, What, and Why of Celebrations of Learning

What Do Teachers Do?	What Do Students Do?	What's the Result?
Create quality learning targets and assessments based on state and Common Core standards. Plan backward to link celebrations of learning to standards.	Understand that the purpose of a celebration of learning is about showing how they have met standards.	Students are able to articulate how their learning and the celebration of learning are tied to standards. Families and community members see the standards come alive at the celebration of learning.
Choose a structure and format for the celebration (e.g., gallery showcase of student work, presentation for community audience, dramatic performance) and make plans transparent to students.	Invest early in the plan for the celebration of learning and understand the importance of hard work and preparation. Take leadership roles in planning the event.	The plan for the celebration of learning becomes a driving force for engaging students in the curriculum.
Create a schedule and agenda for the celebration of learning that meets the needs of families and community members. Ensure that they feel welcomed and that they understand the learning targets and standards addressed at the event. Create a format that enables audience participation.	Participate in communication with families and community members about the purpose of the celebration of learning. Present high-quality work and explain what they learned in creating it.	Teachers, families, students, and community members understand the purpose of the celebration of learning and the student learning that it represents. They become stronger allies with the school as a result.
Design curriculum that calls on students to develop high-quality work that is worth sharing. Provide a structure for drafting, critique and feedback, and revision.	Invest in doing strong work and putting effort into revision to improve quality.	Students produce high-quality work in preparation for sharing it with a public audience.
Plan a schedule well in advance that includes preparation time for students, communication with families and community members, and setting up and breaking down the event.	Understand how structure and preparation for the celebration of learning will help make it (and the students) successful.	Celebrations of learning are focused and productive and lead to greater student achievement and engagement.

(continued)

Table 6.2 Continued

What Do Teachers Do?	What Do Students Do?	What's the Result?
Plan ample time devoted to practicing (e.g., running through presentations, being a gallery tour guide). Use the Common Core speaking and listening standards (SL.4, SL.6) to develop learning targets for the students' role. Give students multiple opportunities to practice in small groups and to give each other feedback based on criteria for success.	Practice. Provide kind, specific, helpful feedback to peers.	Students are confident in their public speaking skills and can present their own work and that of their peers.
Follow an agenda for the celebration of learning and ensure that students understand their role.	Follow the agenda and use it to support communication of achievement and reflection.	Students are able to articulate their learning and work through a structured process.
Allow ample time to reach out to families and community members. Advance planning will permit maximum participation. Use multiple communication formats (e.g., e-mail, website, phone, mailings) to remind families and community members of upcoming celebrations of learning.	Assist teachers in communicating with families and community members.	Family and community participation at celebrations of learning is high.
Give families the opportunity to provide written feedback. Use questionnaires or comment cards.	Assist in collecting feedback from families and guests.	Families and guests feel encouraged to contribute. Students and teachers use the feedback in the reflection process.
Debrief the celebration of learning with students through group discussion and individual writing.	Participate in the celebration debrief and reflect on ideas for improvement.	Students and teachers share ownership for a successful celebration of learning.

SCHOOLWIDE IMPLEMENTATION

Celebrations of learning are tremendous opportunities to build bridges among the school, families, and the community. A clear vision and strong leadership will help ensure that the events aren't merely celebrations of student *work*, but that they go deeper to celebrate student *learning*. School leaders have an important role to play in setting the vision and connecting celebrations to increased achievement and engagement. It is also important that school leaders hold the logistical vision for the events—everything from setting the calendar, to coordinating staffing, to ensuring that thematic threads are apparent from class to class. In schools where teachers are transforming their classroom events, such as open houses, into more large-scale celebrations of learning, school leaders can help bring lessons learned on this small scale to grease the wheels for schoolwide celebrations. We have highlighted some of the key leadership actions that will support smooth implementation of celebrations of learning throughout a school.

Lay the Groundwork

- Set the purpose and vision for implementing celebrations of learning as part of a student-engaged assessment system. Emphasize the importance of making student learning public.
- Collect data on current communication practices and analyze data with faculty members (e.g., how many families and community members attend school events and celebrations of learning?). Use the data and discussions with faculty members to create a plan and set goals.
- Decide on a calendar and possible themes for schoolwide celebrations of learning. Provide administrative support for organizing, scheduling, and communicating celebrations of learning.

Build Teacher Capacity

- Support teachers to make all public displays of learning, even classroom bulletin boards, reflective of standards and the learning journey. Help all teachers move past displays of work to displays of learning.
- Provide professional development on the connections between celebrations of learning and state and Common Core standards. Help teachers see the celebrations as another way to support students to meet standards.
- Provide the time and materials teachers need to plan celebrations of learning.

Communicate with Stakeholders

- Define and communicate the schoolwide expectations for celebrations of learning to faculty members. Include expectations for student work, involvement, and preparation.

- Communicate the vision for celebrations of learning with families and community members.
- Reach out to key district or charter leaders with special invitations to celebrations of learning.
- Support community and media connections to bring the community into the school and spread the word about the school's success.

Support Teachers to Deepen Their Practice

- Facilitate opportunities, such as a gallery walk structure, for teachers to view and discuss their work. Build traditions and protocols for staff around giving and receiving feedback.
- Document and reflect on celebrations of learning, including successes and challenges. Use these data to grow and improve.

Strategy Close Up: Teacher-to-Teacher Feedback

At Evergreen Community Charter School in Asheville, North Carolina, teachers give each other feedback on their displays prior to the school's annual exhibition night. Teachers use a gallery walk, or walk-about structure, to view all of the displays and then discuss what they see in different classrooms that demonstrate big ideas, guiding questions, and evidence of learning. Teachers complete a response sheet for each classroom they visit. Ona Armstrong, a kindergarten teacher says, "It is a great structure because it is created for teachers and allows us to see the work that is happening in different classrooms and at different grade levels. It is also a great opportunity to give and receive feedback." This structure also helps teachers to make last-minute revisions to displays, documentation panels, and representations of student learning prior to the exhibition night.

Case Study

Improving Teacher Practice through Celebrations of Learning at King Middle School in Portland, Maine

At King Middle School student work is celebrated at a schoolwide celebration of learning where all of the students' work is publicly displayed. Parents, community members, and members of the school department come to see student work and talk to students about it. "It began twenty-two years ago when we had erratic practice here," says principal Mike McCarthy. "We had some teacher practice that was good and some teacher practice that was not very good. One of the purposes of the celebration of learning was to make variance in practice obvious to the staff and obvious to the parents and community members. Whenever teacher practice and teacher work is transparent and public, it improves. It was a strategy to help the school improve by saying here is what we do now and here is where we want to be for all of our teachers and all of our kids."

When King first adopted a project-based approach, it was criticized by some in the community for focusing on having students produce high-quality final products. Once the celebration of learning was introduced that attitude changed. "It became very difficult to criticize because the work on display was clearly good work, had gone through multiple revisions, and was done by 100 percent of the kids. That was a game changer," explains McCarthy.

As celebrations of learning became a tradition at King, it changed the landscape of the school and teachers quickly became aware that reform was happening. Initially teachers were very nervous, and clear parameters needed to be defined. According to McCarthy, "The celebration of learning changed practice because it was a public event. Gaps in teacher practice became obvious, and everyone could see what was happening in classrooms. The idea that this event would happen every year changed the work. We were celebrating our work, but we were also putting a mirror up to our practice."

McCarthy states that there are three reasons to celebrate student work: "To celebrate how well students have done in the classroom and the quality of their work, to improve the practice of the teachers, and to make our universal practice public to other teachers within and beyond the school."

WHAT TO EXPECT

Making learning public at a celebration of learning is an opportunity for students to take pride in their work and demonstrate what they have learned, how they did it, and how it reflects their progress toward meeting standards. For school communities getting started in hosting celebrations of learning, it is important to remember their purpose—to give students the opportunity to reflect on learning. With this in mind, teachers should give themselves permission to start small. Bringing the spirit of what it means to make learning public to a classroom open house (versus a schoolwide event with hundreds of people), for example, is a perfectly acceptable way to start. Focusing students on describing their learning is the key ingredient.

Over time, and especially with support from school leaders, the events can become schoolwide celebrations that involve the community and give students the opportunity to connect across grade levels around common learning themes. Bringing the celebrations into the community—to museums, auditoriums, and other public spaces—is a worthwhile goal because it helps students connect their schoolwork to the work of professionals in the field. Such opportunities help students feel that their community supports their learning.

We have identified some of the benchmarks that teachers and school leaders can expect at the beginning, intermediate, and advanced phases of implementing celebrations of learning in their classrooms and schools.

Beginning

- Teachers and school leaders make the key decisions and set up the structures and systems to support successful celebrations of learning.
- The events may be small at first (e.g., in one classroom during an open house).
- Students have the opportunity to practice presenting their work and learning to an external audience.
- Families and community members receive invitations to the event and participation is good.
- Celebrations of learning are typically held at the school as opposed to other public venues.

Intermediate

- Invitations to celebrations of learning preview high-quality work and emphasize the student learning that will be on display. Students take special care to invite community members and professionals who have helped them improve their work.
- Schoolwide or grade-level celebrations are often connected by a theme or common set of learning goals.
- Students are prepared to talk not only about their own work but also about the work of their peers.

- Students take their work through multiple revisions to ensure that it is high in quality.
- Students engage in various protocols to practice their presentations. They participate in dress rehearsals.
- Rather than just describing their work, students describe their learning.
- Students create documentation panels that tell the story of the learning journey, including standards and learning targets.
- Teachers and students prepare materials that will engage the audience in understanding the student learning on display (e.g., surveys, reflection questions).
- Attendance is high. The community-school relationship is strengthened.
- The celebration of learning may happen outside of the school (e.g., at a local gallery).

Advanced

- Student work is clearly linked to standards, quality assessments, and habits of scholarship.
- Teachers plan backward from the celebration of learning to ensure that the event is a demonstration of student proficiency on standards.
- Students internalize the difference between formal and informal speech (directly tied to Common Core standard, SL.6) and can seamlessly adjust their speaking for a public audience.
- Student presentations of learning reflect deep conceptual understanding. Students are able to think on their feet, respond to questions, and make connections to other areas of study or concepts.
- Students study and understand the professional roles they may play at the celebration of learning (e.g., the role of a docent, the role of a master of ceremonies).
- Teachers' professional growth is supported through reflection on the student learning evidenced through the celebration of learning.
- The celebration of learning communicates the identity and culture of the school.

- Family and community participation remains high. Students, families, and community members understand the purpose and importance of celebrations of learning.

COMMON CHALLENGES

Not Enough Time Allocated to Prepare for the Celebration of Learning

Don't rush it. A successful celebration of learning needs careful planning and cannot be put together at the last minute. The events have multiple components that need to be planned for, including student preparation, communication with families and the community, scheduling, and rehearsing. The purpose and type of the celebration of learning need to be determined early so that they have meaning and can be executed successfully.

Celebrations of Learning That Lack High-Quality Work

High-quality work speaks volumes. An integral part of making a successful celebration of learning is that students share high-quality work that they are proud of. The work should reflect learning targets and standards and be linked to quality assessments and habits of scholarship.

Celebrations of Learning with Poor Logistics, Presentation, and Hosting

No detail is too small. Guests at the celebration of learning should be amazed by how beautifully planned and set up the event is and how gracious and articulate the students are. Celebrations of learning require coordination among teachers, staff, families, and community members. Teachers need to have a clear vision of all parts of the celebration of learning and list and prioritize all of the details. Teams need structures for managing tasks and communication. Schools can incorporate such structures by requiring teachers and teams to account for details and logistics in their planning.

Celebrations of Learning with a Poor Balance of Teacher-Created Displays and Student Work

Keep the focus on the students. Celebrations of learning are not a time for teachers to showcase their ability to create a visually impressive display of student work. It is essential that the displays and performances be visually impressive and of high quality, but it must all be student work. Include students in the creation of displays and other pieces linked to a celebration of learning, such as programs and invitations.

Students Describing Their Work Rather Than Their Learning

Learning is the focus. It is essential that when students talk about their work with their families or other guests that they can describe what they learned, including what standards and learning targets they met. Preparing for the celebration of learning can be a powerful learning experience in its own right, because the connections among lessons, projects, standards, and learning targets are reinforced for students.

Poor Preparation for Public Speaking Requirements

Practice, practice, practice. Celebrations of learning are multifaceted, intensive events. It's easy for teachers and students to find themselves consumed with preparing work products and handling logistics. It's important, however, not to neglect the necessary work that goes into preparing students to be confident and effective public speakers. Students need skill building and practice. It's worth the effort—students will feel prepared, families and community members will be impressed, and teachers will help their students master key Common Core standards.

Neglecting the Debrief

Reflection is important. The power of debriefing the experience as a staff or team should not be overlooked. Reflecting on what worked well and what did not work well helps teachers and school leaders in planning future celebrations of learning. It is also important for students to reflect on their experience. Include their feedback in the teacher debrief.

A Celebration of Learning That Is More Like a Party Than a Reflection on Learning

The event is not the cast party—it is the show. Although suffused with joy and pride, a celebration of learning features students communicating achievement, sharing work, and reflecting on the learning process. Sometimes a reception can follow a presentation that provides students with another opportunity to connect with adults and celebrate success.

A Significant Adult or Community Member Cannot Come to the Celebration of Learning

Always have a plan B. Be flexible and anticipate that some students will not have a parent or significant community member to share their work with. One way to plan ahead is to invite staff members such as guidance counselors, administrators, custodians, office staff, librarians, and enrichment teachers to the celebration and connect them with students who need an audience. Ask students ahead of time to get a head count to ensure that there is an adult for every student. The important thing is that every student has the chance to share his or her work with a significant adult.

Chapter 7

Passage Presentations with Portfolios

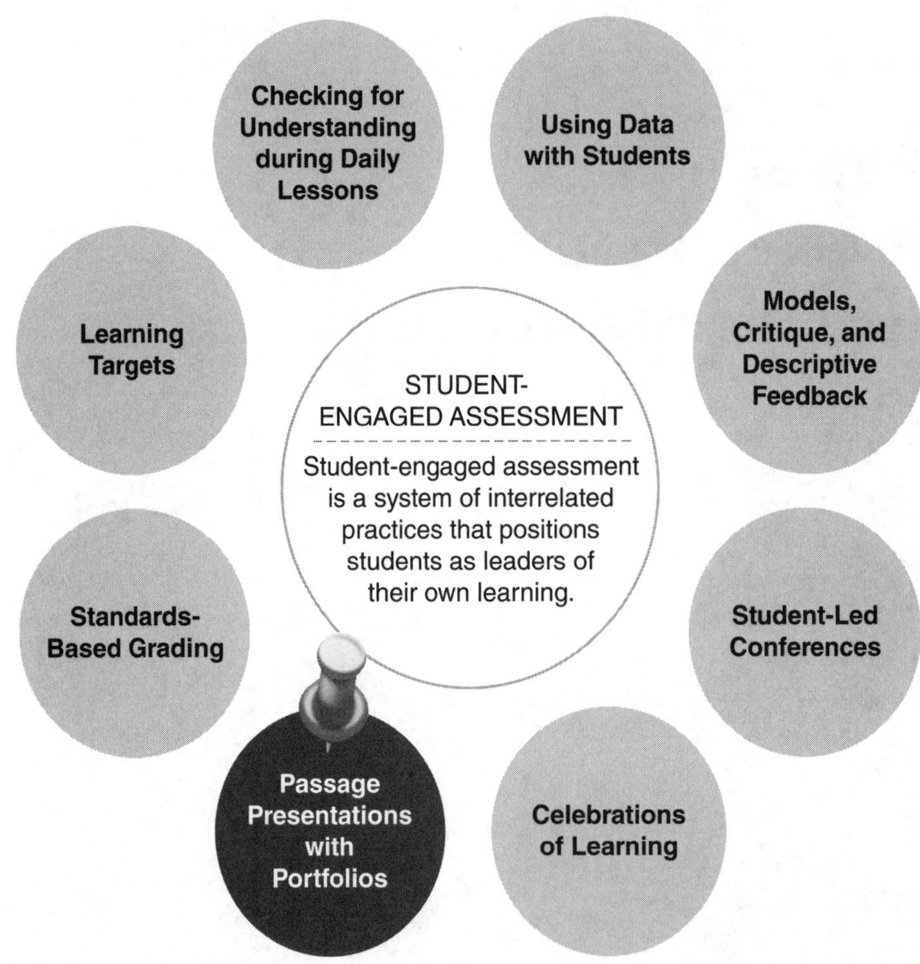
Checking for Understanding during Daily Lessons
Using Data with Students
Learning Targets
Models, Critique, and Descriptive Feedback
STUDENT-ENGAGED ASSESSMENT
Student-engaged assessment is a system of interrelated practices that positions students as leaders of their own learning.
Standards-Based Grading
Student-Led Conferences
Passage Presentations with Portfolios
Celebrations of Learning

There are still towns in the United States where all the students, K–12, go to school in the same place, where one campus houses the elementary, middle, and high school. I was fortunate to work with one such school in a small farming community in upstate New York, where an exciting change was taking place for students. The middle school had decided to implement a new high-leverage practice to raise standards in all subject areas—passage presentations for eighth-graders. In a small town, a new community event like this was a big thing.

From the beginning of the year, the stakes were high. Would they be ready? Would they have high-quality work to show? Would every single student be able to articulate his or her thinking and learning—strengths, challenges, and goals in all subjects—with depth and clarity? Teachers stepped up their game—they improved the quality of their learning targets and the sophistication of their assignments and projects. Students worked harder at everything, always considering what pieces they would be able to show as examples of mastery.

In June, I was a panelist for a full day, sitting with a community member, a teacher, and a high school student, as eighth-graders presented evidence of their learning. Identical presentations were simultaneously going on throughout the library. All day long, I was impressed with the courtesy, seriousness, and honesty of students as they shared evidence of meeting their learning targets and of their readiness for high school. One of the most memorable presentations of the day was by a young man for whom the work had not come easily.

Taylor was a big boy. He entered the room clutching his portfolio tightly. He reached across the table with a giant, calloused hand and shook our hands politely. He was nervous. He opened his portfolio with care and explained to us that he was a "different" learner. He shared that he received significant special education services and that his brain didn't quite work the same as other students. He explained that he worked hard at his academics, but that his work would not look the same as most of what we had been seeing that day. His goal, he said, was to become a car mechanic, like most of his family. He already worked in a repair shop with his relatives.

He shared his work from the year, including clear evidence of meeting learning targets. Near the end, he showed us his research project and presentation on muscle cars. We asked many questions and he was thoughtful in responding to each. At the conclusion of his presentation he looked at us intently. "I have many challenges with my brain," he said, "but I think I can become a productive member of society. I believe I can become a good mechanic—someone you can trust to do a good job. I have promised my family I will make it through high school, and I'm working hard to make sure that I do. I needed help to reach some of my learning targets this year, but I met them." He picked up his portfolio carefully, and shook each of our hands again. "Thank you for taking so much time with me. It means a lot to me that you care how I am doing."

—Ron Berger

Providing Evidence of Growth and Learning

At the end of the school year, students in schools all around the country bring home bags and bags of papers and projects. In some households, mounds of student work accumulate over the years—worksheets and crayon drawings, first attempts at writing, dioramas, models of the solar system, rough drafts and typed essays, vocabulary lists and math problem sets. It is precious material, but it can also be confounding. What does it all say about what a student has learned throughout the year? Can one tell if the student has mastered standards? What does it mean to the student?

Some schools take a different approach. Collections of student work are thoughtfully organized in student portfolios. At the end of the year, instead of bringing home a seemingly random assortment of work, wrinkled and torn from weeks or months at the bottom of a locker or cubby, students can present evidence of their learning in a meaningful way. Portfolios display work that is curated over the course of the year and that illustrates achievement of state and Common Core standards, learning targets, and character growth. Students write reflections on how their work shows evidence of their learning, and they prepare for formal presentations of the portfolios.

A **portfolio** is a selected body of student work—with reflections—that provides evidence of a student's progress toward standards, learning targets, and character growth. **Passage presentations** are benchmark presentations at the end of pivotal transition years (i.e., fifth, eighth, twelfth). During passage presentations, students use their portfolios as evidence to demonstrate their readiness to move on to the next level of their education.

In some schools, portfolios take on a special meaning for students at the end of pivotal transition grades (e.g., primary to intermediate grades, elementary to middle school, graduation). Student portfolios are the anchors for passage presentations during which students—with nervousness, excitement, and pride—stand up before panels that may be composed of teachers, parents, other students, or community members and present evidence of their readiness to move on to the next level of their education. Portfolios and passage presentations, although distinct practices, are complementary—the portfolio is in fact an essential tool in the passage presentation.

Ted Sizer first proposed graduation by exhibition (i.e., passage presentation) in 1984 in his seminal work *Horace's Compromise.* Deborah Meier (1995) and faculty at Central Park East Secondary School in Harlem pioneered the practice in the 1980s and early 1990s. Central Park East students were not certified for graduation simply by minimally passing classes—they had to show evidence that they had learned the key content, concepts, and skills of the disciplines, as well as scholarly habits of mind, by presenting a portfolio of their work to a panel. Almost every student from Central Park East graduated and attended college—a stark contrast to other neighborhood schools—and the structure of portfolio presentations has since spread across the country and internationally.

Together with student-led conferences, celebrations of learning, and standards-based grading, passage presentations with portfolios are a key structure for documenting and communicating learning within a system of student-engaged assessment.

Why These Practices Matter

Passage presentations with portfolios require and empower students to take the lead role in their own learning, building the dispositions and skills they will need to succeed in college and in life. Creating a portfolio and sharing it with a caring but critical audience is a powerful rite of passage for students. It expands the impact of common school passage traditions (e.g., prom, varsity sports) to include ones that celebrate academic growth and achievement, putting scholarship for every student at the center. Passage presentations with portfolios give students the opportunity to demonstrate their achievement and growth and underscore the link among assessment, learning, and student engagement.

Student Engagement

Students in schools of art care deeply about the work they do. They know that their portfolios of work will determine their admission to art programs and future careers. When every student in a school keeps a personal portfolio of his or her academic work across the disciplines, and that work helps determine promotion, graduation, and college acceptance, it has a similar power. Students begin to care much more about quality and take greater pride in their work.

> "The quality of the work goes up when they know that it is going to be shared with a panel of community members."
>
> —*Sally James, fourth-grade teacher, Kettle Falls Elementary School, Kettle Falls, Washington*

Responsibility, Organization, and Decision Making

Students have ownership of much of the process and are required to make many key decisions of what to include in their portfolios and what to share. They are compelled and supported to understand themselves as learners and advocate for themselves, a foundation for college and career success. They learn higher-order skills of metacognition and analysis, because they reflect on their work and learning and assess their own strengths, challenges, and next steps.

A Culture of Evidence

Students are required to provide evidence of their learning and their progress toward state and Common Core standards. This affirms and teaches the evidence-based academic mindset that is at the center of the Common Core. Passing classes is not about pleasing a teacher; it is about providing evidence of understanding and skill.

A Growth Mindset

The first step in building a growth mindset is to help students understand that their brains will grow stronger with practice. Portfolios and passage presentations, with their retrospective focus on growth over time and multiple drafts of work, provide students with evidence that their brains are growing stronger, highlighting the understanding that we all get better at what we do over time, through practice, coaching and critique, and more practice. Students articulate their areas of growth through examining examples of their work and assessments over time, and use this awareness to set goals for future achievement. The portfolios and presentations highlight the character traits—the academic mindsets and learning strategies (e.g., perseverance, collaboration) that are essential for successful scholarship.

Community Pride and Commitment

Passage presentation panels build bridges between the school and community—local civic and business members, community leaders and citizens. Community members take on an authentic, helpful role when they engage with student work. Rather than simply being observers of a school event, community members contribute to the growth of students.

Meaningful Rites of Passage That Celebrate Learning

The most memorable events in the lives of young people and their families are often rites of passage that occur as children grow up. These events—first communions, bar and bat mitzvahs, quinceañeras—are times that relatives come together—to shed proud tears and take photos to frame—to celebrate a child and consider his or her growth. Too often, these rites of passage are related to non-academic pursuits. Passage presentations, however, pull together an audience that includes some of the most important people in a child's life—extended family, friends (within and beyond their grade level), and former teachers—to mark their growth as a person and a young scholar.

Common Core Connections

- Portfolios are archives of evidence of meeting standards. Students own the process of identifying work that demonstrates their learning. Their understanding of and comfort with the standards is heightened as a result.
- Unlike a yearly test, which is divorced from student ownership and reflection, the portfolio provides a clear, ongoing picture for students of what the standards look like when embodied in their own work.
- Passage presentations require that students reflect on their progress toward meeting standards. They can identify strengths and struggles and make plans to ensure they are on target to meet all standards.
- Passage presentations directly meet Common Core speaking and listening standards.

GETTING STARTED

Developing Robust and Dynamic Portfolios

Strong portfolios are key to strong passage presentations. Developing dynamic portfolios that are updated regularly and that paint a picture of student learning over one, two, or three years should be the first priority for schools getting started with passage presentations. The skills of reflection that are necessary to make portfolios truly meaningful and accurate assessments of student learning (e.g., identifying thinking and problem-solving strategies, synthesizing learning, noting patterns and areas of growth) can be nurtured in the youngest of students and gain traction as students grow older. A coordinated, schoolwide approach will produce the best results for students, teachers, schools, and families and will help the practice take root in the school. Whether in the classroom or throughout the school, there are many decisions to make before getting started.

Even the youngest students can use portfolios to mark their growth as learners.

Key Decisions for Portfolios

What Is the Purpose of Keeping Portfolios?

Portfolios are not a new idea in schools; however, they don't always serve the same purpose from school to school. As part of a student-engaged assessment system, their primary purpose is to engage students in assessing their growth and learning. Reflecting on their work and how it demonstrates mastery of or growth toward standards, learning targets, and strong character is primary. It is important for each school to be clear about why it is investing significant time and energy into the practice. What follows is a sample purpose statement.

Purpose of Portfolio—Excerpted from the Passages Portfolios and Presentations Overview of Washington Heights Expeditionary Learning School (WHEELS) in New York City

Our mission at Washington Heights Expeditionary Learning School is for all students to receive a college preparatory education that combines academic rigor with a range of support systems to ensure success. We create a safe, secure, and nurturing environment for adolescents.

At WHEELS, subject area portfolios and Student-Led Conference portfolios are the places where students house evidence of intellectual achievement. Students use these portfolios to present their learning at Student-Led Conferences throughout the year. Teachers analyze those portfolios and other classroom assessments to determine progress toward academic and character learning targets, which they share in report cards and conferences.

WHEELS's Habits of Work and Learning describe aspects of Character that we value in their own right and believe are essential for a student's intellectual achievement and academic success. The Passage Portfolio and Presentation are opportunities for students to showcase their progress and demonstrate readiness for high school success.

What Is the Organizing Principle for Our Portfolios?

Portfolios almost always include an introductory statement or reflection of some sort, but beyond this, there are many choices to be made regarding the organization of the body of the portfolio. They are typically organized in one of the following ways:

- By discipline (e.g., biology, history, music, physical education)

- By student roles that cut across disciplines (e.g., myself as a writer, myself as a historian)
- By habits of scholarship (e.g., collaboration, revision, service)
- By a combination of these three characteristics. Figure 7.1, a sample letter from Genesee Community Charter School in Rochester, New York, describes an organizational structure for portfolios that is a combination approach. In addition to a section that includes work from each academic discipline, students at Genesee write reflections on the history of Rochester; their elementary years; themselves as mathematicians, writers, and artists; and the metaphor that best represents their sixth-grade year.

Within this overarching structure, each section is typically further subdivided. For example, if the portfolio is organized by discipline (or at least has a section that is organized by discipline), a math section might be subdivided by the major standards (often expressed as learning targets) covered during a marking period or year, such as geometric measurement or probability.

What Will Be Included in Our Portfolios?

The first thing to consider is whether the portfolio is a stand-alone document or a tool to aid a verbal presentation. This decision determines a great deal about what goes into the portfolio. A stand-alone portfolio will need written documentation for each piece that describes the reason it was chosen for inclusion, as well as contextualization and reflection. Further explanation of the assignment, as well as rubrics and other criteria, may need to be included. Related to this decision is to what degree the portfolio will give a general overview of a student's performance in a subject versus a snapshot of strong or weak work or work that shows evidence of growth.

Schools should consider the following questions:

- How will students select work for their portfolios? Will they be required to include work that evidences their mastery of specific state or Common Core standards or will they choose the standards to represent within a content area? Are there mandatory pieces from content areas that must be included? The following portfolio checklist is one way to make expectations for what goes into the portfolio clear to students, teachers, and families.

Eighth-Grade Portfolio Checklist—Adapted from the Springfield Renaissance School in Springfield, Massachusetts

Student: ______________________________ Crew: ______________________________

These are things you need to include. They are not necessarily in order.

- ❑ A table of contents
- ❑ A personal reflection letter (letter to high school teacher)
- ❑ College visit reflection
- ❑ A résumé (optional)

Work that shows learning target mastery:

- ❑ A piece of work from ELA with reflection
- ❑ A piece of work from science with reflection
- ❑ A piece of work from math with reflection
- ❑ A piece of work from social studies with reflection
- ❑ A piece of work from elective or intensive with reflection

Work that shows the following qualities of a Renaissance graduate:

- ❑ A piece of work that shows communication with reflection
- ❑ A piece of work that shows craftsmanship and quality with reflection
- ❑ A piece of work that shows creative thinking and expression with reflection

Additional requirements:

- ❑ A binder with a clear plastic sleeve cover to insert name page
- ❑ A decorative name page for front of binder cover
- ❑ Plastic inserts for binder

- Will the portfolio include only final products? What about early drafts and planning documents?
- Will students write reflections for every assignment or rather for learning targets that apply to multiple assignments?
- Should students focus on craftsmanship of the portfolio itself (e.g., create an artistic cover)?
- How will the portfolio be personalized? Is there a student introduction, résumé, or personal or extracurricular information? For example, at Four Rivers Charter Public School in Greenfield, Massachusetts, twelfth-grade portfolios include documentation of a junior internship, a senior learning expedition, best work, and evidence of service and character.

Figure 7.1 Sample Letter to Families Preparing Them for Passage Presentations from Genesee Community Charter School in Rochester, New York

Dear Sixth Grade Families,

The Passage Presentation is a rite of passage for our students as they move from elementary into middle school. The experience gives students an opportunity to reflect on their years at GCCS and on their growth academically, socially, and emotionally. The process helps them gain a greater understanding of themselves as learners and members of a community. The portfolio preparation also gives students experience completing a major individual project.

During the second half of sixth grade, students prepare a number of components for their Passage Portfolio. Students' preparation culminates in a 45-minute presentation to a panel, during which they highlight their accomplishments and share their challenges. The components include:

1. Letter of Introduction to the Community
   This component requires students to write a two-three page letter to the community that describes themselves as individuals and crew members. Students share their assessment of their work habits, their areas for improvement, and their most significant accomplishments to date. Students also explain in what ways they are prepared to be actively contributing members of their community as they move into adolescence and young adulthood.

2. Reflection on the History of Rochester
   GCCS's curriculum focuses on the social, economic, and natural history of the Rochester region, and this component requires students to reflect back on their previous expeditions. Students write a two-three page essay that answers the question, "What do you think was the most important factor contributing to the development of Rochester?" Students may choose one of any number of factors, and then explain how that person, event, movement, or natural resource contributed to Rochester's growth.

3. Reflection on the Elementary Years
   GCCS's program provides students with a range of opportunities designed to deepen their academic and social development. Students write a two-three page essay that answers the question, "What part of your education at GCCS do you think contributed the most to your growth during your elementary years?" This component allows students to reflect upon the experiences they have had and the people they have worked with, and to consider how one of those contributed to their academic and social development.

4. Academic Portfolio
   Students prepare an academic portfolio that includes work samples that demonstrate accomplishment of math, reading, writing, and expedition learning targets.

5. Myself as a Mathematician, Writer, Artist
   Students reflect on their particular skills and approaches to mathematics, writing, and either visual arts, dance, or music. They write a one-two page essay describing their strengths, weaknesses, accomplishments, and dispositions in regards to each of these disciplines.

(continued)

6. Metaphor
   Students create a metaphor to represent their sixth grade year. The metaphor becomes the centerpiece of students' passage presentation; students describe their journey through sixth grade and give examples of how the metaphor illustrates their experience.

Students write most of these components as home learning assignments. Time is set aside each week for teachers to conference with students and monitor their progress. If a particular component seems especially challenging for your child, please alert the teachers so that they may provide extra clarification and assistance.

Portfolios are distributed in advance to the members of the committee. Committee members include at least one current classroom teacher, at least one former teacher, the School Leader or Curriculum Specialist, a Board member, parents, and a community member.

The format of the presentation is:

- Introductions (5 minutes)
- Student description of metaphor (5 minutes)
- Student discussion of academic and social preparedness for middle school (10 minutes)
- Student responds to questions from the Committee (15 minutes)
- Committee deliberates (5 minutes)
- Committee informs student of outcome (5 minutes)

At the conclusion of the presentation, the committee determines if the student has adequately met the criteria of the passage, or if revisions are required. Rubrics have been developed for assessing student performance on the Passage Portfolio and Presentation. Students receive the criteria for "Passed with Distinction," "Passed with Honors," "Passed," and "Failed" as they are given the assignment for each component. Students who fail the Passage are given additional time during the summer to complete this requirement.

We will use the web-based "Sign-up Genius" for the sign-ups for passage presentation times. Here's how:

- Go to www.SignUpGenius.com/
- Enter the password
- Choose your time slot for Thursday, June 9 (There are two slots available at each time)
- Click the "sign up" box
- Click the radio button for "I don't want an account. I'll just enter my name."
- Type your child's name in the box
- Click "sign up"

If you do not have access to a computer, please write your desired time on the attached form and send it back to school with your child.

You will receive a reminder one week before your child's passage presentation.

Thank you!

- Will character growth or habits of scholarship be reflected in the portfolios? Some schools opt to use their habits of scholarship as the organizational structure for their portfolios; others use academic learning targets.
- Will learning that takes place outside the school be included (e.g., jobs, sports, dance, church activities, skills learned from hobbies)? Allowing students to showcase and describe, even briefly, some of their interests or talents that may not be connected to school can add an important component to the portfolios by allowing each student to shine with his or her particular passions. The following snapshot is an example of how one school honored its students' non-academic achievements.

Snapshot: Honoring Students' Achievements outside of School

Within a Flathead Indian reservation in a rural community in Montana is a school that honors the skills and traditions that are important to students outside of school, such as horseback riding, farming, and traditional Indian crafts. When they set up their portfolio system, the faculty members decided that student portfolios should reflect more than just proficiency in core academic subjects. Student portfolios feature knowledge across many dimensions, showcasing talents and interests that are important in their culture. Because of this, student pride and ownership in the process is high.

The school also has a long-standing tradition of excellence in wrestling—photographs of student champions fill the hallways—and, for many reasons, being physically strong is highly valued. The portfolios contain three measures of student fitness—maximum bench press, number of sit-ups in a minute, and time for a mile run. Although these student fitness measures comprise a tiny section of each student's portfolio binder, they are treated with great importance. Visitors to the school are struck by how quickly students—both boys and girls—share their best mile times or bench press numbers, explain their growth since ninth grade, and point out other students in the hallways whose achievements made them proud.

For a student whose passion is piano, computer repair, ballet, basketball, or fishing, the ability to share that passion as a part of his or her portfolio can make all the difference in feeling pride and ownership over the portfolio process.

What Is Our Schoolwide Portfolio System?

Schools should identify how many layers their portfolio system will include. Many schools use working folders in each class or for every subject area. These working folders contain all assignments and reflections and can then be used to pull work from for the more formal portfolio. Schools may also add an additional layer to the passage presentation portfolio for work culled from previous grade-level portfolios. These examples point to the nested layers of expectations and sophistication that can be built into the portfolio system.

Whatever the system, the portfolio should be a living document within the classroom. Students can and should select work, write reflections, and assess progress on an ongoing basis. Portfolios may also include the multiple drafts, self-reflections, feedback, and rubrics to tell the story of the growth of the student as a learner.

> "Our ongoing challenge is trying to make portfolios a living process. Portfolios are not always seen as critical throughout the year, but we are trying to find ways to make them relevant and meaningful on an ongoing basis, not just for student-led conferences or passage presentations."
>
> *—Karen Dresden, head of school, Capital City Public Charter School, Washington, DC*

There are many decisions to make regarding what shape the portfolios will take.

How Will Portfolios Be Used to Teach Reflection?

In order for portfolios to be a tool for student-engaged assessment, including formative and summative assessments, they must be a regular part of classroom conversation, not a static collection of student work. They should be used on a daily or weekly basis for reflections on progress, self-assessment, and ongoing analysis of student work. In this way, they are an important data source for documenting progress. At the Springfield Renaissance School in Springfield, Massachusetts, students follow a structured reflection process that includes these questions:

- What does the learning target mean?
- Describe the work and all the steps that you took to complete the work:
    - What did you have to learn? How did you learn it?
    - What did you have to practice? How did you practice?
    - How did you put the pieces together to complete the assignment?
- What does this piece of work say about who you are as a learner?

How Will Student Work Be Stored in the Classroom or School?

Hammering out the logistical details of how to store, organize, and access student work in the classroom and the school will help the process go more smoothly for students and staff. Some of the key questions include the following:

- Where are portfolios kept in a classroom or school?
- Are portfolios kept across years or sent home each year?
- What kind of binders, folders, bins, or boxes are used?
- Will students use physical portfolios, digital portfolios, or both?
- If portfolios are digital, how will students be supported to manage files effectively? Who will have access to those files?
- How much do students get access to their portfolios? How often do they engage in portfolio tune-ups?
- How is 3D work and multimedia work stored?

Case Study

Making the Key Decisions for Portfolios at Capital City Public Charter School in Washington, DC

At Capital City, every student in grades pre-K–12 has a portfolio. The staff has grappled with many important decisions over the years so that expectations and processes are consistent across the entire school. Head of School Karen Dresden details some of these decisions.

> In order to be successful, portfolios must have rubrics from each piece so students (and teachers) can identify the learning targets and choose appropriate pieces to reflect the mastery of those learning targets. The portfolios are a mix of student-selected pieces, especially in creative writing, and some essential pieces (e.g., one important science project that everyone needs to present).
>
> We have considered the question of how much of the portfolio should be about showing mastery versus showing progress over time. There is always tension there. We have often gone more for mastery at grade-level skills, but I think generally there are a few pieces that we would collect at the beginning and the end to show how students have grown over the course of a grade level. Our early childhood teachers focus more on growth—the teachers have identified that this is incredibly important for that age group.
>
> All portfolios are presented in student-led conferences. Grades 3–12 present in February and June. Students choose three to five pieces that they want to present. There are often two parts to these conferences—one part is the student presenting work and the other part is discussing assessment on standardized measures. Passage presentations are done in eighth and tenth grades. Students are sharing their work, but they are presenting it to a panel and the stakes are higher.
>
> The process of putting together a portfolio, choosing pieces, and then presenting it is a valuable process for students. There is a lot of value in having students return to their work over time and reflect before they present it to an outside audience.

Developing Meaningful Rites of Passage

Introducing passage presentations to a school community signals a commitment to honoring student growth and celebrating rites of passage. For students, teachers, families, and community members, they are highly valued traditions, taken seriously by everyone. Stephen Mahoney, the principal of the Springfield Renaissance School in Springfield, Massachusetts, emphasizes the weight the presentations carry in his school when he recounts the phone call he received one afternoon from a distraught eighth-grader. A rare tornado had just passed through the city and torn the roof off of the community center where the student was playing basketball. His distress that afternoon came not from witnessing such a horrific event, but from the fact that he lost his passage portfolio when his backpack was destroyed by the tornado. We can't underestimate the meaning the presentations can hold for students. To honor the importance of such significant rites of passage, schools must thoughtfully set up the structures and expectations to make them successful.

Key Decisions for Passage Presentations

What Is the Purpose of Passage Presentations?

As with portfolios, schools must determine the primary purpose of passage presentations, of which there may be many:

- To build student investment in high-quality work
- To foster a commitment to schoolwide goals or habits of scholarship
- To build oral presentation skills
- To assess the skills and knowledge of students
- To provide families and communities with an understanding of the standards, learning goals, and habits of scholarship at the school
- To give students an opportunity to synthesize their learning and reflect on their progress
- To require students to demonstrate preparedness to advance to the next level of formal schooling

Articulating the purpose for students, families, staff, and community members is the first step in implementing the practice in a school. The following excerpt of passage objectives is a succinct, clear statement of purpose for staff, students, and families.

Objectives of Passage—Excerpted from the Passage Presentation Handbook of Kettle Falls Elementary School in Kettle Falls, Washington

Objectives of Passage

- To increase student accountability concerning character development
- To hone student verbal communication and critical thinking skills

- To emphasize Kettle Falls Elementary School's philosophy that all students are capable of achieving their CREW learning targets through rigorous academics and service
- To teach students how to use evidence to substantiate their claim that they have met CREW targets

What Is the Overall Vision of Student Success?

In some schools, every student presents his or her portfolio of work at the passage presentation, and as long as it is presented thoughtfully, every student passes (with helpful feedback for future growth). In these schools, students in danger of not being promoted would know well ahead of the passage presentation and would have the opportunity to address the issue(s). In other schools, the process has more teeth to it—there is a reasonable chance that a student will not pass on the first try and will have to revise his or her work. (*Note:* If revision and resubmission of evidence is likely to be a regular occurrence, the school should schedule presentations with substantial time before the year's end to give students the opportunity to revise.) In the accompanying video, we see how three different schools organize and set expectations for passage presentations.

Watch video: "Passage Presentations in Secondary Schools"

What Are the Best Points in Time for Passage Presentations?

Schools should consider how frequently a student will complete a passage presentation. Many schools identify key transition years for the passage process (e.g., elementary to middle school, middle to high school) and others do them at the end of every two-year loop. Schools should also consider if passages are a mandatory requirement for all students or an option for students who wish to meet *exemplary* work.

Who Will Be Part of the Passage Panel?

The panelists can be parents, teachers, other students, and community members. Schools may wish to increase the stakes of passage presentations by changing the panel to include a less familiar and more formal group as students advance in grades. For example, although third-grade passage panels may include a student's teacher, the school principal, and a parent, an eighth-grade passage panel may include a teacher from a different grade level, community members, or district personnel. Parent participation on the panel is an important question to consider. Most schools do not include the student's parent on the panel to prioritize a more objective assessment. In other schools, particularly with younger students, the parent or family member is suggested. Some schools allow an audience of interested spectators—the students' parents and other family members are invited to be part of the audience but not on the panel. Schools may extend this to former teachers or even students who have gotten permission to attend. Schools should also consider the logistics involved in coordinating passage panels:

- How many volunteers are needed from the community for the passage panels?
- How long will panelists have to commit to the passage process?
- Will teachers at the school have time to sit on passage panels?
- Will all students present to the same panel?

As students get older, passage presentations often become more formal.

- Can multiple passage panels take place at the same time?
- Will passage presentations be videotaped?

How Will We Prepare Students for Passage Presentations?

Preparing students for passage presentations should happen throughout the school year. Teachers should help students understand how they will be assessed, analyze examples of strong and weak passage presentations from the past, and give them time to practice for their own presentation. The process of practicing for presentations is also an opportunity for students to practice giving and receiving descriptive feedback, asking strategic questions, and revising their work. Some schools may also identify opportunities for peer feedback between grade levels to have older students mentor younger students in going through the passage process. Many schools support students to talk about their work by creating documents with presentation tips—guidelines for posture, tone, or eye contact, and helpful phrases to describe work (e.g., "I chose this piece because it is a good example of my growth in . . ."; "I want to point out this aspect of the work because it demonstrates . . .").

How Will Passage Presentations Be Structured?

Determine how much time you will need to allocate for the passage presentations and be sure to communicate clearly with panelists about time requirements. An agenda or outline for the presentation will help students plan their time and organize their materials. What follows is a sample outline.

Passage Portfolio Presentation Outline—From the Springfield Renaissance School in Springfield, Massachusetts

Part 1—Introduction (two minutes)

- Crew leader thanks guests for coming and explains the rubric.
- Introduce yourself.
- Explain the purpose of passage portfolios.
- Introduce your invited guests and thank them for coming.

Part 2—Personal Reflection (five minutes)

- Introduction of purpose of reflection (letter to a high school teacher or college essay)
- Reading of personal reflection (probably just pieces of it)

(continued)

Part 3—Presentation of Work (fifteen minutes)

- Explain what this part of the presentation is about.
- For each piece of evidence (choose two or three to discuss in detail here):
  - State the learning target and explain it in your own words.
  - Explain the work in detail and the steps you took to complete the work.
  - Explain what the work shows about you as a learner:
    - How does the work show that you met the learning target? Do some teaching here so your audience sees specific examples from the piece of work. For example, use the whiteboard to show how a Punett square is used to predict offspring traits.
    - How does the work show a Quality of a Renaissance Graduate?

Part 4—Closing Statement (one to two minutes)

- Why I am ready for high school or eleventh grade—explain to your audience how your portfolio proves that you are ready to move on.

Part 5—Questions and Answers (five to ten minutes)

How Will Panelists Be Supported and Their Roles Clearly Defined?

Whether panelists are teachers, family members, students, or community members, they will need support in understanding their roles in the passage presentation. What follows is an excerpt from a letter sent to passage panelists from the Odyssey School in Denver. It outlines the expectations and responsibilities of the panelists.

Passage Presentation Panelist Responsibilities—Excerpted from a Letter to Panelists from the Odyssey School in Denver

A very important responsibility is to honor students by looking carefully at their work and listening to them deeply. You are the authentic audience, and by participating in the process, you give student[s] a chance to prepare and share their work and reflect on their progress in a genuine and formal venue; it is an experience they will never forget.

You will be given a specific protocol to follow with your panel, which will outline a step-by-step process during your two days. However, here's a big-picture overview of your responsibilities:

- Working well with your passage team, upholding Odyssey's norms of:
  - valuing all ideas and questions
  - fostering a safe environment for sharing

- assuming best intent
- being fully present and actively engaged

- Looking carefully at students' portfolios for evidence of the criteria
- Capturing your observations, questions, and targeted suggestions on a provided note catcher that will support each student in preparing for his/her presentation
- Determining the most important questions to ask of each student during his/her presentation linked to each Habit target
- After the presentation, writing a letter to the student following a format provided by the school

The notes you take on your note catcher and the letter you write not only support the student by providing him/her with specific feedback, they are also critical pieces of evidence that help the staff in making their final decision about whether or not the student has qualified for passage.

What Will Be Assessed in the Passage Presentation?

Before embarking on implementing passage presentations, schools need to clearly define what will be assessed and what role the panelists play. It is a given that teachers will assess students' mastery of standards and learning targets—both academic and character learning targets. Some schools also equip passage panelists to assess mastery of standards and academic learning targets. This may require panelists to have time to thoroughly review the portfolio pieces, rubrics, appropriate state and Common Core standards and reflections to help determine if a student has met expectations. Other schools ask panelists to assess oral presentation skills, usually providing rubrics that guide panelists to consider public speaking criteria. Still other schools assess habits of scholarship as demonstrated through student presentations of reflections and portfolio pieces. In a case like this, teachers will assess the portfolio for academic content mastery before or after the presentation, whereas passage panelists are looking and listening for evidence of meeting habits of scholarship (e.g., perseverance, respect, revision).

Once schools are clear on what will be assessed in passage presentations and who will be assessing the presenters (teacher or passage panelists), schools should develop the assessment criteria and tools. Rubrics, checklists, and narrative letters are some examples of how students receive feedback from panel members. Schools should also consider the next steps following this assessment for students who do not meet the criteria for passage. Will students be allowed to redo the passage portfolio and presentation? When will they revise? Will they be allowed to move to the next grade if they do not meet expectations? Is there a ritual or tradition to celebrate students who have passed their passage presentation? How will the passage assessment be communicated to the student, parents, and the district (if graduation or promotion is at stake)?

Table 7.1 is a rubric created by the Springfield Renaissance School that passage panelists use to assess student portfolios. They use a separate rubric for the presentation.

What Happens If a Student Doesn't Pass?

If the passage panel decides that a student has not met the criteria for a quality passage presentation, schools must have a clear process in place to support the student in his or her next step. In some schools, students work with their teacher(s) to revise their passage presentation and then present to another panel at a later date. Other schools craft a contract with the student, parents, and teachers for the next year, stating what needs to be accomplished or demonstrated for that student to master the passage requirements.

Setting Up Structures

In order to ensure student success, teachers must have a clear picture of the structure, process, and expectations for passage presentations and accompanying portfolios. These must be discussed at a schoolwide level so that schoolwide consistencies and grade-level discrepancies can be considered. Once the school structures are in place (e.g., how portfolios will be organized, what a passage presentation entails, how students will be assessed, who will make up the passage panel)—ideally laid out in a handbook—then teachers can develop a plan and timeline to communicate with families and prepare students for portfolios and passage presentations.

Communicate with Families

In some schools, student-led conferences with families will have laid the groundwork for the more challenging, high-stakes process of passage presentations. But when introduced for the first time, passage presentations are very different structures than many families and students are used to. Particularly when the passage presentations have high stakes—movement to the next grade level or

Table 7.1 Tenth-Grade Passage Portfolio Rubric

	4	3	2	1
Table of contents	Table of contents is organized, includes support for required elements, and follows a logical sequence that supports the focus of the student's reflection.	Table of contents is organized and includes all required elements.	Table of contents is inconsistently organized or missing required elements.	Table of contents is incomplete and does not follow any format.
Letter of reflection	Letter contains a thoughtful, well-written reflection of time at SRS, how student has grown, and identifies future goals.	Letter contains a reflection of how the student has grown over the years at SRS and personal goals for the future.	Letter contains some references to the student's growth and either the SRS experience or personal goals.	There is no evidence of the student's reflection on his or her growth.
Up to seven pieces of work revised to high quality	Each piece of work demonstrates mastery of a learning target, is well presented, and has an insightful written reflection.	Each piece of work references a learning target and had a well-written reflection that explains the work.	Portfolio may be missing work and some reflections; work may be disorganized and may not demonstrate mastery.	Portfolio is missing many pieces of work, and reflections lack an explanation about why the work was chosen.
Up to four pieces of work that demonstrate habits of scholarship	Each piece of work demonstrates mastery of a learning target and a well-written reflection that explains a clear connection to the chosen criteria.	Each piece of work presents course work and its relation to a learning target. The reflection explains a clear connection to the chosen criteria.	Each piece of work presents course work and a reflection that may not make a connection to one of the required criteria.	Work is missing and may not clearly identify the learning target. The reflection is either missing or shows no connection to required criteria.
Résumé	Résumé is well organized, including support for all elements.	Résumé is consistently organized, including all elements.	Résumé is inconsistently organized or missing elements.	Résumé is incomplete and does not follow any format.
General résumé and table of contents appearance and organization	Binder is complete, presentable as a published piece of work, organized as described in the table of contents, and shows attention to detail and audience.	The binder is complete, presentable, organized as described in the table of contents, and shows respect for work and the audience.	The binder is mostly complete and presentable.	The binder is missing components, lacks organization, or may not demonstrate respect for the work or the audience.

Source: Springfield Renaissance School.

Investment from families is key to a successful launch of passage presentations.

graduation—families will need lots of up-front information to build their understanding and support. From the beginning, it is important for schools to inform families about the vision and plan for passage presentations so they know why they are important and what to expect. Clear guidelines, together with a flexible approach, will lead to high attendance and investment in the process. The sample letter to families in figure 7.1 is a good example of how schools can inform and support families.

Preparing Students to Develop Strong Portfolios

Teachers should introduce portfolios to students at the beginning of the year, explaining how they will be organized and how students will gather work to fit within that organization (e.g., by academic learning targets). The teacher must explain which things are required components of the portfolio and which are up to the students, outline expectations for craftsmanship, and review the audiences and purposes for the portfolio.

Teachers should provide space and materials for students to collect evidence of their learning and store it in working folders or binders. Many classrooms establish a set time each week for students to move work from working folders into portfolios, write reflections, and self-assess work using rubrics.

Before student-led conferences, passage presentations, or other portfolio-sharing forums can occur, students will need practice presenting their portfolios. A structure of peer feedback can be helpful.

Preparing Students for Passage Presentations

As discussed previously, preparation for passage presentations should be ongoing throughout the passage year. When implementing passage presentations for the first time, teachers should introduce the plan in the beginning of the year and ensure that students are clear about the expectations and purpose. If possible, it helps to show students videos of passage presentations from previous years. They may benefit from looking for evidence of past students meeting the Common Core speaking and listening anchor standard, SL.4: *Present information, findings, and supporting evidence such that listeners can follow the line of reasoning and the organization, development, and style are appropriate to task, purpose, and audience.*

If special pieces, such as résumés, are required as part of the passage presentation, students will need clear criteria and time for developing them. Teachers should review the criteria that will be used to assess passage presentations and accompanying portfolios and create a schedule for peer critique and one-on-one conferences to ensure that all students are ready for their passage presentations.

> "It has been really helpful to videotape exemplars from previous years to give students strong models of passages and portfolio conferences in action."
>
> —*Karen Dresden, head of school, Capital City Public Charter School, Washington, DC*

Figure 7.2 is a reflection letter guide developed by the Springfield Renaissance School in Springfield, Massachusetts. This guide includes all of the required components of the letter as well as helpful questions to guide student reflection.

Figure 7.2 Sample Reflection Letter Guide from the Springfield Renaissance School in Springfield, Massachusetts

The Springfield Renaissance School
10th Grade Passage Portfolio Reflection Letter Guide

(Use these questions to help organize your thinking for your reflection letter.)

Address your letter to the faculty and the community at large. This is an application for the additional freedoms and responsibilities of upper division.

Your letter must include:

- Self-introduction
- Why you chose this school
- Effect of OB/fieldwork/intensives/expeditions/kickoffs/other EL structures on your growth
- Analysis of self as learner – strengths and weaknesses and strategies learned and support needed
- Strongest/most growth character trait
- Analysis of your Habits of Work
- Long terms goals – (upper division years/college/career)

Use these questions to help guide your letter.

Who are you?

Why are you at the Springfield Renaissance School rather than another high school?

Think about the Outward Bound trip, fieldwork, intensives, expeditions, kickoffs – which has been the most valuable/important for you?

Tell one story about your learning target performance from freshman year. What did you do? How did you grow?

Tell one story about your learning target performance from sophomore year. What did you do? How did you grow?

In which of the character traits are you the strongest? In which of the character traits have you shown the most growth? Tell a story that provides evidence.

In which of the Habits of Work are you the strongest? Which of the Habits of Work is the most challenging for you? Give an example.

Who are you as a learner? What are your strengths and weaknesses? What strategies have you learned? What support do you still need to be successful?

Imagine yourself in your last two years of high school, in college, in your life after college. Describe one or two long term goals – where you're preparing to be and when. Long term can be upper division high school, college or career.

2008 – 2009

IN PRACTICE

Deepening Student Reflection and Learning

There are many logistical details and challenges involved in the early stages of passage presentations. As those are resolved and implementation becomes smoother, schools have an opportunity to deepen student reflection and learning through the passage presentation process.

The following sections—creating a developmental progression of portfolio and passage presentation requirements, using portfolios as a tool for college admissions, using technology strategically, and linking portfolios and passage presentations to standards—are all facets of taking portfolios and passage presentations to the next level.

Creating a Developmental Progression of Portfolio and Passage Presentation Requirements

As students progress through the grades, it is important that portfolios and passage presentations evolve with them and challenge them in new ways. The practices will lose their power if students feel that they are going through the motions of a tradition that does not have meaning. Striking the right balance of celebrating and reflecting on progress throughout the year and challenging students to push themselves academically and personally is key.

The primary and early elementary grades are a natural place to introduce reflection and instill in students the habit of collecting work that demonstrates evidence of learning and growth. Simple reflection sheets completed at the conclusion of lessons or assignments can help students get into the practice of reflecting on what they've learned and setting goals for improvement. Figure 3.5, "Sample Goal-Setting Worksheet," is a good example. In the later elementary grades, schools may place a greater emphasis on standards and learning targets as students gain understanding of the standards and what mastery means. Table 7.2 shows one set of character learning targets from the Odyssey School that illustrates the developmental progression from second grade to eighth grade and focuses on evidence, a key to meeting Common Core standards. Odyssey organizes their passage presentations around these character learning targets and students reflect on them during the presentation.

The Springfield Renaissance School, which organizes their passage presentations around a combination of academic and character learning targets, decided after a few years of passage presentations at the eighth- and tenth-grade levels that the tenth-grade students were not being challenged enough. As a result, they

Table 7.2 Sample Habits of Scholarship Targets

Inquiry	
Grades 2–3	Grades 2 and 3 teachers are responsible for introducing the inquiry process to students. Students will be able to name the process that learners go through when studying a topic deeply: develop questions, find resources, develop conclusions, and report conclusions.
Grades 4–5	I can pose quality questions that help me study a topic deeply. I can find resources that help me confirm or deny my theory. I can interpret the information that I have. I can report and defend my findings to an outside audience.
Grades 6–8	I can develop deep, probing questions and theories based on initial research and background knowledge. I can locate diverse and quality resources that help me answer my questions and deepen my understanding. I can evaluate and synthesize the information and evidence I found. I can report findings in a way that helps my audience access the information.

embarked on a pilot program with fifteen to twenty tenth-graders. To engage these older students on a deeper level, they added a physical challenge and a service challenge to the passage requirements. Students were required to conduct twenty hours of community service and set a serious physical goal for themselves that would improve their health. They then wrote reflections about how their efforts with these challenges reflect the qualities of a Renaissance learner:

- Inquiry and investigation
- Critical thinking and analysis
- Creative thinking and expression
- Problem solving and invention
- Communication
- Craftsmanship and quality

In addition, they instituted a new requirement for all tenth-grade students that they write a college essay in English language arts class to be used as an opening for their passage presentation. The requirements of this pilot became standard for all tenth-graders the following year.

As students make the important personal transitions from childhood to adolescence and adolescence to young adulthood, the rite of passage dimension of the passage presentation often takes more prominence. Rather than diluting academic challenge, adding adventure, service, artistic, or physical challenge components to portfolios and passages presentations at key developmental stages affirms the multi-dimensional reality of students' experience.

The composition of passage presentation panels is another vehicle for increasing the challenge and rigor of the learning experience over time. Beginning with panels of classroom teachers and parents, schools add layers of formality and challenge with teachers who do not teach the presenter, students from earlier grades, and outside experts from the community.

The following case study from Four Rivers Charter Public School in Greenfield, Massachusetts, exemplifies the school's special efforts to challenge seniors in new ways as they prepare for the most important passage of their schooling thus far: graduation from high school.

"I like to see an overall progression in student ownership from ninth through twelfth grades, when students build reflection and presentation skills. Ninth- and tenth-grade students get direct support in constructing and presenting a quality portfolio and upperclassmen have more autonomy on what and how they present. The crew leader becomes the guide in the higher grades."

—Eric Levine, instructional guide, Tapestry Charter School, Buffalo, New York

Case Study

A Progression of Portfolios and Passage Presentations at Four Rivers Charter Public School in Greenfield, Massachusetts

At Four Rivers, portfolios and passage presentations are organized around and framed by the portraits of a Four Rivers graduate: investigators, critical thinkers, creative thinkers, problem solvers, and communicators. Passage presentations take place in eighth, tenth, and twelfth grades.

The eighth-grade passage presentation, framed by the questions, "Who are you? What shapes you? Who do you want to be?" is called the rite of passage. This presentation is the culmination of a yearlong investigation of transformation in all academic disciplines. The audience consists of teachers, parents, community members, and additional audience members selected by the student.

(continued)

The tenth-grade passage presentation is framed by the question, "Who are you becoming and what's next?" The faculty members have recently worked to ensure that the tenth-grade presentations build on the eighth-grade experience. Previously the process was very prescriptive—all students answered the same questions—and every passage presentation sounded alike. Now the students are required to generate the questions. As Susan Durkee, assistant principal and cofounder, puts it, "When everyone follows the prescription, it's like reciting vows that don't have any personal meaning. We want kids to write their own vows."

Senior year is the culmination of the portfolio and passage progression at Four Rivers. Beginning in eleventh grade, Durkee says, students start to work on a mastery—or graduation—portfolio. "They pick their best work that illustrates the schoolwide learning targets. They learn to talk about the work and learning all along the way, but twelfth grade is mastery more than process."

The senior learning expedition is the central focus of the graduation portfolio. From the senior expedition guide comes this description:

> Four Rivers strives to graduate and promote students based on what they actually know and can do. That's what you've been showing us through years of Passage Portfolios and Presentations. A successful Senior Expedition is a graduation requirement, but more important, it is an opportunity to demonstrate your highest level of learning at Four Rivers. Senior expedition is about learning through your interests and building your skills as a more independent learner. It's about choosing a field and defining a problem, a concern or an idea that is of importance to you, becoming a budding expert in your chosen field, and creating solutions.
>
> **The Basic Requirements**
>
> - Choose a topic that interests you.
> - Develop essential questions around it.
> - Learn all about your topic and become an expert on it.
> - Further develop your knowledge through fieldwork and hands-on experiences and use it to create something useful.
> - Give a presentation to the community on what you have learned, how you learned it, and what you did with your knowledge.
> - In all aspects of this expedition, you are to demonstrate excellence—what we for years have been describing as high-quality work.

As Durkee describes it, the senior learning expedition is a powerful culminating academic assessment confirming graduates' abilities to conduct independent research and present findings. However, staff found there was a missing dimension—it was too much about the project, and not enough about where students were ending up as people. Drawing on what the school learned from fellow EL Education schools, Casco Bay High School in Portland, Maine, and Codman Academy in Boston, they created a "final word" reflection as a requirement of the senior passage presentation. Students needed to address the question, "How do you see the seeds of your future self in what you have done?"

Durkee explains, "The presentation of the senior learning expedition starts with an overview of 'Here's what I set out to do' and an overview of themselves (i.e., what I know about myself and why I chose this topic). They present their project and product and share the process. There's applause and they take some questions. Then they show their portfolio. Finally, they step back and add the new part—the 'final word.' It's a written piece that they also deliver as a speech. One thing seniors were concerned about was would they receive a written grade for the 'final word'? We'll say no for now, but the piece has to be real and substantial. When they're done this year, students and staff will get to weigh in whether or not the 'final word' should be graded going forward. We videotape each presentation to use for critique, reflection, and revision of process."

Using Portfolios as a Tool for College Admissions

The work that students put into developing and maintaining a portfolio that reflects their growth and learning over time is substantive. A portfolio prepared for a senior passage presentation may well be the best collection of work a student will ever compile. Full of high-quality work, thoughtful reflections, and evidence of rigorous learning, such a portfolio should be considered a tool for students to bring along to college admissions interviews or to draw from when writing applications. The portfolios can be organized to include all of the information a college admissions counselor would want to see and students should start creating them at the start of ninth grade.

At Harborside Academy in Kenosha, Wisconsin, the introduction alone of the tenth-grade passage portfolio includes a four-year plan, transcript, a résumé, and a reference letter. The portfolio also houses all state assessment results, ACT scores, examples of work that meets learning targets, character statements, and academic reflections. Students write profiles of themselves as writers and readers and reflect on such skills as their scientific literacy and historical knowledge. It is a comprehensive profile of nearly everything a college needs to know to determine a student's readiness for the next level of his or her education. Schools will do their students a service by considering the college admissions officer a target audience for students' passage portfolios.

Using Technology Strategically

Technological tools have the potential to enhance portfolios and passage presentations—they build student skills with presentation software and design, add interest for students drawn to the tools, and can be a solution for schools that want to store student work from previous years, but don't want to take up physical space to do so. It is also necessary for all students, K–12, to meet the Common

When used strategically, technology can add depth to passage presentations.

Core writing anchor standard, W.6: *Use technology, including the Internet, to produce and publish writing and to interact and collaborate with others.* Portfolios and passage presentations are a perfect opportunity for students to meet these standards and to approach technology each year with the increased sophistication and skill demanded by the standards. But there are also potential pitfalls—an over-reliance on tools may detract from quality reflections or bog down the process for those less adept. It is important for schools to weigh the pros and cons of this approach.

Snapshot: A Technology Evolution at Tapestry Charter School in Buffalo, New York

Tapestry Charter School has gone through distinct phases in using technology to develop their portfolio and passage presentation system. Students go through passages in tenth and twelfth grades. At first they used three-ring binders for their passage portfolios, but they wanted to have a more professional structure, so they decided to switch to a web-based passage portfolio.

They first used iWeb, an Apple product, but it was so slick that student portfolios sometimes looked deceptively good. Also, the staff began to feel that the process was too cumbersome. Students spent too much time scanning and uploading documents and not enough time on the presentation itself. As a result, they decided to switch the platform again—this time to Google Apps.

After five years of doing tenth-grade portfolios and passage presentations this way, they again realized that some of the embedded components of the passage presentations, such as the oral defense of their readiness for the next phase of high school, were being overshadowed by technology. They switched to Prezi presentation software and have been happy with the professional, authentic look of student presentations. As Eric Levine, Tapestry's instructional guide, put it, "In the future, students will need to use a variety of software and other tools for presenting information. Prezi is one of many dynamic choices in a larger toolkit for communication that will keep growing. This is an important college- and career-readiness connection for our students."

Linking Portfolios and Passage Presentations to Standards

All parts of a student-engaged assessment system should be integrated and relate clearly to standards. A standards-based grading system ensures that grades clearly reflect whether or not students have mastered the standards (see chapter 8 for more information). Standards-based grades should also be aligned with assessments of portfolios and passage presentations. It sounds self-evident, but it takes time and is quite complex. Often portfolios remain supplemental tools for reflection rather than core to standards and assessment. The following activities offer different ways of linking the portfolios more closely with standards and other assessments.

Organize Portfolios by Grade-Level Standards

"In the video, 'Kindergarten Student-Led Conference,' first referenced in chapter 5, we see kindergartner Trinity from Delaware Ridge Elementary School in Kansas City, Kansas, walking her parents through her portfolio during her student-led conference. In the reading section, she reads the learning target, "I can stretch out words to hear all the sounds," which corresponds to Common Core phonics and word recognition standards for kindergartners. The paper in her portfolio includes her careful spelling of the word *egg*, which she reads slowly to her parents, stretching out each sound: *e-g-g*.

The portfolios and passage presentations that most clearly demonstrate mastery of standards are organized by standard as opposed to being organized by subject or some other structure. If portfolios are organized around character learning targets or habits of scholarship, the connection to academic standards must be clear. For example, it is important to avoid a situation in which a student who is not meeting standards in writing or mathematics is assessed as *exemplary* for a portfolio organized around character learning targets. Table 7.2 is a good example of character learning targets that are closely aligned with the academic rigor of the Common Core.

Ensure You Have Benchmark Exemplars

One way that schools deepen the alignment of portfolios, passage presentations, and standards is by documenting benchmark exemplars of work that reflects key standards. Archives of exemplars can be used as models to guide student work. This is helpful to teachers and students. For teachers, the conversations required to determine which exemplars reflect a particular standard are key to ensuring that everyone shares the same understanding of the standards at each grade level. This goes a long way to ensuring a consistent portfolio and passage presentation approach from class to class and grade to grade. Questions to consider include the following:

- What does *quality writing* look like in ninth grade versus twelfth grade?
- What is an exemplar of work that meets a standard of *proficiency?*
- What is an exemplar that shows how a student may *exceed* a standard?

Particularly when passage presentations have high stakes (such as moving on to the next grade level), this is a critical activity.

The goal of these practices always is to engage students more deeply in understanding the standards and applying them to their own work and learning. Examining exemplars that reflect standards is a way of making the standards real and concrete for students.

Use Learning Target Trackers and Rubrics to Guide Students' Creation of Portfolios

Learning target trackers—on which students record their progress toward meeting learning targets—and rubrics can help flesh out students' understanding of standards and guide them in making selections for their portfolios. Because trackers capture the different stages in a student's effort to meet a particular learning target or standard, they are valuable tools for capturing the learning process. Students can see, for example, that an initial draft reflected a lower rating on the rubric and through revision a higher score was earned.

Critical Moves for Deepening Student Engagement

Passage presentations, with their accompanying portfolios, are opportunities for students to present evidence of their learning and their progress toward meeting standards to an important audience. They have student engagement at their core. Students make the key decisions about what evidence to include and make connections between their experiences and their learning. Table 7.3 illustrates the

Table 7.3 The Who, What, and Why of Portfolios and Passage Presentations

What Do Teachers Do?	What Do Students Do?	What's the Result?
Define a clear purpose and organizing structure for portfolios that is linked to learning targets and state and Common Core standards.	Understand that each lesson and learning activity is connected to learning targets, and that their portfolios will document their progress in meeting them.	Students meet standards and have greater engagement and ownership of learning. Students can use their portfolios as a body of evidence to demonstrate meeting standards.
Engage students in classroom discussion about how and why portfolios will be created. Examine benchmark exemplars together.	Participate in classroom discussions and understand how to show evidence of meeting learning targets in a portfolio.	Students understand the purpose of portfolios and what it means to provide evidence of learning.
Determine how habits of scholarship and out-of-school or elective pursuits will be documented in the portfolio.	Engage in selecting evidence of their progress in habits of scholarship and out-of-school interests.	Students grow more committed to character learning targets because they are expected to document evidence of meeting them. They feel that their interests and passions are valued at school.
Prepare students to be reflective about their work and learning. Make reflection an ongoing classroom practice—set up daily or weekly reflection times and a reflection form or template.	Engage in reflection and set goals for improvement.	Over time, students' reflections grow deeper and more self-aware. The results can be seen in improved achievement and engagement.
Create a structure and space for students to begin building portfolios and collecting evidence of their learning.	Take responsibility for the creation of their portfolios, taking care to select and keep good evidence of their learning.	Over time, portfolios become anchor points in the classroom, frequently referenced and reflected on. A culture of evidence is fostered.
Determine how portfolios will be shared: frequency, format, and audience. Create a passage presentation process as a culminating structure for sharing portfolios.	Develop ownership of their portfolios and skill in presenting them to a variety of audiences.	Students are more engaged in the portfolio process when they have experience sharing them with meaningful audiences.

(continued)

Table 7.3 Continued

What Do Teachers Do?	What Do Students Do?	What's the Result?
Plan a schedule for passage presentations well in advance that includes preparation time for students, communication home, and presentations with debriefs. Define clear guidelines for panelists' role in passages.	Understand how structure and preparation of the passage presentation will help make it productive.	Passage presentations are focused and productive and lead to greater student engagement and achievement.
Allow ample time to reach out to passage panelists and schedule the presentations at times that work for them. Use multiple communication formats (e.g., e-mail, website, phone, mailings) to remind panelists of upcoming presentation times.	Assist teachers in selecting and inviting panelists.	Participation on passage presentation panels is a positive experience for the panelists.
Develop learning targets for the passage presentation tied to Common Core speaking and listening standards (SL.4, SL.6), develop criteria for a successful presentation, and review roles with students. Plan at least one class devoted to modeling a presentation. Allow students to practice and give and receive feedback.	Engage in preparation for the passage presentation and understand their role in making it a success.	Students have a clear understanding of their role in the presentation and are confident and well prepared.
Prepare panelists for their role with oral and written guidelines.	Interact with panelists with impeccable courtesy.	Panelists feel valued and prepared.
Give panelists the opportunity to provide written or verbal feedback. If a student does not pass a passage presentation, make sure the follow-up steps are clear and actionable.	Students listen to feedback and use it to frame goals or, if necessary, to make revisions.	Panelists feel encouraged to contribute and participate—they understand that students will be held accountable for their work. The relationships among families, communities, teachers, and students are strengthened.
Debrief the passage experience with students through group discussion and individual writing. What aspects of the format worked well? What did they learn? What could be improved?	Participate in the passage presentation debrief and share ideas for improvement.	Students and teachers share ownership for effective passage presentations.

who, what, and why of passage presentations with portfolios and their power to increase engagement and achievement.

SCHOOLWIDE IMPLEMENTATION

Implementing passage presentations requires strong leadership. The practice demands schoolwide consistencies and clear communication with families, particularly if passages determine whether or not a student moves on to the next grade or graduates. Leaders must present a strong rationale—tied to increased engagement and achievement—and hold everyone accountable for his or her part in the process. Frequent opportunities to reflect on implementation and ask probing questions with the staff about the efficacy of the practice are important. Does the organizational structure chosen for portfolios make sense (i.e., by learning targets versus content areas, the frequency of updates, how and when the portfolios are used in classrooms)? Do any shifts or revisions need to happen? After the first round of passage presentations, it's important to consider how the process can be improved for the next time. Was the panel composed of the right people? Were students sufficiently challenged? Did they present evidence of their growth and learning? We have highlighted some of the key leadership actions that will support smooth implementation of passage presentations throughout a school.

Lay the Groundwork

- Start with the standards. Provide professional development time for teachers to know them deeply and understand what it means for students to demonstrate mastery.
- Set the vision and create the sense of purpose for passage presentations and portfolios. Embed the practices in a broader plan for student-engaged assessment and make the link to standards clear. Lead faculty discussions on the criteria for passage and how students will be held accountable.
- Create a master schedule that allocates time for planning, preparation, and implementation of passage presentations.
- Provide necessary supplies and equipment for collecting and storing portfolios (e.g., folders, boxes, online portfolios).
- Collect data on current assessment and communication practices and analyze data with faculty members (e.g., how many teachers currently use work folders

and reflection strategies with students? Goal setting?). Use the data and discussions with faculty members to create a plan.

- Create a clear progression and alignment of portfolio and passage presentation requirements across the grade span of the school.

Build Teacher Capacity

- Provide models of portfolio systems and presentation structures from other schools to jumpstart the planning process and clarify the vision with concrete examples.
- Ensure that teachers have time and support to craft long-term and supporting learning targets from standards and to align the portfolios and passage presentations with the learning targets.
- Create professional development time and support for teachers to prepare for portfolios and passage presentations and to create the necessary tools (e.g., rubrics, letters to families).
- Create time and structure for faculty members to share sample portfolios, presentation videos, student reflections, and benchmark exemplars. What is the quality of student work and reflection? Do the faculty members agree on what it means to provide evidence of mastery?

Communicate with Stakeholders

- Communicate with families early and often. Encourage all families to attend as panelists or audience members, depending on the structure for family involvement set up by the school.
- If failure is an option (i.e., students risk not being promoted if they fail the passage presentation) make sure that families are well informed, well ahead of the event. Provide families and students with all necessary information to meet requirements ahead of time and, if the student cannot meet the requirements, options for remediation after the fact.
- Invite community members to be a part of the passage process and provide them with information about the expectations for their participation.
- Consider inviting district or charter leaders to participate on panels.

Support Teachers to Deepen Their Practice

- Support a portfolio culture throughout the building by incorporating student portfolio evidence into discussions and decisions about curriculum, instruction, and student achievement. Consider using teacher portfolios as a tool for supervision and evaluation.
- Celebrate success. Track data about portfolios and passage presentations and document successes as well as challenges. Share student, family, and community stories and insights.
- Facilitate faculty member conversations about lessons learned from implementing portfolios and passage presentations—themes that emerge from the work students present and ways to strengthen the process.
- Analyze passage presentation video clips during professional development time and create a process for peer observation.

WHAT TO EXPECT

Passage presentations are a fairly advanced student-engaged assessment practice, built on a foundation of student reflection, alignment of learning targets and assessments, and the dynamic use of portfolios. Because they are such powerful traditions for students and families, they deserve intensive preparation. A well-tended (i.e., regularly updated) portfolio of student work, including rubrics, reflections, and evidence of meeting standards, is essential to success with this practice. Students must be able to use their portfolio of work—which sometimes contains work spanning two or three years—to demonstrate evidence of their readiness for passage.

Schools just getting started with this practice should focus first on developing a robust portfolio practice. With this in place, passage presentations can be tailored in many ways to honor different aspects of students' lives in addition to their academic growth and achievement, such as athletic or artistic accomplishments, habits of scholarships, and interpersonal relationships. As schools gain experience with passage presentations, these kinds of decisions will strengthen the experience for everyone involved.

We have identified some of the benchmarks that teachers and school leaders can expect at the beginning, intermediate, and advanced phases of implementing passage presentations with portfolios.

Beginning

- Basic portfolio processes are established and students have regular opportunities to update and reflect on evidence of their learning.
- Teachers and students have rich conversations about state and Common Core standards and what evidence of proficiency looks like. Student portfolios and passage presentations clearly reflect evidence of meeting standards.
- Students practice their presentations with teachers and each other.
- The school communicates early and often with families about the passage process, particularly when there is a possibility that a student will not pass.
- Family attendance at passage presentations is high.
- School leaders, teachers, and students debrief the passage process and make adjustments as necessary.

Intermediate

- Student reflections on their strengths and struggles lead to new learning goals and personal growth.
- Teachers and school leaders have conversations about the evidence of student achievement observed through the passage process and the implications for instruction.
- Students and panelists are well prepared for passage presentations and understand their roles. Panelists ask probing questions and are prepared to assess students in pre-identified areas.
- New teachers are introduced to the portfolio and passage presentation system early on and are supported in implementing it.

Advanced

- A growing archive of exemplars of student work at different benchmark levels support students to show evidence of meeting standards in their portfolios and passage presentations.
- Students engage in deep reflection on their progress toward learning targets and standards in all classes and stages of curriculum.
- Students take greater ownership of their portfolios, updating them, and making key decisions independently.

- The school increases the challenge and rigor of the process as students get older—they present their portfolios to a wider range of panelists, such as older students, future teachers, and community members, and they include increasingly sophisticated work in the portfolio and presentation.
- All of the forms of communicating learning—standards-based grading, student-led conferences, celebrations of learning, and passage presentations with portfolios—are aligned and reflective of a deep understanding of standards.

COMMON CHALLENGES

Confusion over Goals or Organization of Portfolios

Purpose and learning targets must be clear. The evidence collected in a portfolio should reflect mastery of or progress toward learning targets that the students understand. Whether the portfolio is organized by academic learning targets alone or by habits of scholarship (or both), the student's reflections should make clear connections between the evidence and the learning targets.

Portfolios That Teachers Care about, but Students Do Not

It's all about the students. Students should consider themselves the authors of their own portfolios. For portfolios to serve as a record of learning and a dynamic snapshot of students' lives, students must have a sense of ownership over the process. Although there are some non-negotiable items students must include, many of the aesthetic decisions about the portfolio and its assembly may be left entirely to students. The portfolios should not be entirely dry and generic—personal touches (e.g., journals, creative writing, personal photos, accomplishments in sports and arts, outside interests, and talents) can help students feel ownership.

Lacking Meaningful Work

Work must be worthy. For student work to serve as evidence of mastery of standards and learning targets, the work must not only be high quality but it must also demonstrate the learning that brought students to achieve this work. As such, not every piece of good work satisfies these criteria. The selection process for including work in a portfolio requires addressing a cycle of questions: Does the work demonstrate mastery of a standard or learning target? Which standards or learning targets does the work show mastery of? Does the work provide evidence of the learning involved in mastering the standard or learning target?

Reflection as Afterthought

Make reflection truly a daily practice. Portfolios can't sit on a shelf all semester and get pulled out for a presentation at the end—they should be living parts of classroom practice—used often for reflection and discussion and tuned up regularly. If reflection is saved for the end of the learning process and reserved for final portfolio preparation it will lack depth and quality.

> "One area we are working to improve is to link day-to-day instruction to the reflection process. It always seems like a rush at the end to get reflections done and, if the work was completed a while ago, the reflection is not fresh and sometimes not authentic feeling."
>
> —*Eric Levine, instructional guide, Tapestry Charter School, Buffalo, New York*

Students Describe the Work Rather Than How Work Reflects Learning

Focus on the learning. Describing the work is a natural pitfall, and one teachers should expect to address regularly as students develop their portfolios. It is understandable, particularly within a school culture that values high-quality student work, that students will tend to showcase the work as opposed to the learning that went into the work. To keep portfolios from becoming static repositories, remind students at frequent intervals about the purpose of portfolios as a record of learning, perhaps instructing students to answer this question for each piece: What skills and content did I need to master in order to produce this work? Regular reflections on work and learning help students to consider growth and progress. Finally, showing students models of portfolios that underscore these differences will provide the clearest demonstration of all.

Not Allocating Enough Time to Plan and Prepare

Time is of the essence. Neither portfolios nor passage presentations can be thrown together at the last minute. Each requires forethought and planning. Rehearsing for passage presentations is essential. Observing videos of past presentations, participating on panels, and conducting practice runs are all good ways to help students prepare and know what to expect.

Overly Prescribed Format

Make room for individual voice. As described in the Four Rivers case study ("A Progression of Portfolios and Passage Presentations at Four Rivers Charter Public School in Greenfield, Massachusetts"), it is possible to make passage presentation or portfolio reflection requirements so prescriptive that they all sound alike. Guard against that by varying the formats used, changing or adding to requirements as students progress in grades, asking students to create their own questions, and providing examples of strong student voices. Allow students opportunities to share their interests and talents beyond class assignments.

Lack of Clear Developmental Progression

Get the sequence right. Portfolio reflections and passage presentations should reveal greater depth and scope of learning and reflection over time. They should not become rote exercises in "meeting requirements."

Technology as Distraction

Technology is a means not the end. It is easy to be swept away by technological toys and neglect the content of what is being presented. Guard against wasting time and money by selecting technology for its usefulness in storing and sharing strong evidence of learning.

Panel Members Who Are Unprepared or Not Applying a Critical Lens

Prepare for rigor. Take time to carefully prepare and orient panelists. Give them the tools they need to understand the standards, the context for learning, and the best process for providing feedback.

Not Having a Plan in Place for Students Who Don't Pass the Passage Presentation

High stakes demand clear follow through. Schools need to have a clear plan for what happens if a student fails to meet expectations of passage presentations.

Chapter 8

Standards-Based Grading

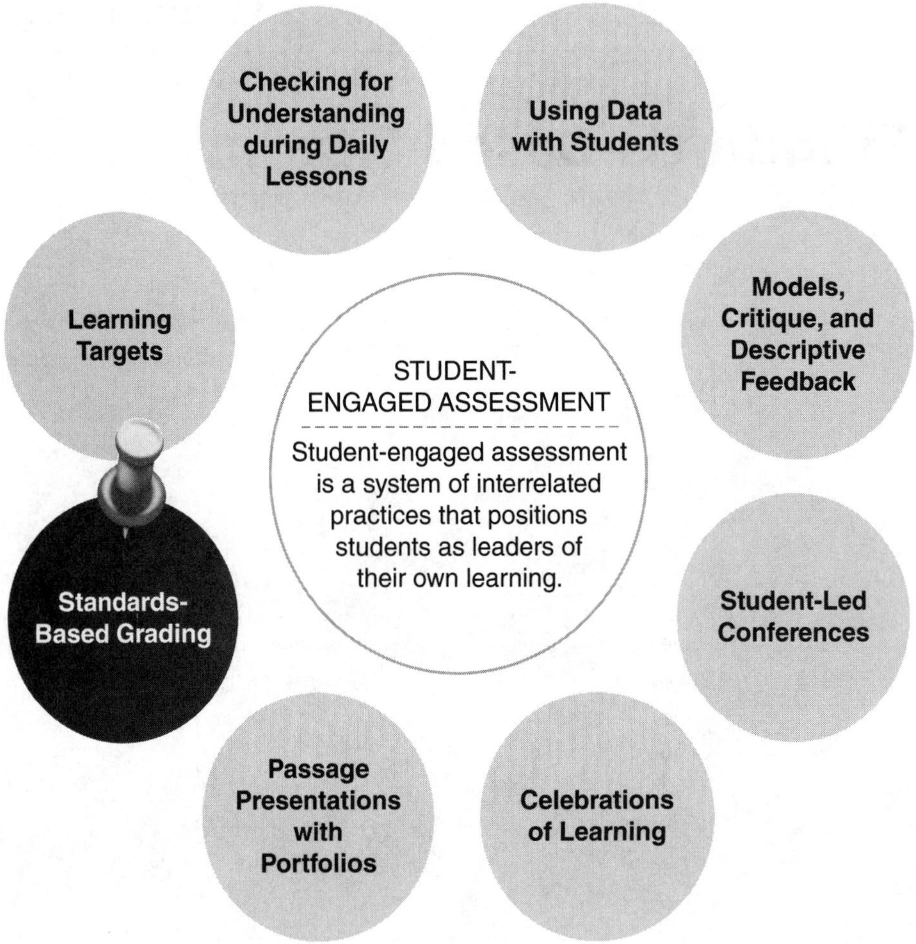

Checking for Understanding during Daily Lessons

Using Data with Students

Learning Targets

STUDENT-ENGAGED ASSESSMENT

Student-engaged assessment is a system of interrelated practices that positions students as leaders of their own learning.

Models, Critique, and Descriptive Feedback

Standards-Based Grading

Student-Led Conferences

Passage Presentations with Portfolios

Celebrations of Learning

If we, as adults, received grades regularly for our actions and work in our professional and personal lives, we might remember how strange and dispiriting they can be. Grading students in school theoretically does a number of things to promote learning: it gives feedback to students regarding their effort and performance, it provides incentive to work hard, and it ranks students so that they can be grouped or sorted. Except that much of the time grading, as it is usually done, does none of these jobs well, and it undermines learning more than promotes it for a good portion of students.

As a teacher, I had intake meetings with parents when a new child moved into town and entered my classroom. Often, parents talked about grades from the student's prior school as a serious problem. When Donte's mother met with me, she had tears in her eyes. "He doesn't like school," she said. "He is always a D student. He says there is no use in trying. He's just a D student. That's who he is."

Cady's foster parents said to me that she stayed home from school much of the time in her last school with stomachaches because she was worried about grades. When I asked if she received bad grades, they said no, except in attendance. But she always worried about it, because she always felt that people didn't like her, and she really had no idea how grades were determined—they just seemed like teacher opinions and she never felt that anyone would have a good opinion of her.

Maria's mother had an almost opposite concern. Her daughter always got excellent grades in her last school but didn't seem to have learned much. She was a "good student" with neat handwriting and sat up front and always behaved politely. But on state tests, she performed poorly. The teacher last year said she just had test anxiety. But Maria's mother felt that her daughter didn't really understand math well and was not a strong reader.

If we are going to give grades to students—and we should always consider carefully if grades are warranted—we had better be sure that the grading system we use actually promotes understanding and learning, communicates to students and their families exactly where they are in their progress toward concrete goals, and offers useful information about how students can improve.

—Ron Berger

Reporting on Student Growth and Achievement

In a brief scene from the musical *You're a Good Man, Charlie Brown* (Gesner, 1999), Sally marches on stage holding a pathetic, mangled coat hanger "sculpture" and implores an unseen teacher to explain how she could have gotten a C on the assignment. "A 'C'? A 'C'? I got a 'C' on my coat hanger sculpture? How could anyone get a 'C' in coat hanger sculpture? May I ask a question? Was I judged on the piece of sculpture itself? If so, is it not true that time alone can judge a work of art? Or was I judged on my talent? If so, is it right that I be judged on a part of life over which I have no control? If I was judged on my effort, then I was judged unfairly, for I tried as hard as I could! Was I judged on what I had learned about this project? If so, then were not you, my teacher, also being judged on your ability to transmit your knowledge to me? Are you willing to share my 'C'? Perhaps I was judged on the quality of the coat hanger itself out of which my creation was made . . . Now is this not also unfair?" An unintelligible teacher voice is heard squawking off stage, to which Sally replies, "Thank you, Miss Othmar." She then winks at the audience, "The squeaky wheel gets the grease!"

Sally Brown's persuasive abilities expose the shaky foundation of a grade that is based on a teacher's mixed judgment, using hazy criteria for effort, materials, skills, and final product. Unfortunately, this scene, written in 1967, is hardly a thing of the past. The traditional grading system in use in the vast majority of schools today produces results all too similar to Sally's experience. Getting a C in algebra could be based on the same kind of shaky criteria on which Sally's sculpture was graded. We simply can't know what a traditional grade means because it doesn't provide enough information about what students are learning or what they need to do to improve.

Along with student-led conferences, celebrations of learning, and passage presentations, standards-based grading is key to communicating student learning within a standards-based grading system. The transparency of standards-based grades—a counterpoint to Sally Brown's C—engages students in knowing where they stand and what they need to do to progress. Table 8.1 provides a snapshot of standards-based grading as compared to a traditional grading system.

Making the change from a traditional system to a standards-based grading system is hard work and is a difficult adjustment for most teachers. Of all of the student-engaged assessment practices in this book, none requires as much commitment to change and collaboration as this does. The system is different in many ways.

Table 8.1 A Tale of Two Grading Paradigms

Traditional Grading	Standards-Based Grading
Final grades are an average of performance, effort, homework completion, and other criteria developed by the teacher. As a result, what final grades communicate might be unclear and will likely vary from teacher to teacher.	Final grades describe a student's progress toward specific course standards (or learning targets). The specificity enables students and families to clearly identify strengths and areas for improvement.
A certain average (e.g., 70 percent) is required to pass a class and receive credit. Students may not have mastered a large portion of the material but will still receive credit.	To receive credit, students must meet criteria for each and every course standard within a class.
Grades are viewed as rewards or punishments for overall school performance.	Grades are viewed as a tool for communicating student progress toward specific course standards (or learning targets).
Work habits, such as homework completion or on-task behavior, are averaged in with course grades. This practice can raise or lower grades without clarity as to why.	Habits of work are reported and graded separately and are evidence and skill based. They are viewed as equally important as academic grades.
Grading is something done by teachers to students and is generally not well understood by students.	Students play an active role in understanding learning targets, tracking their progress, identifying next steps, and communicating their progress.

Source: Adapted from the *Family Grading Guide* at Casco Bay High School in Portland, Maine.

Teachers must shift from making decisions about student grades alone in their classrooms to working within a cohesive schoolwide grading system. The system demands that there be no more "easy" or "hard" graders. From classroom to classroom, grades must have a consistent meaning for students. Grades for meeting academic learning targets are kept separate from grades for meeting character learning targets, making it more clear if students understand the material and whether they have strong work habits. Academic grades are no longer an average of student performance over a grading period, but a measure of whether or not they can show mastery at its closure.

Like many things that are difficult, however, these shifts are worth the effort. Students will make progress toward meeting more rigorous standards and they will understand how their work habits influence their grades. And, the school will make a huge leap in communicating with families about what students are learning.

Principles That Guide Standards-Based Grading[1]

Although the topic of grading may seem dry and technical on the surface, grades and the grading process can pack an emotional wallop. All of us have been shaped to some extent by our experiences being graded throughout our school careers. Were we A, B, or C students? Were we traumatized by an F on a math test in seventh grade? Literature and movies are full of examples of good and bad grades, report cards, and the attending rewards and punishments. Changing the grading paradigm requires a substantial cultural change. For this reason, it is paramount to adopt clear principles to guide a school's effort in developing a new grading system.

The primary purpose of **standards-based grading** is to communicate about student achievement toward well-defined learning targets. Habits of scholarship are graded separately from academic content, and student engagement is key to the grading process.

Grades Must Accurately Describe a Student's Progress and Current Level of Achievement

Final grades that show up on a report card or progress report should describe a student's progress toward a set of learning targets. Report card grades should reflect a student's current level of academic achievement—this means focusing on trends in student work, especially the most recent work connected to a particular learning target, versus averaging all of the scores in a term. Students should have multiple opportunities to make and show progress toward learning targets through multiple quality assessments. Inherent in this principle is the belief that all students can meet high standards, given appropriate support.

Habits of Scholarship Should Be Assessed and Reported Separately

Reporting on habits of scholarship, such as effort, timeliness, and class participation, is as important as reporting on academic achievement. Progress on

[1] These principles derive in part from the work of the Assessment Training Institute and in particular from Ken O'Connor's book, *A Repair Kit for Grading: 15 Fixes for Broken Grades.*

habits of scholarship, assessed through character learning targets, should be determined and reported separately. Habits of scholarship are important and distinct, and they deserve their own learning targets. The Common Core State Standards point to the importance of habits of scholarship in the English language arts portrait of students who meet the standards and the math practice standards, making it imperative that teachers provide instruction on habits of scholarship, give students feedback, ask them to self-assess, and collect evidence of progress.

Grades Are for Communication, Not Motivation or Punishment

Grades should truly serve the purpose of communicating progress toward standards and should not be used as motivation or punishment. Many believe that students will learn to "work harder next time" if they receive low grades. The reality is that students who receive low grades tend to continue receiving them—or give up. For example, if a student accumulates enough unexcused absences to jeopardize passing a class, what will be the motivation to start doing the work? In a standards-based grading system, those absences will be reflected in the habits of scholarship grade and the student will still have the opportunity to meet the academic standards and pass the class. If students understand from the beginning what they are aiming for and how they will be assessed, they will be more inclined to keep trying.

Student Engagement Is Key to the Grading Process

If students understand their learning targets up front, they can be involved in communicating about their progress. Teaching students how to effectively self-assess their learning and progress is a critical part of the learning process. Self-assessment contributes to students' sense of self-efficacy (the belief that they will be successful at learning), because it gives them a means by which they can accomplish goals. They learn to observe and interpret their own performance and determine what they need to do next. This is a real source of motivation, counterpoint to the imagined motivation of good and bad grades.

Why This Practice Matters

Our work is rooted in the ethic that all students can get to the top of the mountain or meet challenging standards for achievement if the appropriate supports are in place. If everyone is to meet the same high standards, then students and teachers must learn to assess progress by comparing individual performance to standards, not by comparing students with each other. Standards-based grading is a critical component of a school's student-engaged assessment system because grades and report cards send powerful messages to students and families about what is valued at school.

Communicating Clearly about Achievement

We want what's important—student achievement—to be clearly communicated to students and parents. When grades are averaged, when effort is factored in, when targets aren't named, or when students get bonus points for bringing in their pencils, students and parents can't really tell what counts or what has been learned. In the accompanying video, Susan McCray, an English teacher at Casco Bay High School, uses the analogy of learning to ride a bike when talking about standards-based grading. "When you're learning to ride a bike, you are going to fall . . . a lot. If I average together all of your attempts and falls, you are going to fail bike riding. Or, after a time, I can look at your riding. Are you still a little wobbly? Are you steady? Can you pop wheelies?" A standards-based grading system accounts for the early mistakes and enables students to obtain the opportunity to learn and improve.

Watch video: "Why Use a Standards-Based Grading System"

Engaging Students

In a standards-based grading system, students have an active role to play in understanding the learning targets and reflecting on their progress. Rather than being passive recipients of grades they barely understand, students become partners with their teachers in understanding and working toward standards. When targets are clear, and progress toward them is clearly communicated, students and parents can become much more engaged in conversations about learning and achievement. Without the clarity of standards-based grading, most parents don't know how to assess whether a grade reflects understanding of the material, good behavior, or "hard" or "easy" graders.

Holding Students Accountable

Standards-based grading provides teachers with a means to track and hold students accountable to academic and character learning targets at all grade levels and in all subject areas. As Cindy Kapeller, principal at Delaware Ridge Elementary School in Kansas City, Kansas, says, "A huge mistake is that schools don't talk to kids honestly about their progress. Once they turn work in to the teacher, they feel as if it's not theirs anymore. 'We don't have time' is frequently the reason given. The time you put into having the conversations and doing the reflection is more valuable than anything else you could do." Kapeller believes that this reflection about standards should begin in kindergarten. "Setting that standard in kindergarten is the best time. They learn to advocate for themselves. When they are responsible for their learning, they are not going to sit quietly and not ask a question."

Common Core Connections

- Assigning grades to standards (as opposed to averages of overall performance) provides students with a clear understanding of their learning strengths and struggles. Understanding their progress toward specific learning targets empowers them to take charge of meeting standards.
- In addition to being such an important structure for communicating student learning, the process of learning to use standards to self-assess progress builds students' self-awareness, understanding of the standards, and skills of reflection. These are essential traits of a successful learner.
- Standards-based grades bring families into the grading process in a way that enables them to better support students in their academic and character growth.

GETTING STARTED

Building on a Foundation of Student-Engaged Assessment Practices

To be most effective, standards-based grading should be implemented schoolwide and with the support of the school district and community. Short of full district and community support, however, there are strategies that individual teachers and teams can use that will make grading more accessible and useful to students and families. This chapter addresses implementation within classrooms and teams, as well as schoolwide implementation.

A strong foundation for a schoolwide system of standards-based grading includes the following elements:

- A practice of developing and using learning targets to guide curriculum, instruction, and assessment. Learning targets are standards written in student-friendly language. They are the primary means by which teachers assess learning and report progress.
- Clearly defined habits of scholarship, which reflect the school's code of character with specific, evidence-based skills and actions. Habits of scholarship may be known by a variety of other names such as *habits of work (HOWs), habits of work and learning (HOWLs), character and habits of work (CHOWs), habits of mind,* and many others. The examples included in this book could easily be referred to by any of these names.
- A commitment to student-engaged assessment broadly, and a variety of practices to involve students in the work of assessing their learning

Laying the Groundwork with a Faculty Grading Guide

Often schools form a grading team, use a subcommittee of the leadership team, or use the entire leadership team to establish the common structures and make the important decisions necessary to get started with standards-based grading. Formulating and publishing a faculty grading guide is an essential component of the process. This guide ensures that the important decisions are made at the outset and is an anchor for grading consistency across a school. When teachers grade consistently across the school, students spend less time trying to figure out what each teacher expects or values, and more time focused on learning.

Although a faculty grading guide is essential for schoolwide consistencies, individual teachers will also find the concepts and examples outlined in the following sections helpful as they get started in their classrooms. A faculty grading guide provides important support for teachers implementing a standards-based grading system. It guides teachers in the following key areas.

Ensuring That All Grades and Subjects Have Prioritized Standards and Powerful Learning Targets

Starting with state and Common Core standards, the school should develop a clear progression of academic content and skills as students move through the grades. A well-developed curriculum map ensures that grade-level standards are met and prevents unnecessary repetition of content across grades. Although curriculum maps are typically separate documents, the faculty grading guide creates a bridge from curriculum to grading by identifying the essential standards and the recommended number of learning targets expected per term per course. In some schools, curriculum maps give teachers the flexibility to create their own learning targets based on the prioritized standards at each grade level. In other schools, the learning targets are developed for teachers.

Developing a Common Language and Definitions for Proficiency on Learning Targets

Developing clear and consistent schoolwide criteria for meeting or exceeding proficiency on learning targets is key to engaging students and families in the grading process. If what a score means is a mystery, it will be more difficult for students to make progress. Grades will remain arbitrary judgments made by teachers. An example of common schoolwide criteria follows.

Sample Criteria for Standards-Based Grades—Excerpted from the Faculty Grading Guide of Casco Bay High School, Portland, Maine

Each Casco Bay High School course is built around ten to fifteen course standards. A course standard is a description of a learning target that can be achieved during a particular course, representing the essential things all students must know or be able to do in a course. Our standards-based grading language and scale is consistent with the scale that the state uses for the Maine High School Assessment and is comparable to the 4.0 scale that is used in many schools and colleges.

1 = Does not meet the standards

2 = Approaches the standards

3 = Meets the standards

4 = Exceeds the standards

(continued)

For each major assessment, teachers will develop rubrics (often with student input) that make clear the criteria that a student will have to meet in order to receive a 2, 3, or 4.

1 = Does not meet the standards: A 1 is given when, in the absence of extenuating circumstances (e.g., an excused absence), a student does not demonstrate substantive progress toward meeting the standards or criteria of a given assessment by an established deadline. This may mean that a student has not met the majority of performance indicators or criteria for that assessment, or he or she has not genuinely attempted to meet the rubric criteria. This is not a passing grade.

2 = Approaches the standards: A 2 is given when a student has demonstrated a substantive attempt to meet the standards of a given assessment by the established deadline, but needs more time to achieve competency. This may mean a student has met the majority (51 percent) of the performance indicators or criteria for that assessment or genuinely attempts to meet the rubric criteria. This is not a passing grade.

3 = Meets the standards: The student's work fundamentally meets the standard being assessed and the assessment requirements. It is competent work that demonstrates the essential skills and knowledge for that grade level or course. All of the criteria for meets the standard (e.g., in the rubric) are demonstrated in the work. This is a rigorous standard and a passing grade.

4 = Exceeds the standards: The student's work goes substantially above and beyond the course standards in quality. The work may not be perfect, but it includes complexity, sophistication, originality, depth, synthesis, and application that clearly exceeds what would be expected to meet the standards in this assessment. Sometimes, a student will have to opt to complete a particular task(s) or prompt(s), not required of all, in order to be eligible for an exceeds the standard rating. All of the criteria for exceeds the standard (e.g., in the rubric) are demonstrated in the work. This is a rigorous standard and a passing grade.

Determining Progress toward Long-Term Learning Targets

Standards-based grades are based on multiple quality assessments for long-term learning targets. The number of long-term learning targets assessed per term, per course, is detailed in the faculty grading guide. The guide also lays out expectations for teachers to build a body of evidence by which they can determine students' progress toward each long-term learning target. Teachers develop a cohesive set of supporting learning targets, which build the skills and content knowledge necessary to meet the long-term learning targets. A series of formative and summative assessments gives teachers important information by which they can assess the needs of the class and adjust instruction if necessary to support all students to meet supporting and long-term learning targets. What follows are sample guidelines for determining progress toward learning targets.

Sample Guidelines for Determining Progress toward Learning Targets—Excerpted from the Faculty Grading Guide of Homestake Peak Middle School, Eagle-Vail, Colorado

- Teachers break long-term learning targets into supporting targets that help scaffold students' progress. Assessments are then linked with the supporting targets to build a body of evidence that provides information about a student's progress toward meeting the long-term target.
- To meet a long-term learning target, every component of the target should be demonstrated at some point. This may not all happen with the same assessment; it may happen over time. Teachers must be deliberate and clear in identifying the supporting targets that lead to meeting a long-term learning target.
- In order to meet a long-term learning target, a student should be able to demonstrate that she or he can reliably demonstrate that target when it is assessed. Meeting a long-term learning target reliably does not mean meeting it perfectly.
- Gradually building toward meeting a long-term learning target throughout the trimester, demonstrating growth along the way, and then finally meeting the target during the last possible opportunity for demonstration is acceptable. However, a student who demonstrates the target once early on and then never demonstrates it again has not met the long-term learning target.
- A comprehensive body of evidence is necessary for the teacher to accurately assess student progress toward a long-term learning target. In order to be comprehensive, a body of evidence must include multiple quality summative assessments that ideally offer a student more than one method of demonstrating proficiency.

Calculating Grades at the End of the Term

Faculty grading guides make a distinction between determining overall student progress on learning targets and calculating grades at the end of the term. The faculty grading guide describes what is required to pass a class. In some schools, grades are tied to reaching proficiency on all identified learning targets in every course—students do not pass until they demonstrate proficiency on every learning target. In other schools, grades are based on an average of proficiency scores on long-term learning targets, and it is possible to pass a course without reaching proficiency in one or more learning targets. What follows is sample language from two schools with two different policies for grade calculation.

Sample Guidelines for Calculating Grades—Excerpted from Two Faculty Grading Guides

Example 1: Homestake Peak Middle School, Eagle-Vail, Colorado

Calculating Trimester Grades

To calculate trimester grades, the scores representing progress toward each long-term learning target are averaged together; the average represents the level of progress toward the set of targets as a whole. Note that this is different from determining students' progress toward each individual learning target because the teacher is relying on his or her professional judgment of each target completed at the previous stage.

Example 2: Casco Bay High School, Portland, Maine

What Does It Means to Pass a Course at Casco Bay High School?

In order to pass a course, a student must meet each and every course standard [long-term target] at the "meets the standard" (3) level or above. This does *not* mean that a student has to pass each and every assessment. It does mean that a student has to pass at least one assessment (and sometimes more) for each and every course standard.

> "This system ensures that so-so is not enough. You have to do quality work. I think it helps instill in students what it means to do quality work—the level of excellence it entails—as well as the habits of doing good work. You can't just skate by, because we're going to say, 'do it again.'"
>
> —*Derek Pierce, principal, Casco Bay High School, Portland, Maine*

Figure 8.1 is an excerpt of a standards-based report card with final grades determined by averaging scores on all long-term learning targets in a marking period.

Reporting on Habits of Scholarship

Just as the faculty grading guide builds a bridge from the school's curriculum map to the grading process, it also builds a bridge from the school's habits of scholarship to the grading process.

Figure 8.1 Sample Standards-Based Report Card with Averaged Learning Target Scores Using JumpRope Software

Progress Report for

ALGEBRA 9 TRM 3 OF 3	3.1
Intro to Graphing	3.9
Overall Academic Mastery	3.9
- I can distinguish between independent and dependent variables. (Power Law)	3.9
- I can graph and find equations of direct and inverse variation functions.	4.0
- I can plot points on a graph.	3.8
- I can use a graphing calculator.	3.9
- I can write equations to model situations. (Max Value)	4.0
- I know the vocabulary of and can identify a coordinate plane (Power Law)	3.5
Overall Character Mastery	1.3
- I can complete my work on time.	1.3
Slope and Linear Equations	2.6
Overall Academic Mastery	2.6
- I can compare slopes (positive vs. negative, parallel vs. intersecting, zero vs. undefined)	3.4
- I can check whether a point is on a graph.	2.2
- I can find a slope using two points.	2.6
- I can find equations of lines given information about the graph.	1.9
- I can find slope and intercepts from any form of linear equation.	3.7
- I can graph from equations, data tables, or situations.	2.3
- I can transform equations from one form to another, and can identify the three forms (standard form, slope intercept form, and point slope form).	2.4
- I can translate data table growth rate into slope.	3.1
- I can write equations to model linear situations.	1.7
Overall Character Mastery	3.6
- I can complete my work on time.	3.6

ENGLISH 9 TERM 1	2.8
The Classical Epic	2.8
Overall Academic Mastery	2.8
- I can analyze authors use of imagery, figurative language, symbolism, plot structure, character development, and thematic content.	3.0
- I can complete my work on time.	4.0
- I can develop my vocabulary by acquiring new words through context clues, dictionary use, and analysis.	3.0
- I can employ correct spelling, punctuation, and grammar in my writing.	2.3
- I can use active reading skills to make personal connections, compare with other texts, and use inquiry questions.	2.3
- I can use informal response journal to probe and make connections to readings.	2.0
- I can write well organized essays incorporating textual evidence.	3.5

"[Doing this] makes us look at each habit to ensure that it is teachable and assessable. How can we quantify courage?"

—Mary Alice McLean, principal, St. George School, Tenants Harbor, Maine

The faculty grading guide should describe accountability for meeting character learning targets, including consequences for not meeting them and recognition for consistently exceeding them. The guide should also include a rubric that supports schoolwide consistency. What follows is sample language for assessing habits of scholarship.

Assessing Habits of Work (HOW)—Excerpted from the Faculty Grading Guide of Casco Bay High School, Portland, Maine

- We recognize that quality habits of work (HOW) are essential for students' future success in school and work. Students receive a distinct HOW grade in each course.
- Our habits of work grade assesses how you interact with others, how you approach learning challenges, and how you participate in class.
- Habits of work are regularly assessed in each course and each marking period, using the same grading scale (1–4).
- There is a HOW honor roll for all students who earn a 3 or higher for a HOW grade in every class. "HOW Students of the Week" are also recognized at school meeting.
- A student with a HOW of 3 cannot fail. At the end of the trimester, a student with a HOW of 3 or higher who has not met standards will receive an incomplete. This means that the student will be granted additional support and time, typically two weeks, to meet remaining standards.

Identifying the Support Structures or Processes for Students Who Do Not Meet or Exceed Their Learning Targets

Inevitably, some students will struggle to meet their learning targets. The faculty grading guide must detail the school's policies and procedures for identifying and supporting these students. The "In Practice" section of this chapter will provide further detail on a variety of approaches to help all students meet standards. What follows is sample language related to supporting struggling students from the faculty grading guide of a school that is in the process of moving from a traditional grading system to a standards-based system.

Accountability for Meeting Learning Targets and Habits of Work Targets—Excerpted from the Faculty Grading Guide of St. George School, K–8, Tenants Harbor, Maine

Our goal is for each student to be "accomplished" on habits of work targets and academic targets in all subjects. St. George will support students and hold them accountable for achieving this goal with the following procedures:

- In weekly team meetings, teams discuss students who are at risk of not being proficient in habits of work and academic targets. Teachers will identify the plan for immediately increasing support (i.e., during the rest of the term) for each student at the meeting. A student support checklist (which identifies the issues and the plan) should be completed at the meeting.
- Teachers will offer students regular opportunities for self-assessment on habits of work targets and academic targets.
- If, at the end of a term, a student continues to struggle, she or he will engage in the SIT (student intervention team) process.
- A mid-level team will provide intensives at the end of each term to give students more support and time as needed for reaching targets.

For most students having the same target as their classmates with accommodations and support will be sufficient, however, in some cases, students will need to have different targets. These will be developed with the classroom teacher and special education services.

Additional Considerations

The faculty grading guide should address the school policies for such things as homework, makeup work, and *exemplary* or *honors* designations so that teachers have a consistent approach.

FAQs on Homework and *Exemplary* Grades—Excerpted from the Faculty Grading Guide of Homestake Peak Middle School, Eagle-Vail, Colorado

What Is the Role of Homework in Determining Students' Grades for a Course or Assessment?

Homework that is used as practice should be used primarily as assessment *for* learning and *not* be included in a student's body of evidence toward meeting a long-term

(continued)

learning target. However, whether or not students complete homework in a timely manner will affect their habits of work (HOW). When students complete longer-term work at home, this type of homework is most often related to an assessment of learning that will be entered into the grade book.

What Does It Mean to Be *Exemplary*?

Accomplished or B-level work reflects proficient achievement that is solid, capable, and appropriate. *Exemplary* or A-level work reflects excellent achievement that is exceptional and of high quality. This designation is not intended to be impossible to achieve or even rare; it is intended to recognize when a student's work on a particular assignment or in the class overall reflects a high degree of sophistication and craftsmanship achieved through revision, preparation, and careful execution.

Do Teachers Provide the Possibility for Achieving *Exemplary* on All Summative Assessments?

Yes. It is important that students have the opportunity to reach *exemplary* on every summative assessment and every long-term learning target. Teachers are expected to craft long-term targets in such a way that students know what it means to meet them *and* achieve *exemplary*.

Prepare and Support Teachers

Having a faculty grading guide ready at the outset provides an anchor for quality and consistency of implementation, but it does not replace the need for professional development. Individual teachers and teams can do a great deal with the classroom practices described in the following sections, but to have the greatest impact on student learning and achievement, schoolwide implementation and district support are important.

> "Have a plan for reassuring people that it's a step in the right direction. You are not going to implement this system perfectly at first. We need to remember that it's better than the old way, even if it's not perfectly implemented."
>
> —*Mary Alice McLean, principal, St. George School, Tenants Harbor, Maine*

School leaders can lend significant support to teachers and the overall quality of implementation of a standards-based grading system by focusing on the following schoolwide practices.

Dedicate Significant Professional Development Resources and Ample Time to Take in the Principles and Practices of This New Grading Paradigm

Teachers must have time to study, reflect, and wrestle with the principles of standards-based grading—not to mention the Common Core standards themselves—if they are to internalize and fully embrace them. Most of us were not graded in this way or trained in these practices, and it is easy to revert to the old structures and approaches. Having a common goal as a school and a structure of collaborative accountability also helps with the transition.

Teachers can begin to assess more efficiently when they design and use only those assessments that effectively measure student achievement toward well-defined learning targets. Schools should provide significant professional development time for teachers to develop quality standard-target-assessment plans. Such plans should reflect Common Core, state, or district standards aligned with the school's skill and content maps (if available), high-quality learning targets that are aligned with those standards, and a set of formative and summative assessments that give students multiple opportunities to meet the learning targets. Having plans in place at the outset will ensure that teachers are giving their students the best chance possible to meet standards.

Table 8.2 is a sample standards-targets-assessment plan from Susan McCray's humanities class at Casco Bay High School. McCray taught and assessed this set of writing learning targets through an interdisciplinary public policy project. She assessed how proficiently students wrote expository papers by asking them to write two pieces: a literary analysis, and a research paper. Having these two contexts for writing gave her a broad body of evidence with which to determine student progress. McCray broke down each writing skill and each step of the writing process during the creation of literary analysis papers. She provided students with a great deal of scaffolding during this first piece of writing. By the time they got to the research paper, she expected them to be able to use writing traits and the writing process more independently. This is evident in the assessment column—there are more formative assessments overall for the literary analysis than the research. Her plan also enabled the literary analysis summative assessments to be used in formative ways when they embarked on writing the research paper. In the video "Descriptive Feedback Helps All Students Reached Proficiency—Standards-Based Grading," first referenced in chapter 4, we see McCray's class in action.

Table 8.2 Sample Standards-Targets-Assessments Plan

<table>
<tr><th>Standards</th><th>Targets</th><th>Formative Assessments</th><th>Summative Assessments</th></tr>
<tr><td rowspan="2">Common Core literacy standard, W.11–12.2: Write informative, explanatory texts to examine and convey complex ideas, concepts, and information clearly and accurately through the effective selection, organization, and analysis of content.
Subcategories:
• Introduce a topic; organize complex ideas, concepts, and information so that each new element builds on that which precedes it to create a unified whole; include formatting (e.g., headings), graphics (e.g., figures, tables), and multimedia when useful to aid comprehension.
• Develop the topic thoroughly by selecting the most significant and relevant facts, extended definitions, concrete details, quotations, or other information and examples appropriate to the audience's knowledge of the topic.
• Use precise language, domain-specific vocabulary, and techniques such as metaphor, simile, and analogy to manage the complexity of the topic.
• Establish and maintain a formal style and objective tone while attending to the norms and conventions of the discipline in which they are writing.</td><td colspan="3">Long-term learning target:
I can write quality expository papers (literary analysis and research) about our expedition topic. This means I can effectively use all six writing traits to match the type of writing I'm doing.</td></tr>
<tr><td>Supporting learning target:
(1a) I can develop a central idea or thesis that can be supported with evidence.</td><td>• Thesis development chart
• Introduction template
• Evidence planner
• Draft introduction paragraph and draft body paragraph
• Introduction paragraph
• Outline</td><td>• Thesis for literary analysis (assessed on ideas strand of quality expository writing rubric)
• Literary analysis paper draft one (based on expository writing rubric first page)
• Literary analysis paper final draft (based on entire expository writing rubric)
• Research paper final draft (assessed using entire expository writing rubric)</td></tr>
</table>

Table 8.2 Continued

Standards	Targets	Formative Assessments	Summative Assessments
	Supporting learning target: (1b) I can use passages from my text(s) to effectively support my ideas.	• Evidence planner • Draft introduction paragraph and draft body paragraph	• Literary analysis paper draft one (based on expository writing rubric first page) • Literary analysis paper final draft (based on entire expository writing rubric) • Research paper final draft (assessed using entire expository writing rubric)
	Supporting learning target: (1c) I can organize my writing with a clear sequence of ideas that builds.	• Evidence planner • Draft introduction paragraph and draft body paragraph	• Literary analysis paper draft one (based on expository writing rubric first page) • Literary analysis paper final draft (based on entire expository writing rubric) • Research paper final draft (assessed using entire expository writing rubric)
	Supporting learning target: (1d) I can develop a voice in my writing based on purpose and audience.		• Literary analysis paper final draft (based on entire expository writing rubric) • Research paper final draft (assessed using entire expository writing rubric)
	Supporting learning target: (1e) I can choose words and structure sentences to effectively convey my ideas.		• Literary analysis paper final draft (based on entire expository writing rubric) • Research paper final draft (assessed using entire expository writing rubric)

Develop Schoolwide Habits of Scholarship and Structures to Track Student Progress toward Meeting Them

Habits of scholarship take time and effort to develop; however, it is worth the effort because they enable schools to communicate clearly with students and families about work habits and behavior that may be influencing academic grades. When teachers set up good systems for tracking student progress toward habits of scholarship, there are few surprises for students and families when report cards come out, and it is easy for everyone to see correlations between habits of scholarship grades and academic grades.

In traditional grading systems, a certain portion of course grades are based on participation, behavior, or effort. This means that the single grade students receive sometimes communicates confusing information. For example, a student who knew all the content in a course but came to class late or showed less than appropriate effort might earn a C. At the same time, in the same class, a student who didn't understand the content but came on time, participated in class, and made every effort might also receive a C. These students and families would be hard-pressed to understand progress toward meeting standards or what behaviors might be affecting their grades. In the accompanying video, watch a school leader, teacher, parent, and student discuss the benefits of separating habits of scholarship from academic grades.

Watch video: "Habits of Work Prepare Students for College—Standards-Based Grading"

In an effort to communicate more clearly with students and families about progress in academics and habits of scholarship, schools should give students a separate grade in each area. Each school should develop a set of character learning targets, and teachers should provide students with instruction, give them feedback about their progress, require them to self-assess their progress, and collect assessment evidence related to character. It is common, especially in elementary schools, to identify the code of character that guides all students in the school, but to further identify specific character learning targets that are distinct for each grade level (to account for developmental differences among students). In Table 8.3, we see character learning targets from the Odyssey School in Denver.

Table 8.3 Sample Habits of Scholarship Targets

1. Responsibility	
Grades 2–3	I can complete quality homework on time. I can maintain my focus in class. I can identify which crew courtesies are easy for me to hold up and which challenge me.
Grades 4–5	I can explain how I use targets to support myself as a learner. I can use my planner to support myself as a learner. I can complete quality first-draft work. I can consistently demonstrate focus and participation in class.
Grades 6–8	I can demonstrate consistent use of strategies (e.g., my own notes, participation in class, before- and after-school help sessions, RTD, etc.) to fully engage in my learning. I can complete quality classwork on time. I can act as an intentional up-stander (i.e., stand up for others).

Source: Odyssey School, Denver.

These character learning targets for grades two through eight are associated with the schoolwide character trait of *responsibility.* Student report cards reflect grades for each character learning target.

Support Teachers in Setting Up Grade Books (Including Online Grade Books) by Long-Term Learning Targets Rather Than by Assignment or Assessment

Table 8.4 shows how Susan McCray of Casco Bay High School sets up her grade book to track progress toward the long-term learning target, "I can write quality expository papers (literary analysis and research) about our expedition topic. This means I can effectively use all six writing traits to match the type of writing I'm doing." The full standards-targets-assessment plan is detailed in Table 8.2. McCray walks us through her grade book in the accompanying video.

Watch video: "Understanding Grades in a Standards-Based Grading System"

Develop a Report Card That Is Standards Based and Includes Character Learning Targets

Figure 8.1 and figure 8.2 show two sample standards-based report cards. The report card in figure 8.2 uses PowerSchool software, common in many school

Table 8.4 Grade Book Excerpt

Target	Assessment	Grade
WRITING #1A	Formative assessment: thesis chart	2
WRITING #1A	Formative assessment: intro template	2
WRITING #1A	**Summative assessment: lit analysis thesis (central idea rubric)**	**2**
WRITING #1B	Formative assessment: evidence planner	3
WRITING #1A, B, C	Formative assessment: draft intro/body	3
WRITING #1A, B, C	**Summative assessment: draft lit analysis paper (rubric front)**	**3**
WRITING #1A–F		**3.25**
WRITING #1A, B, C	Formative assessment: outline: research paper (rubric front)	2
WRITING #1A	Formative assessment: intro paragraph: research paper (central idea rubric)	3
WRITING #1A–F	**Summative assessment: final research paper (whole rubric)**	**3**
WRITING #1 Final Grade		**3**

McCray organized her grade book by linking assessments to her writing targets. First, she labeled the writing targets on her assessment planner. That way, she could use codes in her grade book rather than writing out whole targets.

McCray used the boldfaced, summative assessment to determine the student's final grade for the long-term writing target, which was communicated on the second trimester report card.

This student did not meet the target on the first summative assessment—the thesis statement for his literary analysis paper—despite having received feedback on both his thesis chart and introduction template beforehand. He received additional feedback from peers and McCray before turning in his draft lift analysis paper, which helped him progress to a 3 on his second summative assessment. He also met (or exceeded) the target on the final two summative assessments. In looking at his progress over time, McCray noted a trend toward meeting the target, despite his score of 2 on this first summative assessment. She determined his final grade for the report card's quality writing section would be a 3, or "meets the target."

Figure 8.2 Sample Standards-Based Report Card Using PowerSchool Software

Period 4	COURSE: Art 6 (Q1) TEACHER:	MP 1	MP 2	Final
		B		
	Learning Target Average:	*3.00*		
LT1:	I can effectively use the elements and principles of design.	3.00		
LT2:	I can demonstrate my knowledge of the media, materials, and techniques unique to the visual arts.	3.00		
LT3:	I can create art that represents a concept.	3.00		
LT4:	I can demonstrate my ability to observe, abstract, invent, and express.	3.00		
HOW1:	I come to class ready to learn.	3.00		
HOW2:	I actively and respectfully participate in class.	3.00		
HOW3:	I assess and revise my work.	3.00		
HOW4:	I contribute to the success of groupwork.	3.00		
Period 5	**COURSE: Science 6 (YR) TEACHER:**	**MP 1**	**MP 2**	**Final**
		C		
	Learning Target Average:	*2.66*		
LT1:	I can gather and record qualitative and quantitative data.	2.80		
LT2:	I can read contour maps of Earth's physical features.	2.50		
HOW1:	I come to class ready to learn.	2.50		
HOW2:	I actively and respectfully participate in class.	3.00		
HOW3:	I assess and revise my work.	2.00		
HOW4:	I contribute to the success of groupwork.	3.00		
Period 6	**COURSE: Social Studies 6 (YR) TEACHER:**	**MP 1**	**MP 2**	**Final**
		B+		
	Learning Target Average:	*3.20*		
LT1:	I can locate landforms and countries in Latin America, Europe and Africa.	3.70		
LT2:	I can categorize aspects of culture in Latin America and Europe.	3.00		
HOW1:	I come to class ready to learn.	3.00		
HOW2:	I actively and respectfully participate in class.	2.50		

districts and adapted in this case for standard-based grading, whereas figure 8.1 uses JumpRope software, which is specifically designed for standards-based grading. Both demonstrate the clarity with which standards-based report cards communicate progress on academic and character learning targets.

Prepare and Engage Students

In order to engage students in the assessment and grading process, teachers need to teach them how to understand learning targets, how to be good trackers of their own progress based on assessment information, and how to identify next steps and goals to help them reach the targets. Common tools such as student progress trackers, goal-setting templates, and student-friendly assessment planners can help create consistency and ownership. Table 8.5 is an example of a student progress tracker for Nancy Hagstrom's Spanish class at Casco Bay High School in Portland, Maine. Casco Bay teachers also use a website called *Infinite Campus,* which enables them to continually update progress trackers online. Students and families can log in to check on their progress in all of their classes.

At first, a standards-based grading system can seem strange and unfamiliar to students, but given the right information they quickly get up to speed. As Michael, a junior at Casco Bay High School puts it in the previously referenced video "Why Use a Standards-Based Grading System," "You can't just pass with a 78 and not know half the material. In middle school I passed science with a B– and when I came to Casco and we had physics, I didn't know half the material we were supposed to know in middle school, because that was the half I didn't do well on."

The principal, Derek Pierce, and a few students at Casco Bay put on a short skit for a whole-school community meeting to introduce the concept in a fun, student-friendly way. Pierce used a cookie metaphor to communicate the standards-based grading scale (1–4). He bit into and discussed the quality of four different chocolate chip cookies (e.g., the 2 was half-baked). At the end of the skit, Pierce revealed the big ideas of standards-based grading: that the equivalent of Cs and Ds didn't exist because all students would need to meet

Table 8.5 Sample Student Progress Tracker

Supporting Learning Targets	Evidence and Next Steps	Evidence and Next Steps	Evidence and Next Steps	Summative Assessment
I can use *-ar* verbs consistently and correctly in written sentences.	Date: 9/13 "I can identify the 6 conjugations of *-ar* verbs—I get them."	Date: 9/15 "I got a 3 on *-ar* verbs quiz."	Date: 9/20 "I wrote 4 sentences with 4 different subjects, Hagstrom ok'd them."	1. Quiz—"got a 3."
I can use *-er* and *-ir* verbs consistently and correctly in written sentences.	Date: 9/30 "I played 'battleship' without my notes and knew the conjugations."	Date: 10/5 "I have done all my HW and have understood warm-up sentences in class."	Date: 10/12 "I took the *-er* and *-ir* verbs quiz—got a 2, will make up at block 7 this week; need to study."	1. Quiz—"got a 2." 2. Quiz makeup—"got a 3." 3. Writing assessment—"3.25"

Learning Target Process Reflection

- Looking back at the long-term and supporting learning targets, why were you successful at achieving the learning targets? Why not?

  "I did my homework and paid attention in class. I figured that if I could do each part individually, I could do them together. I went to block 7 so that I could make up the quiz that I didn't meet standards on."

- What are some strategies (tangible steps) that you used to achieve the supporting learning targets that can be applied to a new learning target?

  "Did my homework, participated in class, studied for quizzes and writing assessments."

Teacher Feedback

"Great job keeping up with the homework and participating in class! I encourage you to consistently try the exceeds option, I know you can do it."

the standards, that all students would likely get a 2 at some point but that was part of the learning process, that the school would be there to support students, and, that if students received grades of at least a 3 on their habits of scholarship, they would have almost unlimited opportunities to meet or exceed the standards. The teachers then followed up with students in their classrooms.

Communicate with Families and College Admissions Offices

Family members bring their own experiences with grades and with how report cards are supposed to look to their children's schooling. As principal Derek Pierce says, "parents sometimes have more unlearning to do about what grades mean than their kids." The school should proactively share information with parents about what to expect within a standards-based grading system and, more important, the reasons why a standards-based system is more effective. Many schools develop a family grading guide that makes the process transparent. High schools must also take care to explain their grading system to prospective colleges in their school profile. What follows is a school profile excerpt from Health and Science School in Beaverton, Oregon.

> "In the end, everyone will get a 3 or a 4. It's just not really an option for kids to slip by. It just doesn't happen that a kid will get a 1 on a project and not change it."
>
> —*Eleventh-grade student, Casco Bay High School, Portland, Maine*

School Profile for College Admissions Offices—Excerpted from Health and Science School, Beaverton, Oregon

Letter grades on transcripts are derived from proficiencies on learning targets; weighted grades are in bold.

A: Student must achieve at level 3 for all learning targets of the course. (See levels 1–3 below.)

B: Student must achieve at least two 3s for every one 2 on the learning targets, and none at level 1.

C: Student must have a majority of learning targets at level 3 and none at level 1.

I: Student has work that is incomplete or missing or below expectations for grade level and the course.

A proficiency-based three-point system is used to assess students on learning targets in their courses.

Level 1: A beginning or basic understanding of a complex body of knowledge or concept

Level 2: A more detailed level of understanding of knowledge and facts, but not fully proficient

Level 3: Meets or exceeds the target, using higher-level thinking (application, justification, synthesis)

IN PRACTICE

Ensuring a Comprehensive Approach to Standards-Based Grading

Developing a strong standards-based grading system is complex work. It takes time, commitment, leadership, and professional development. In the early stages, schools often focus on laying the groundwork: developing a faculty grading guide, strong learning targets, and a system for determining grades, and tracking progress toward habits of scholarship. Also in the early stages, many schools hone these practices internally before developing external communication tools, such as standards-based report cards.

Later on, as implementation deepens, schools add layers to the work:

- Deepening student-engaged assessment practices
- Reviewing and refining standard-target-assessment plans to ensure quality
- Refining schoolwide structures and staffing roles to help students who need additional support

Deepening Student-Engaged Assessment Practices

There are many interlinking practices that engage students in assessing their work and learning and communicating their progress toward standards. Teachers engage in regular formative assessments, give students descriptive feedback on their progress and require multiple revisions of work. Formal presentations of learning, student-led conferences, and passage presentations involve students in communicating their progress to a wider audience. A standards-based report card is like the part of an iceberg that is visible above the water. What lies beneath are thoughtful standard-target-assessment plans, quality assessments, a common understanding of what evidence of learning looks like, and a school culture in which all students are expected to do quality, meaningful work in school.

Table 8.6 Assessing Thesis Statements

Supporting learning target: I can develop a central idea or thesis that can be supported with evidence.				
Traits	**1–Not Yet***	**2–Approaching**	**3–Meets**	**3.25–4–Exceeds**
Central idea (thesis)	*Not yet showing the qualities listed for *approaching*	• Central idea exists and is either too broad or too obvious. • Needs to establish a position or take a stand. • Central idea can't be supported.	• Contains a clear central idea that establishes a position or thesis. • Central idea can be supported. • Supporting points build and develop so that the position is clearly explained.	• Central idea or thesis is fresh and compelling. • Supporting points flow and expand to deepen the readers understanding and to provoke thinking.
Structure of thesis statement	*Not yet showing the qualities listed for *approaching*	• Statement includes details and direct reference to the text (needs to stay universal). • Statement needs to include title and author of text.	• Statement is universal in nature (does not include reference to the text directly). • Statement includes title and author of text.	
Write your thesis statement here:				
Self-Assessment Score:		**Why?**	**Peer Feedback Score:**	**Why?**

Susan McCray at Casco Bay High School engages her students in assessing their work against established criteria for meeting learning targets, as shown in table 8.6. They must also assess the work of a peer. In each case they point to evidence in the work that explains the given score (from 1–4). This practice builds student skills in citing evidence, a key to meeting Common Core standards, and also makes assessment something that students understand and participate in.

Case Study

Engaging Students in Tracking their Learning at Casco Bay High School in Portland, Maine

In Susan McCray's eleventh-grade humanities class at Casco Bay, students focus on expository writing learning targets during the second trimester, which are based on Common Core writing standard, W.11–12.2: *Write informative/explanatory texts to examine and convey complex ideas, concepts, and information clearly and accurately through the effective selection, organization, and analysis of content.* Student progress toward these targets is reported in the quality writing section of the report card.

Students write two different types of expository papers during the second trimester. The first is a literary analysis paper and the second is a research paper. Students are expected to effectively use all six traits of writing in each of these papers (as described in the book *6+1 Traits of Writing* by Ruth Culham [2003]).

The literary analysis paper comes first and is thoroughly scaffolded by McCray through mini-lessons, ongoing assessment practices such as giving descriptive feedback, and opportunities for revision. In other words, it is chunked, or broken down, into smaller components. Each supporting learning target is focused on during the literary analysis phase. For McCray this is part of a strategy of ongoing formative assessment, "How do I know how you are doing well before report cards?" She and her colleagues have instituted the use of entrance and exit slips to check for student understanding on a daily basis. "We ask them to reflect, 'Here's the learning target, how do you feel you are doing on the target today?' I can look at the responses and say, 'Oh I've got to adjust what I'm doing.' Sixty percent of the kids are saying they don't get it and the rest are saying, 'Please stop talking. I know what I'm doing.'"

When the students move on to the research paper, they are expected to produce quality writing more independently. This shift from teacher guidance to student independence is apparent in the standards-target-assessment plan in table 8.2. For the literary analysis, there are more formative assessments in general. Additionally, the first two summative assessments for literary analysis—the thesis and the first draft—are also used in formative ways (even though they count toward the final grade on this target). McCray uses the four summative assessments—including the final research paper—to determine overall progress toward the long-term target.

The standards-based grading practices do not just represent a more accurate picture of what the students know and can do; the clarity and specificity of the assessment practices help students reach the standards. In the previously referenced video "Understanding Grades in a Standards-Based Grading System," McCray walks us through her process for determining grades.

Reviewing and Refining Standard-Target-Assessment Plans to Ensure Quality

Over time, faculty members can work together to tune their standard-target-assessment plans to ensure their quality and consistency. It is also important that faculty members engage in a calibration process so that they are on the same page about what makes a 2 a 2, a 3 a 3, and so on. The following checklist is a useful tool for standard-target-assessment plan refinement.

Revision Checklist for Quality Assessment Plans

Standards and Learning Targets

- ❑ Do the standards and learning targets align with one another?
- ❑ Do the learning targets meet the criteria for quality (standards-based, one clear verb, identify the intended learning, divided into long-term and supporting targets appropriately)?
- ❑ Are targets written in student-friendly language with an "I can" stem?
- ❑ Are there a variety of kinds of learning targets—reasoning, knowledge, and skill?
- ❑ Do knowledge and skill learning targets prepare students for reasoning targets?
- ❑ Are content, literacy, numeracy, and character all accounted for, with purposeful decisions about including or excluding character and craftsmanship targets?

Summative Assessments and Assessments of Learning

- ❑ Are there multiple opportunities for students to do on-demand assessments and demonstrate mastery of each long-term learning target?
- ❑ Is there clarity around the assessment tool to be used for assessments of learning (e.g., rubric, criteria, checklist, test)?
- ❑ Do the learning targets and assessment methods align with one another (i.e., have you selected appropriate methods to enable you to make a decision about student mastery of the learning target)?

- ❑ Are assessments varied in format and type?
- ❑ Are the assessment experiences designed to motivate and engage students?
- ❑ Have you included smaller assessments that can be used with students in formative ways?
- ❑ Are assessments designed to support student success on state assessments aligned to the Common Core?

Formative Assessments

- ❑ Do assessments for learning dominate the assessment plan (more assessments for learning than of learning), with assessment for learning opportunities for each supporting learning target?
- ❑ Do your assessments for learning practices prepare students in form and content for culminating assessment(s) of learning?
- ❑ Have you attended to a variety of learning styles in the range of assessments for learning opportunities you have provided for students?
- ❑ Are assessments for learning experiences crafted to maximize student motivation?
- ❑ Do assessments for learning provide students with a clear vision of the learning targets and ensure regular opportunities for descriptive feedback?
- ❑ Do assessments for learning strategies involve students through self-assessment, peer revision, and reflection at regular intervals?

Refining Schoolwide Structures and Staffing Roles to Help Students Who Need Additional Support

The goal of a standards-based grading system is for all students to meet rigorous standards. But, as every teacher knows, not all students learn at the same pace, and they require different kinds of support. It is therefore important that schools develop a variety of structures to support students who need additional time and support to meet standards, as well as extension opportunities for students ready to go beyond the standards. Systems must be in place to provide students with feedback on an ongoing basis to help them advance. Strategic interventions and structures—from after-school tutoring to standards-based summer school—provide opportunities for students who need additional time for support or enrichment to receive it.

Intensives in Secondary Schools

Intensives are courses lasting four to eight full school days during which students are engaged in either an in-depth study of a topic or intense, targeted academic support in areas where learning targets have not been met. Schools usually offer intensives at the end of grading periods (usually twice per year). Students who are passing all courses can select from a menu of elective intensives. If a student is failing one or more classes, he or she will be enrolled in an academic makeup intensive to earn back lost credit. In support intensives, students are given a range of supports, including one-on-one conferences with teachers, small-group instruction, ongoing descriptive feedback, and help from English as a second language or special education teachers.

Although there is no one right way to do it, determining who needs an academic support intensive may follow a process similar to this:

- Two weeks prior to the end of the term, teachers take a day to assess each student's work and organize end-of-term feedback.
- By the following day, students are clear about which targets they have met and which they need to focus on for the rest of regular class time.
- During the last regular week, academic classes continue and students work to meet the remaining targets. At the end of that week all academic work is due.
- Also during the last week of the term, students cull work from working folders for subject area portfolios and prepare for student-led conferences. At these conferences, students discuss their work with their parents, go over their trimester reports, and review their plans for the upcoming intensive.

Other Support Structures

Many schools have found that in addition to intensives they must provide other kinds of support structures that can be more consistent throughout each term in order to fully support all students. It can also be logistically complicated to create a calendar that gives the flexibility to conduct intensives. What follows are several examples of other kinds of support structures.

Support structures like intensives give teachers the time to work one-on-one with students.

Examples of Support Structures at Casco Bay High School in Portland, Maine

Block seven: On Monday, Tuesday, Thursday, and Friday, all students are encouraged to stay for block seven, from 2:20–3:30. This after-school block is intended for students to use for extra help, for "exceeds" work, for quiet study, or for cocurricular activities or special events. Each teacher designates at least one block seven per week to work with students.

Mud season school: Mud season school provides students with a 3 on their habits of work or a 2+ on academic standards (or learning targets) an opportunity to meet standards they have yet to meet from previous trimesters. A 2+ means students are very close to meeting the standard and just need a bit more time to demonstrate this in their work. Students participate by teacher invitation. Teachers from each grade-level team are available for at least part of the time mud season school is in session to support their students in meeting standards from their classes. Mud season school occurs in March on two consecutive half-days.

Summer standards intensives: Casco Bay offers summer standards intensives in late June for students to complete remaining standards. These intensives are designed for students who have passed two (but not three) trimesters of humanities, math, or science. Students who pass one trimester may also be eligible if they earned a 2+ in the other two trimesters or have teacher permission.

Examples of Support Structures at Codman Academy Charter Public School (High School) in Boston

Extended day schedule: The regular day schedule at Codman is 9:00–4:15 (already seventy-five minutes longer than the average Boston high school). In addition, there is a required ninety-minute wellness period before or after the school day. Students who are struggling academically participate in the morning session of wellness, which enables them to participate in a required study hall from 4:15–6:00 P.M., Monday through Thursday. Codman faculty work an early shift (8:45–5:00) and a late shift (10:30–6:00) to accommodate this schedule.

Saturday classes and tutorials: Codman extends learning time for students through Saturday morning one-on-one tutorials. Codman has also formed partnerships with local colleges and universities to provide an innovative support system for ninth- and tenth-grade students. During Saturday sessions, students meet on college campuses to receive three hours of one-on-one tutoring from undergraduate students who are trained by Codman in effective tutoring strategies in reading, writing, and mathematics. All of the instructors for the Saturday seminar program are hired as adjunct faculty, but the school's dean of enrichment is always on-site during the Saturday program to ensure continuity and to provide support as needed.

Examples of Support Structures at The Crossroads School in Baltimore (Excerpted from Faculty Grading Guide)

Acceleration program: The acceleration program at Crossroads is designed to provide assistance to all students in the areas of reading and mathematics through a small-group intervention designed to improve skills in basic elements of comprehension and computation. Comprehension and computation are essential building blocks for success with more difficult academic work, and many students arrive at Crossroads with deficiencies in both areas.

The acceleration program is not a remediation program. It is designed to be challenging and engaging for students and provides an opportunity for additional time and support as needed. The program is intentionally focused on a very limited number of essential outcomes, and the amount of time that students have to develop mastery in those areas is limited in most cases to six weeks. The acceleration program provides students with the skills necessary to accelerate their learning as they strive to reach grade-level learning targets.

"Think of [our acceleration program] as a support intensive that meets every day of the school year. This structure requires that teachers ruthlessly prioritize their learning targets to make sure that students are getting the most support to meet the targets that are most important in the curriculum. This structure provides students with a double dose of reading or math every day based on their needs. While not a panacea, it eliminates the question of where to pull kids when they need additional support."

—*Mark Conrad, former principal of Crossroads School, Baltimore*

First six weeks math program: During the first six weeks of school, students participate in a focused review of multiplication facts, long division, and subtraction with regrouping. Students are divided into three groupings based on data collected on the number, relationships and computation strand of the fifth-grade Maryland School Assessment (MSA). This data is verified using a pretest that is administered and scored during the first week of school. Students who have demonstrated proficiency in these areas on the pretest and the MSA are provided with an opportunity to extend and enrich content that is currently being explored in the daily math class.

During this time all students are also assessed using the qualitative reading inventory and other tools to determine reading levels. These assessments help to determine student needs for the reading acceleration portion of the first trimester.

Defining the Roles of Learning Specialists

Within a standards-based grading system, every student works toward meeting the same long-term learning targets. Some students will require additional services or supports from special educators or English as a second language teachers to meet these learning targets:

- At the outset of a term, specialists and classroom teachers have focused conversations about how to provide appropriate scaffolding and support for all students to reach the long-term learning targets.
- Decisions about the type of support and the focus of support are based on a common set of targets and priorities shared by the classroom teacher, special educator, and other support staff.
- Students with disabilities may need different supporting learning targets (to get to the long-term learning targets) or just may need more scaffolding for the supporting learning targets already in place.
- When students are in a self-contained setting for a required subject area, their classroom usually has its own set of learning targets.

Specialists work with classroom teachers to create quality assessments linked to specific long-term learning targets for those students requiring these services or supports:

- Identifying accommodations or creating appropriate scaffolding steps for students to complete assignments successfully
- Modifying the assignment, when appropriate
- Identifying different methods or formats all students can use to show they've met the learning target; all students should have more than one opportunity to demonstrate proficiency on long-term learning targets

In some cases, learning specialists assist in determining grades for long-term targets:

- Contributing assessment information to teacher's grade books from pull-out settings
- Discussing students' overall progress and sharing professional judgment by which a final grade might be determined

Critical Moves for Deepening Student Engagement

Although schoolwide structures are critical to ensure quality and consistency, the heart of standards-based grading is in each teacher's classroom practice. When learning targets are clear and students are actively involved in assessing their learning, students and teachers truly become partners in meeting standards and achieving at high levels. Table 8.7 illustrates the who, what, and why of standards-based grading and its power to increase engagement and achievement.

Table 8.7 The Who, What, and Why of Standards-Based Grading

What Do Teachers Do?	What Do Students Do?	What's the Result?
Work collaboratively with school leadership to develop a faculty grading guide.	N/A	The school's grading system is transparent to students and families. Students experience predictable and consistent grading practices throughout the school.
Identify prioritized learning targets, based on state and Common Core standards, and align them to assessments before the term begins. Build a grade book around the learning targets. Share this information with students.	Understand what learning targets their grades will be based on.	Teachers and students have a shared vision of the learning that will take place during any given term.
Design multiple quality assessments to determine student progress toward long-term targets.	Show what they know and can do at multiple points in time, in multiple ways.	Student progress is determined from a diverse body of evidence. Students have multiple opportunities to demonstrate their learning.
Show students what it looks like to meet a standard of *proficient and exemplary.* Build a shared understanding of the criteria for quality work.	Identify their own level of performance and what it will take to improve.	Students are clear about expectations and can identify how to meet learning targets.
Establish routines for guiding students to reflect on current work, identify current level of achievement or progress toward learning targets, and discuss next steps via student-led conferences, passage presentations, or other forum.	Reflect on and assess their own progress toward learning targets. Name strengths and areas for improvement. Search for and present evidence of mastery in different formats.	Students own the learning and assessment process and see how all of the pieces of a student-engaged assessment system fit together. They see assessment and grading as a helpful tool for learning, not as something that happens *to* them.
Respond to formative assessment data gathered from students and adjust instruction as needed to support all students to meet learning targets.	Analyze their own needs and advocate for support when appropriate.	Students are more engaged in the process of tracking their progress toward learning targets. When they see teachers respond meaningfully and effectively to their needs, they feel supported. A positive classroom culture is nurtured.

(continued)

Table 8.7 Continued

What Do Teachers Do?	What Do Students Do?	What's the Result?
Establish reasonable deadlines and structures for revisions or remediation. Consider connecting student opportunities to revise work or retake a test to their habits of scholarship grade (this is often a schoolwide structure, not just an individual classroom structure).	Understand what is required of them and take advantage of opportunities to revise or retake.	Students take more responsibility for their learning because having opportunities for revision makes them feel supported. The system is designed to help them succeed, versus let them fail.
Determine a student's overall progress on a learning target by looking for central tendencies and trends in the assessments that form the body of evidence, prioritizing current level of achievement and using professional judgment.	If allowed, submit a self-evaluation to help inform the grading process.	Grades give an accurate picture of student achievement. Students and families trust that grades are based on a wide range of information, not on a single test at the end of the term. Students no longer say "she gave me this grade" but rather "this is what I achieved."

SCHOOLWIDE IMPLEMENTATION

Of all of the student-engaged assessment practices, standards-based grading is perhaps the most complex. Successful implementation requires strong coordination and communication. It is the leader's role to make a strong case for the practice with the faculty members and to provide them with the professional development they need to implement the practice successfully. Teachers will need a strong foundation in other student-engaged assessment practices—most notably learning targets—and a solid grasp of their grade-level standards. Leaders can support teachers with curriculum maps, a faculty grading guide, standards-based grading software, and communication with

"Holding students to rigorous standards can become a psychological challenge for them. Students who have always passed before might suddenly find themselves just 'approaching a target' (a 2). It can be difficult to focus their attention on making progress toward a target and doing good work, versus being grade obsessed."

—*Derek Pierce, principal, Casco Bay High School, Portland, Maine* families, and district and college officials when appropriate. Leaders will also need to set up systems and structures for academic support and remediation to address student needs. We have highlighted some of the key leadership actions that will support smooth implementation of standards-based grading in a school.

Lay the Groundwork

- Facilitate faculty member conversations about state and Common Core standards. Teachers need to understand the standards deeply before they can assess student progress toward meeting them.
- Create a sense of urgency, build a case, and establish a vision for changing the approach to grading—what does the research and key evidence show about student motivation, achievement, and grading? How are students currently performing in a traditional system? What will it look like when the school takes a different approach to grading?
- Determine a timeline and clear steps toward implementation. Will the school implement a standards-based grading system from top to bottom all at once or plan incremental steps to full implementation?
- Use leadership team, grading team, or leadership team subcommittee to create structures and policies for standards-based grading. Be sure to include a feedback loop for faculty input. Structures and policies should address the following:
  - Establish parent, district, community engagement
  - Write a faculty grading guide (which means establishing policy)
  - Create a common grade book and report card
  - Teach and assess habits of scholarship
  - Identify expectations and templates for learning targets and assessment plans
  - Plan for parent communication
  - Plan for student communication early in school year
  - Create a college communication and transcript guide, and contact local colleges
  - Developing support structures for all students: expectations within classrooms; structures within the schedule, before and after school, and at certain junctures in the year; and remediation and acceleration structures

Build Teacher Capacity

- Create a professional development plan for teachers and allocate time accordingly. Include opportunities to get supportive, collegial feedback on learning targets and assessment plans. And, recognize the need for other types of professional development to support this system, such as differentiated instruction, checking for understanding techniques, and other components of a comprehensive student-engaged assessment system.
- Create an environment of support and healthy accountability for teachers when entering this new system. Ensure that staff are using the grading approaches described in the faculty grading guide consistently.

Communicate with Stakeholders

- Provide a rationale for standards-based grading to parents and students. Explain what's different, what's the same, and how the school will support every student to be successful.
- Advocate and communicate with the district. Identify specific areas of support needed from the district (e.g., to design a report card, to have an electronic grade book or database that supports standards-based grading). For high schools, the district will need to provide leeway to determine graduation requirements, including garnering support for making habits of scholarship grades matter. When a district is unwilling to provide a standards-based report card to the school, the school leadership team will need to set up a system for translating standards-based grades to a traditional report card. The following student handbook excerpt describes one school's approach to standards-based grading within a district that required them to translate grades to a traditional system.

Adapting Standards-Based Grades for Traditional Report Cards—Excerpted from the Student Handbook of The Crossroads School, Baltimore, Maryland

A standards-based system enables students, parents, and other stakeholders to be clear about what the learning targets are—for each class and for each major assessment or project—as well as how a student is doing with each target. A standards-based system is explicit with students (and parents) about what the student has learned and where the student still needs to focus.

Based on Baltimore City Public Schools policy, students at The Crossroads School are required to receive grades in all subjects including language arts, mathematics, social studies, science, and enrichment classes. Although instruction in many of these areas is integrated, students have regular opportunities to practice, master, and apply specific content area skills that are assessed and graded separately.

For the purpose of report cards, we use the following grading scale in all subject areas:

A = Exemplary performance—exceeds expectations (90–100 percent)

B = Strong performance—meets expectations (80–89 percent)

C = Satisfactory performance—some areas for improvement (70–79 percent)

N = Not yet acceptable—needs more time and effort to produce acceptable work.

To determine a student's grade, a teacher averages all of the student's performance levels from a given trimester on all learning targets. For each target the teacher begins with the most recent and reliable evidence of student performance (0–4). The totals for each target are combined and averaged by dividing by the total number of targets. The averages are then converted using the following scale:

3.9–4.0 = A+	3.6–3.8 = A	3.4–3.5 = A−	
3.2–3.3 = B+	3.0–3.1 = B	2.8–2.9 = B−	
2.5–2.7 = C+	2.2–2.4 = C	2.0–2.1 = C−	0–2.0 = N

Case Study

Advice for Adopting Standards-Based Grading from Casco Bay High School in Portland, Maine

Standards-based grading has been a central structure of Casco Bay since its founding in 2005, and it is something they are still continually refining and working on. As one of the founding teachers, Susan McCray, puts it, "Standards-based grading surfaces every important issue and dilemma of teaching and learning."

Principal Derek Pierce advises school leaders working to implement a standards-based system at their school to first build a case for a new grading paradigm. "Conduct staff development that exposes the problems of traditional grading in a nonthreatening way. Leaders need to prove there is a problem. Make the problem transparent and invest the entire school community in solving it." Research should be used to deepen

(continued)

the conversation. "Consider the new wave of Common Core State Standards and how important it is for everything to be standards based."

The structural and organizational pieces are also critical. For example, "Don't have grades be equivalent to 'A-B-Cs.' Try not to run two systems simultaneously. It creates the confusion of standards-based grading without the benefits." For high schools, it is important to educate and build the support of local colleges to make clear that students will not be negatively affected by a different grading system. "We had to survey colleges to show they were supportive to our school community."

During the 2011–12 school year, Casco Bay developed new graduation outcomes. The outcomes prioritize the skills Casco Bay believes will best set their graduates up for success in the postsecondary world, also emphasizing the core values of the school. This global set of proficiencies cuts across all subjects and binds together the discipline-specific course standards.

The school is now working on designing an assessment framework for the new graduation outcomes. This may include a digital portfolio and adjustments to their current presentations of learning (e.g., sophomore passages, freshman finale). Casco Bay hopes to garner the support of the district to use its graduation outcomes and course standards as the basis for a true proficiency-based diploma. See principal Derek Pierce discuss standards-based grading at Casco Bay in the accompanying video.

Watch video: "Schoolwide Structures for Standards-Based Grading"

WHAT TO EXPECT

Standards-based grading is a multifaceted practice. Schoolwide communication and collaboration are key to its success. The faculty grading guide is the essential first step. With this in place, teachers, students, and families will have a common language for talking about grades.

Although some growing pains are inevitable for schools developing a standards-based grading system, everyone involved will quickly see the rewards. Students will know exactly how their grades are derived and can focus their efforts accordingly, teachers will be able to identify patterns and trends in classwide understanding and target instruction to fill in gaps, and families will be able to meaningfully engage with students about their strengths and struggles and the relationship between their habits of scholarship and academic grades. Along with student-led conferences, celebrations of learning, and passage presentations with portfolios, standards-based grading powerfully engages families in student learning.

Generally as a school enters the more advanced phase of implementing a standards-based grading system, which may take several years to achieve, there is general acceptance of the practice by district officials, college admissions offices, and other external stakeholders. When these groups see the power of the practice to accurately communicate what students know and are able to do, and to engage students deeply in understanding themselves as learners, it is hard to not see it as a benefit for all involved.

We have identified some of the benchmarks that teachers and school leaders can expect at the beginning, intermediate, and advanced phases of implementing standards-based grading.

Beginning

- Guided by school leaders, teachers know state and Common Core standards deeply. They can identify priority standards and translate them into long-term learning targets. They design curriculum and instruction based on these learning targets.
- School leaders, with teacher input, develop a faculty grading guide for the school and communicate with students and families about the grading system.
- School leaders provide professional development to support teachers with grading.
- Teachers set up their grade books by learning targets, rather than by assignments.
- Teachers align assessments to learning targets and gather a body of evidence to support a student's grade on any given learning target.
- Students are able to articulate more specifically what they are learning in their classes because their grades are tied to particular learning targets.
- Based on school habits of scholarship, teachers develop character learning targets and assess students on them.
- Families have more detailed information about what concepts and skills their children are learning.

Intermediate

- Standards-based report cards separate academic learning targets from character learning targets.
- Student can identify the relationship between their habits of scholarship and their academic grades.
- Students and families value standards-based grades because they clearly communicate student progress toward learning targets.
- When standards-based grades reveal gaps in student understanding, interventions can be targeted to support proficiency on specific learning targets.
- Students understand exactly how their grades are derived and take ownership of monitoring their progress and understanding what they need to do to succeed.

Advanced

- Faculty members continually review and refine the alignment of standards, learning targets, and assessments.
- Students adeptly track their progress and make decisions alongside the teacher about next steps. They own the learning and assessment process.
- Students view assessments and grades as a way to help them learn, not as something done to them.
- Structures for academic interventions are well established and support students to meet all learning targets.
- Parents, students, and teachers have detailed conversations about students' strengths and areas for improvement. Students can lead these conversations.

COMMON CHALLENGES

Lack of Clarity about Learning Targets

Know where you're headed. Teachers cannot effectively involve students in the assessment process or coherently track student progress themselves if they haven't established clear learning targets before instruction begins.

Using the Same Approach with All Students

One size doesn't fit all. Standards-based grading requires flexible instruction and flexible use of time. When gathering information about how students are doing with specific learning targets, teachers see very clearly the wide range of needs in their classrooms and must learn differentiation strategies to support all students in learning. Not all students are ready to meet the targets at the exact same time, and it's important to manage time flexibly within the classroom and within the weekly schedule and yearly calendar. In a traditional system, time is fixed and learning is flexible. In a standards-based system, learning is fixed and time is flexible. This challenge can be met through differentiated scaffolding and student support and ensuring that students who are done early have meaningful extension tasks.

"Giving kids who deserve more time more time and not enabling other kids is a challenge. Once time is a variable, it leads to negotiating with students in ways that can be positive, but if used improperly, it can create seemingly worse work habits for some kids. Figuring out the right mix of incentives and consequences is a big challenge."

—Derek Pierce, principal, Casco Bay High School, Portland, Maine

Overemphasizing the Group

Don't lose the tree for the forest. Find the appropriate balance between holding all students accountable for meeting rigorous standards and also responding to individual needs. Use the expertise of learning specialists when appropriate and provide support and appropriate scaffolding to maintain a strong focus on each individual student.

Feeling Overwhelmed by Struggling Students

Be prepared. When shifting to a standards-based system, it can feel like there is an increase in students who struggle. There are no averages, bonus points, or A's for effort. Students who used to just scrape by or fly under the radar no longer do so, and schools often reel from having to support so many students on the cusp. Having a clear support plan in place—within classrooms, within the school day or after school, and within the year—will help schools maintain the rigorous expectations of students that a standards-based system demands without feeling overwhelmed.

Slipping Back to Old Ways

Stay the course. It can be challenging to maintain adherence to the principles of standards-based grading. There are pressures of convenience and culture that pull teachers back toward averaging scores over time, grading group projects, and combining effort and academic achievement. Establish strong professional collaborative practices to ensure consistency over time.

Missing the Mark with Student Involvement

View students as partners in the process. It is important to collaborate with students to build their investment in a standards-based grading system. Students can grow weary of self-assessing, reflecting, and tracking progress if they don't feel there is an authentic purpose for doing it. Unless they witness their teachers being responsive to this information and using it to adjust instruction, and unless they need to communicate their progress to a meaningful audience during conferences and other presentations of learning, students will feel this is just another task.

Habits of Scholarship without Power

Teach and assess skills-based habits of scholarship. Grading students' work habits and making this a meaningful endeavor is not easy. The challenge can be met by ensuring that habits of scholarship are skills that can be described, taught, and assessed. Habits of scholarship are not meant to determine whether students are "good" or "bad," but whether they demonstrate collaboration and effective work skills. Making the habits of scholarship or character grade matter is another challenge. In addition to making these habits live through school traditions, it is important for schools to have a clear structure for recognizing students when they demonstrate strong character and holding them accountable when they don't.

Lack of District Support

Rally support. District leaders must guide and support the development of effective standards-based grading systems. Although it is possible, schools—particularly high schools—will have a difficult time establishing standards-based requirements for passing or receiving course credit if they must translate grades into a traditional system of letter grades and seat time.

Conclusion: Transforming Schools

When we began writing this book, our goal was to create a practical guide for teachers and school leaders. By the time we finished, we realized that we had described nothing less than a vision for transforming schools. As we interviewed teachers, school leaders, and students in schools around the country, the power of student-engaged assessment was palpable. They told us that the practices transformed their teaching, improved their schools, and made them more confident and independent learners.

Brett Kimmel, principal of Washington Heights Expeditionary Learning School in New York City, makes this bold statement: "Student-led conferences have tentacles into so many different things that you get tremendous bang for your buck. The student-led conference is a game changer when influencing a kid's trajectory towards college." Similarly, high school teacher Susan McCray at Casco Bay High School in Portland, Maine, told us, "I really do think that the whole system has transformed my teaching." Liza Eaton, instructional guide and teacher at the Odyssey School in Denver remembers a turning point that led to dramatic improvement in students' test scores: "I started realizing it wasn't just about me and my planning. I had been writing the targets on the board, but we weren't necessarily using them. Then I developed a self-assessment tool and in using it, kids started to understand where they were in relation to the target. That year our state test scores went up a ton, and they stayed up. Suddenly we realized the power of our assessment work."

It was the student voices that we heard time and again that made the impact of the practices most concrete for us. Sixth-grade math students at Genesee Community Charter School in Rochester, New York, speak with striking honesty about learning to understand their weaknesses and addressing them by tracking and analyzing data. Rather than demoralizing them with their mistakes, the data seems to energize and empower them. One student declared, "When I get a bad grade it makes me feel 'aw, I did bad,' but I can still make it better." The drive to revise and improve is one thing, but the skills to know how to improve is quite another. A third-grader at Grass Valley Charter School in Grass Valley, California, spoke about rubrics as a tool for improvement: "Rubrics help you understand what quality work is. They tell you the truth. You may have thought you did very good, but then you get your score and you see what you need to work on." A seventh-grader at that same school appreciates the power of models "because they give a visual representation for people who learn better visually than by reading or listening." And finally, an eleventh-grader at Casco Bay High School reminds us of the purpose of all of this work when speaking about standards-based grading: "It's just not really an option for kids to slip by."

Throughout the book, the voices of students, teachers, leaders, and parents express the insight, discovery, and satisfaction that come from engaging in this complex work. They are not making grandiose claims. They are reflecting the reality of what happens when assessment becomes part and parcel of learning itself and a vibrant partnership between teacher and students.

Although there are many entry points and no single map, when teachers and school leaders commit to implementing student-engaged assessment practices in their classrooms and schools, they touch on every aspect of education.

As policy makers, school boards, teachers unions, and countless other groups struggle to reform education, writing this book has left us with a profound realization. If the practices of student-engaged assessment help teachers to transform their approach to instruction, school leaders to transform their approach to professional development and structures, and students to transform their approach to learning, then they will transform schools. School improvement can begin from many places, but in the end, it only succeeds when it is embraced and led by the hearts and minds of the students themselves, by how much they care and understand about their growth as scholars and as members of their school community.

Appendix

Accessing the Bonus Web Materials

Bonus web content, including new videos and teacher tools, can be found at www.elschools.org/leadersoftheirownlearning. Check back periodically for new and updated materials on topics such as these:

- Growth mindset
- School and classroom culture
- Habits of scholarship
- Assessment for learning and formative assessment
- Writing strong learning targets
- Instructional techniques
- Data inquiry
- Rubrics
- High-quality student work
- Protocols

- Communicating with families and other stakeholders
- Templates and forms for student use
- Sample handbooks and guidelines from schools
- Sample report cards
- Sample assessment plans

References

Black, P., & Wiliam, D. (1998, October). Inside the black box: Raising standards through classroom assessment. *Phi Delta Kappan,* 139–148.

Blackwell, L. S., Trzesniewski, K. H., & Dweck, C. S. (2007). Implicit theories of intelligence predict achievement across an adolescent transition: A longitudinal study and an intervention. *Child Development, 78*(1), 246–263.

Brookhart, S. (2008). *How to give effective feedback to your students.* Alexandria, VA: ASCD.

Culham, R. (2003). *6+1 traits of writing.* New York: Scholastic.

Duckworth, A. L., & Seligman, M.E.P. (2005). Self-discipline outdoes IQ in predicting academic performance of adolescents. *Psychological Science, 16,* 939–944.

Dweck, C. S. (2006). *Mindset: The new psychology of success.* New York: Random House.

Dweck, C. S., Walton, G. M., & Cohen, G. L. (2011). *Academic tenacity: Mindsets and skills that promote long-term learning.* White Paper. Seattle, WA: Gates Foundation.

Fisher, D., & Frey, N. (2007). *Checking for understanding: Formative assessment techniques for your classroom.* Alexandria, VA: ASCD.

Gesner, C. (1967). *You're a good man, Charlie Brown* based on the comic strip "Peanuts" by Charles M. Schulz. New York: Random House.

Good, C., Aronson, J., & Inzlicht, M. (2003). Improving adolescents' standardized test performance: An intervention to reduce the effects of stereotype threat. *Journal of Applied Developmental Psychology, 24,* 645–662.

Hess, K. (2009). *Hess' cognitive rigor matrix.* Retrieved from http://static.pdesas.org/content/documents/M1-Slide_22_DOK_Hess_Cognitive_Rigor.pdf

Himmele, P., & Himmele, W. (2011). *Total participation techniques.* Alexandria, VA: ASCD.

Lemov, D. (2010). *Teach like a champion: 49 techniques that put students on the path to college.* San Francisco: Jossey-Bass.

McDonald, J. P., Mohr, N., Dichter, A., & McDonald, E. C. (2007). *The power of protocols: An educator's guide to better practice* (2nd ed.). New York: Teachers College Press.

Meier, D. (1995). *The power of their ideas: Lessons for America from a small school in Harlem.* Boston: Beacon Press.

Moss, C., & Brookhart, S. (2009). *Advancing formative assessment in every classroom.* Alexandria, VA: ASCD.

National Governors Association Center for Best Practices and Council of Chief State School Officers. (2010). *Common core state standards.* Washington, DC: National Governors Association Center for Best Practices, Council of Chief State School Officers.

O'Connor, K. (2007). *A repair kit for grading: 15 fixes for broken grades.* Boston: Pearson.

Oyserman, D., Terry, K., & Bybee, D. (2002). A possible selves intervention to enhance school involvement. *Journal of Adolescence, 25,* 313–326.

Perkins, D., & Blythe, T. (1994). Putting understanding up front. *Educational Leadership, 51*(3), 4–7.

Sizer, T. R. (1984). *Horace's compromise: The dilemma of the American high school.* Boston: Houghton Mifflin.

Stiggins, R. (2005). *Student-involved assessment for learning* (4th ed.). Upper Saddle River, NJ: Prentice-Hall.

Stiggins, R., Arter, J., Chappuis, J., & Chappuis, S. (2006). *Classroom assessment for student learning: Doing it right—using it well.* Portland, OR: Assessment Training Institute.

Vispoel, W. P., & Austin, J. R. (1995). Success and failure in junior high school: A critical incident approach to understanding students' attributional beliefs. *American Educational Research Journal, 32*(2), 377–412.

Walsh, J., & Sattes, E. (2005). *Quality questioning: Research-based practice to engage every learner.* Thousand Oaks, CA: Corwin Press.

Walton, G. M., & Cohen, G. L. (2007). A question of belonging: Race, social fit, and achievement. *Journal of Personality and Social Psychology, 92,* 82–96.

Wiggins, G. (2012). Seven keys to effective feedback. *Educational Leadership, 70*(1), 10–16.

Yeager, D., Purdie-Vaughns, V., Garcia, J., Apfel, N., Brzustoski, P., Master, A., Hessert, W., Williams, M., & Cohen, G. (2013). *Breaking the cycle of mistrust: Wise interventions to provide critical feedback across the racial divide.* Retrieved from http://homepage.psy.utexas.edu/homepage/group/YeagerLAB/ADRG/Pdfs/Wise%20feedback%20-%20Yeager%20Cohen%20et%20al.pdf

Yin, Y., Shavelson, R., Ayala, C., Ruiz-Primo, M. A., Brandon, P., & Furtak, E. (2008). On the impact of formative assessment on student motivation, achievement, and conceptual change. *Applied Measurement in Education, 21*(4), 335–359.

How to Use the DVD

SYSTEM REQUIREMENTS

PC with Microsoft Windows 2003 or later
Mac with Apple OS version 10.1 or later

USING THE DVD WITH WINDOWS

To view the items located on the DVD, follow these steps:

1. Insert the DVD into your computer's DVD drive.
2. A window appears with the following options:

    Contents: Allows you to view the files included on the DVD.
    Links: Displays a hyperlinked page of websites.
    Author: Displays a page with information about the author(s).
    Exit: Closes the interface window.

If you do not have autorun enabled or if the autorun window does not appear, follow these steps to access the DVD:

1. Click Start → Run.
2. In the dialog box that appears, type d:\start.exe, where d is the letter of your DVD drive. This brings up the autorun window described in the preceding set of steps.
3. Choose the desired option from the menu. (See step 2 in the preceding list for a description of these options.)

IN CASE OF TROUBLE

If you experience difficulty using the DVD, please follow these steps:

1. Make sure your hardware and systems configurations conform to the systems requirements noted under "System Requirements."
2. Review the installation procedure for your type of hardware and operating system. It is possible to reinstall the software if necessary.

To speak with someone in Product Technical Support, call 800-762-2974 or 317-572-3994 Monday through Friday from 8:30 A.M. to 5:00 P.M. EST. You can also contact Product Technical Support and get support information through our website at www.wiley.com/techsupport.

Before calling or writing, please have the following information available:

- Type of computer and operating system
- Any error messages displayed
- Complete description of the problem

It is best if you are sitting at your computer when making the call.

Index

D

E

F

G

H

I

J

K

L

M

N

O

P

Q

R

S

T

V

W

Y

Z